Cambridge Texts in Computer Science

Edited by D. J. Cooke, Loughborough University

Also in this series

27 Cambridge Computer Science Texts

An Introduction to Functional Programming Systems Using Haskell

Antony J. T. Davie

Lecturer in Computer Science, University of St Andrews

CAMBRIDGE
UNIVERSITY PRESS

Published by the Press Syndicate of the University of Cambridge
The Pitt Building, Trumpington Street, Cambridge CB2 1RP
40 West 20th Street, New York, NY 10011-4211, USA
10 Stamford Road, Oakleigh, Victoria 3166, Australia

First published 1992

Printed in Great Britain at the University Press, Cambridge

Library of Congress cataloguing in publication data available

British Library cataloguing in publication data available

ISBN 0 521 25830 8 hardback
ISBN 0 521 27724 8 paperback

Contents

Preface

This book is aimed at introducing beginners to the subject of functional programming (also called applicative programming) and the systems that are associated with such programming. The readership is envisaged to include both undergraduates and postgraduate students who wish to obtain a grounding in the arts of programming, analysing and implementing. The computer literate layman should find it simple enough to understand fairly detailed ideas about one of the most interesting aspects of modern computing.

The functional language Haskell is used as the main vehicle for teaching both the rudiments and finer points of functional technique. Haskell is a recently emerged internationally agreed functional language the design of which incorporates the following goals:

- It should be suitable for teaching, research, and applications, including building large systems.
- It should be completely described via the publication of a formal syntax and semantics.
- It should be freely available. Anyone should be permitted to implement the language and distribute it to whomever they please.
- It should be based on ideas that enjoy a wide consensus.
- It should reduce unnecessary diversity in functional programming languages.

The present text has similar aims but does not attempt in any way to be a defining document for Haskell. For that, readers should refer to the Haskell report [huda91][1] from whose preface the above goals were quoted. In contrast this book is introductory and, although covering most of the features of Haskell, is not *fully* comprehensive in the way that the report is. The book is, however, more explanatory than the formal report.

---

[1]The language Haskell is under constant development. This was the latest language definition at the time of writing. A version with some minor changes will be published in SIGPLAN notices in early 1992.

In addition to the programming aspects of Haskell, this book introduces readers to the concepts necessary for analysing and implementing functional programs. The former is represented by chapters on proving correctness of programs and on transforming them in various ways; the latter is dealt with by chapters on applicative order and normal order evaluation and on parallel evaluation of functional programs.

The author encourages serious readers to try to obtain an implementation of the Haskell language to accompany their study of the book. A number of such implementations are available, details of four of which can be obtained by writing to:

- John Peterson, Department of Computer Science, Yale University, Newhaven, CT 06520, USA (electronic mail address `peterson-john@cs.yale.edu`). Available on Sun-3, Sun-4 and Apollo computers.

- Will Partain, Glasgow University, Lilybank Gardens, Glasgow, Scotland G12 8QQ (electronic mail address `haskell-request@dcs.glasgow.ac.uk`). Available on Sun-3 and Sun-4 computers.

- Lennart Augustsson, Department of Computer Sciences, Chalmers University, Göteborg, Sweden (electronic mail address `augustss@cs.chalmers.se`). Available on Sun-3, Sun-4 and other computers.

- Mark Jones, Programming Research Group, 11 Keble Road, Oxford University, Oxford, England, OX1 3QD (electronic mail address `Mark.Jones@prg.oxford.ac.uk`). Available on Sun-3, Sun-4 computers and on PC's.

A common electronic mailing list for technical discussion of Haskell is also available by sending requests to `haskell-request@dcs.glasgow.ac.uk` or to `haskell-request@cs.yale.edu`.

The author gratefully acknowledges help from a number of colleagues both in helpful discussions about many aspects of functional programming and in proof-reading. In particular David McNally, Ron Morrison, Stef Joosten, Sahalu Junaidu, Mike Livesey, Gerald Ostheimer, Norman Paterson and Rachel Harrison can be singled out though many others contributed. I particularly want to thank Peter Burgess for his help with the finer points of LaTeX even though I eventually decided not to use it as the typesetting system for the book.

A.J.T.D. January 1992

Chapter 1

Introduction

1.1 THE VON NEUMANN BOTTLENECK

In 1978 J.W.Backus was invited to give the Turing Award lecture, one of the Association for Computing Machinery's highest honours. His title asked the question — 'Can Programming Be Liberated from the von Neumann Style?' [back78a]. The discussion of this question identifies a real problem with current machines and programming languages. It provides a good starting point for explaining why we wish to consider a method of describing and discussing algorithms which is radically different from the usual method of programming computers.

First then, what is it that we need to be liberated from? What is the von Neumann style of programming? In 1945 John von Neumann prepared the 'First Draft of a Report on EDVAC' ([vneu45] and [burk46]). This draft was never completed and we cannot now be certain of the provenance of the various ideas set out there. However it did describe, probably for the first time, the concept of a stored program computer which is the one now widely accepted. Such computers have become known as *von Neumann computers*.

To quote from Backus' lecture:

> 'When von Neumann and others conceived it [the von Neumann computer] over thirty years ago, it was an elegant, practical, and unifying idea that simplified a number of engineering and programming problems that existed then. Although the conditions that produced its architecture have changed radically, we nevertheless still identify the notion of "computer" with this thirty year old concept.
>
> In its simplest form a von Neumann computer has three parts: a central processing unit (or CPU), a store, and a connecting tube that can transmit a single word between the CPU and the store (and send an address to the store). I propose to call this tube the *von Neumann*

1

> *bottleneck.* The task of a program is to change the store in a major way; when one considers that this task must be accomplished entirely by pumping single words back and forth through the von Neumann bottleneck, the reason for its name becomes clear.'

Backus goes on to discuss the problems inherent in the majority of the programming languages that we use to code algorithms today. These are modelled on the above architectural features in that they use *variables* to mimic the individual cells in the store and *assignments* (:=, = or ←... depending on the language) to model the forcing of data and addresses up and down the bottleneck. In addition these basic assignments are constrained to be executed in a certain controlled time-order. Backus calls such languages *von Neumann languages*. They are also known as *imperative* or *command* languages.

1.2 VON NEUMANN LANGUAGES

The von Neumann languages commonly divide the domain of interest into two types of grammatical construct — the *statements* (or *imperatives*) which are requests to the CPU to make some change to the store and the *expressions* which are much simpler in that they merely describe (or *denote*) a value which has to be calculated by the CPU. (In fact the word 'statement' is a misnomer and perhaps we should use 'command or 'instruction' instead, but we will stick to the common parlance.) To complicate matters even further, many languages allow, during the evaluation of expressions, the calling of subroutines or procedures which may have statement-like *side effects* embedded in them which change the state of the store during the evaluation of the expression. Thus expressions may not only be descriptive but also, if one is not careful, imperative as well. We may even find situations where expressions such as x=x do not yield the value True. Just substitute random or readinteger for x to see why. The trouble is caused by those constructs which cause a change in the store (mainly assignments) and the fact that these do not *commute*. That is, we cannot arbitrarily change their order. Programs written in von Neumann languages are heavily order dependent. The fact that equality is no longer reflexive means that *we can no longer use the ordinary rules of conventional mathematics* to reason about programs in typical von Neumann languages. This book is about *functional* programming, also known as *applicative* programming (we shall use the terms as complete synonyms of each other) and we shall see that functional programming languages restore reflexivity and preserve the rules of mathematics, so that proofs become easier to apply when establishing correctness of functional programs.

There are those that maintain that extensive use of side effects is bad programming practice, and that they make minimal use of them. Two replies may be given to them. Firstly — are they sure? Examples of side effects being used even in the 'cleanest' programs abound. For instance many languages, especially the Algol like ones, have constructs like readinteger and readreal which, as well as getting the value of the next number in the input stream, cause a side effect (of moving the input stream on to the next number); readreal + readinteger is unlikely to have the same value as readinteger + readreal if indeed both of them have legal results at all. Secondly, would it not be an advantage if the very structure of a language were to discourage the use of such practices? Von Neumann languages actively encourage them by being *fundamentally* side effect driven. One of the cornerstones of conventional programming is the while loop whose specific task is to perform side effects repeatedly while a condition remains satisfied. It is fair enough to say that *controlled* use of side effects (such as only assigning to local variables) is reasonable usage but the fact remains that it is the dynamic changing of the store which causes problems with both the bottleneck and mathematical reasoning about programs.

1.3 PARALLELISM

Perhaps the most obvious way we could set about widening the bottleneck which is based on the single tube connecting CPU and store would be to replace it with several such tubes connected to several CPUs. That is, we could try to utilise *parallelism* and let several processors go to work on a single program. The current cheapness of VLSI hardware relative to software makes this a realistic proposition. It may even be attractive and possible from the point of view of hardware to consider a virtually *unlimited* number of processors being utilised in an analogous manner to the way we are accustomed to think quite freely of a nearly unlimited number of storage cells being available on modern von Neumann processors via the single bottleneck. The means of scheduling large numbers of processors is under consideration by a number of researchers such as [darl81, huda85, kell83, kell85, peyt89b, robi83 and slee80]. See also chapter 11.

A number of projects designed to *extend* von Neumann languages to take advantage of specific pieces of specially designed hardware are being pursued; for instance [char86, flan77, hill86b, kuck77 and ston87]. Other hardware developments, not really parallel in nature, attempt, by anticipating future needs for data and program, to 'pipe-line' ([kogg81, rama77]) several words into the von Neumann bottleneck in advance of the time they will be needed. This allows overlapping the fetching of data and instructions from the store with the processing of earlier data. But this is really a *shortening* of the bottleneck whereas what we really need is a *widening*. Pipelining will only give a speed-up by a constant value in exchange for a very expensive outlay on highly sophisticated special purpose hardware; all we are doing in this way is building faster von Neumann computers. But parallelism with very many processors has at least the potential of actually reducing the functionality of the time-complexity of certain algorithms rather than merely reducing the constant of proportionality. For instance the best methods of sorting n elements using non-parallel methods takes a time of order $O(n \log n)$ while fully parallel methods exist which can do it in $O(\log n)$ [bitt84]. Parallel algorithms exist for many other problems which are significant improvements over more conventional sequential solutions [hill86a].

A method of approach which is allied to those we advocate in this book is called *dataflow*. Its main idea is to make the whole evaluation process data driven. When a piece of data has been evaluated a *flow graph* indicates where it will be of use and the data is made to inform a processing element that it is ready to be used in some further expression. Thus instead of the CPU asking for data from the store, the individual pieces of data ask for processing units, of which there may be many, to carry out some manipulation. While we think this a fertile field of investigation we will not pursue it here but refer the reader to any of [arvi80, denn80, ieee82, veen86 and wats79]. Also related is the work being done on and around the *logic programming* language Prolog ([clar84, cloc81 or kowa79]).

Other approaches include making facilities available to control parallelism directly. Facilities are provided in ADA, for instance, which attempt to allow parallelism to be specified by multi-tasking but this is merely added complexity for the programmer who is already bombarded on all sides with a plethora of 'features' and concepts to be mastered. Programmers have their own problem to think about, be it the simulation of a wind tunnel, the sorting of a large file or automatic parsing of a computer language, without having to be concerned with the minefield of difficulties such as synchronization and inter-process communication connected with multi-tasking. By using the so called applicative style which this book considers, parallelism can be *automated* to a certain extent and taken out of the programmers' hands so that they no longer have to specify just where parallelism is to occur, the system extracting what parallelism it can find for itself. We shall give an indication of how this can happen in the section below on referential transparency and we consider it again in chapter 11.

1.4 MATHEMATICS — A STATIC LANGUAGE

Most of the discrete mathematics and logic available for reasoning about programming is not geared to the time sequence and storage concepts of imperative languages and is not much use for describing commands. Instead mathematics is statically orientated. Even though mathematicians use what they call '*variables*', these entities very seldom vary at all. When a proof mentions, for instance,

let S be the set of odd integers

the prover is very unlikely to make changes to S by deleting members or adding new ones. Later on in the proof one is not liable to find that S is now, for instance, the set of prime numbers. But this is exactly what a von Neumann programmer might try to do if simulating the sieve of Eratosthenes for calculating the primes. Mathematics is a *static* language and mathematicians do not change objects in any way analogous to programmers' assignment. Another unfortunate difference is that classical predicate logic, as used by mathematicians to prove theorems, is not much help to conventional imperative programmers. The logic of commands (e.g. [hoar69, grie81]) has been developed to deal with this situation and parallelism and concurrency can be dealt with using temporal or dynamic logic [mann83] but these have not been particularly popular among practitioners for a number of reasons, one of which is that the proofs of correctness tend to be very much longer and more turgid than the programs themselves and the complex *specifications* (e.g. [haye85, bjor82]) for programs are also often difficult to construct and comprehend. In a static situation, such as the one that we find when programming applicatively, this problem is greatly alleviated.

1.5   THE   COMPLEXITY   OF   PROGRAMMING LANGUAGES

So von Neumann computers contain a hardware bottleneck which may present considerable barriers to efficiency; and the languages which reflect their architecture are difficult, because of their complexity, to reason about.

Most modern programming languages seem to do nothing to alleviate this tendency to complexity — rather the reverse. Compare ADA [some87] with its ancestor Pascal [jens78] or compare PL/I [fike70] to FORTRAN II [back78]. Instead of attempting to clear the air by simplifying, there seems to be a trend in some quarters to add as many bells and whistles as possible to languages under the impression that more concepts means greater strength. This is the unfortunate ascendancy of quantity over quality.

It is the main thesis of this book that a *simplifying* step, the removal of commands from languages leaving only expressions, may go a long way towards assuaging the two problems mentioned above — those of efficiency and of effective reasoning about programs. Consequently we shall be discussing, as the main programming vehicle in this text, a language called Haskell[1] which is static, descriptive and command free [huda91]. Chapters 2 and 3 are devoted to introductory programming in Haskell and give a comprehensive introduction to the applicative style. Chapter 9 talks about how we can reason about and prove properties of applicative programs. Chapter 10 is on transforming applicative programs to different (possibly more efficient) forms while maintaining their correctness. We shall also look at some parallel architectures which attempt to deal with the von Neumann bottleneck in novel ways. This will be dealt with in chapter 11.

1.6 REFERENTIAL TRANSPARENCY

Consider the expression f + g and suppose we wish to calculate the two sub-expressions f and g (which could be very complicated calculations involving among other things many function calls) and then add them. An optimising compiler might decide to calculate f first and then g or the other way round or might, on suitable hardware, try to effect their evaluation at the same time, in parallel. If the effect of calculating one of them was to change the value of the other (via a side effect) then we would be in trouble because the result would depend on the time order of working out the sub-expressions. We would be in a situation in which the value of an expression did not wholly depend only on the values of its constituent subexpressions but on other factors like their order of evaluation.

If however we were to ban side effects completely by designing a system in which they could not take place, then evaluation of any or all of the subexpressions in a formula in any order including in parallel would be safe. The order of evaluation would not matter and they could even be calculated, quite automatically, in parallel if the appropriate hardware were available. A language in which the value of expressions only depends on the values of their well formed subexpressions is called *referentially transparent* [quin60]. Another equivalent way of thinking about this is to say that any well formed sub-expression must be able to be replaced by another with the same value without affecting the value of the whole. Besides the arguments following from parallelism considerations it is also mathematically advantageous to be able to say that an expression is only dependent on the values of its subexpressions because modular methods of proof can then be utilised. It will similarly be possible to prove statements about whole constructs by proving sub-theorems about their constituents and then joining these together using simple and well known logical methods of deduction and proof construction.

For the above reasons applicative languages are constructed so that their programs are referentially transparent.

---

[1]Named after the logician and mathematician, Haskell B. Curry who, as we shall see, was intimately concerned with the theory which lies behind applicative languages.

1.7 HIGHER ORDER FUNCTIONS

If we are not to be allowed to state the time sequence of events explicitly in our programs, what will replace it? We should ask what takes its place in ordinary mathematics. The expression $f(g(x))$ is perhaps useful as an example. It contains some *implicit* sequencing in that we are asked first to apply the function g to x and then to apply f to the result [1]. The expression $f(g(x))$ is sometimes written another way in mathematics — as $(f \circ g)(x)$ — where $\circ$ is the *composition* operator. Here it becomes possible to divorce the function involved from the argument and talk about $f \circ g$ as the function obtained from composing f and g. The composition operator is itself a kind of function but one with functional arguments and producing a function as its result. There is absolutely no reason at all why functions should not act on other functions and produce such as their results. Functions producing or consuming other functions are known as *higher order functions* and they play a prominent rôle in applicative programming. They lead to a very rich programming style.

As another example of the use of higher order functions we can imagine a function *thrice* which, when applied to an arbitrary function, f say, produces another which when applied to its argument gives the effect of f applied three times to it. Thus $(thrice(f))(x) = f(f(f(x)))$ — or $thrice(f) = f \circ f \circ f$. The bracketing structure is rather clumsy in the above example and we can abbreviate $(thrice(f))(x)$ to $thrice(f)(x)$ under the understanding that the application associates to the left. In fact we shall drop further brackets when we come to programming in Haskell.

Once we have accustomed ourselves to realising that functions are valid objects for manipulation in a universe of discourse all sorts of ideas start to spring to mind. For instance we could have a function *for* which when applied to an integer n produces something like *thrice*, only it operates *its* argument n times. Thus

$$for(n)(f)(x) = f(f(\dots f(x)\dots))$$

where the f is applied n times on the right. In particular

$$thrice = for(3)$$

We will see further examples in chapter 3 of the varied use of higher order functions.

One word of warning should perhaps be given about the functional style of programming. It can be extremely terse — on occasion so much so that applicative programmers sometimes catch the 'one-liner' disease which seems to be endemic to programmers in certain languages, for instance APL [iver62]. This is an ailment that we will try to avoid for readability's sake. It is of no great merit to be able to say 'I can code this algorithm in fewer symbols than you'. The similar 'I can code this algorithm more elegantly than you' is perhaps not quite so pernicious as it

---

[1]But this is not the whole story — If f is the function that always returns *3*, say, whatever its argument, is there any point in applying g at all? The real moral of this aside is that it *doesn't matter* in mathematics what order is used. Mathematicians don't actually think about *doing* calculations!

sometimes lends insight to the working of the algorithm itself but it is still a kind of recreation with which it is all too easy to be carried away. What one *would* however like to say is 'I can code this algorithm using less of my employer's valuable time than you' and there is some hope that functional programming is a good medium for prototyping problems very fast (see for instance [hend86, joos89a and joos89b]).

1.8 λ-CALCULUS

In fact there exists a mathematical/logical formalism ready made to talk about applicative programming. In 1941 Church [chur41] presented a notation for functions called λ-calculus which suits itself very conveniently to the underlying theory of applicative programming. Curry and his colleagues [curr58], Barendregt [bare84] and others have developed the syntactical aspects of λ-calculus extensively while work by Scott [scot76] reported more gently by Stoy [stoy77] and Schmidt [schm86] has given the semantics (meaning) of the notation a new respectability which allows us to use it fairly freely.

We are used to such phrases as 'the function $x+3$'; but this is a very loose usage. The expression $x+3$ does not denote a function at all but stands for a number which is got by adding x and 3 together (presuming that $+$ and 3 have their normal usage and x stands for some number). We assume that someone or something (the context of the calculation) will tell us what number x is. What we should really have done is to *abstract* x and to have said 'the function that maps x into $x+3$'. Mathematicians normally *name* such functions so that they might say 'the function f such that $f(x) = x + 3$' or 'the function $f: x \rightarrow x + 3$'. What Church's notation allows us to do is to make functions anonymous. We may say 'the function $\lambda x.(x+3)$' without any mention of f or any other name for the function. This allows us to put functions on a par with other kinds of object. It is perfectly possible to mention nameless real numbers such as 3.14159 (though we *sometimes* give them names such as π) When a definition

$$\text{let } f(x) = x + 3$$

is made, we could just as easily say

$$\text{let } f = \lambda x.(x+3)$$

What is happening is that the λ is used as an *abstraction* operator which tells us that the following x is to be used as a variable (or *formal parameter*) and that a function is being defined together with a way of calculating the result of the function — the $x+3$ — on that variable.

We shall see that Haskell can be regarded as a *sugaring* of λ-calculus in the following sense. Pure λ-expressions (the allowable syntactic forms of λ-calculus — we shall see more of this in chapter 5) can only be in one of three rather restricted grammatical shapes. If however we allow less rigourous but more user-transparent grammatical constructions to stand for some of the more often utilised permutations of λ-expressions we obtain a language which is more friendly (and possibly more familiar to conventional programmers). It will, at the same time, be translatable into λ-expressions by 'desugaring' and consequently it can be put in a form in which mathematics can be applied. In chapter 5 we shall investigate λ-calculus and its relationship to Haskell more fully.

1.9 IMPLEMENTATION OF FUNCTIONAL LANGUAGES

We have laid some emphasis in this chapter on parallelism and suggested that parallel hardware would be one way to ease the von Neumann bottleneck. We must however have some reservations about that since parallel facilities for functional programming are not widely available commercially and even to research academics represents the frontiers of the work being carried out in this field. Although we do talk in chapter 11 about some of the work being done with novel architectures this will not be available to many of the readers of this book and we therefore devote some time to discussing various implementations of applicative languages on conventional machines in chapters 6 and 8.

1.10 AREAS OF APPLICATION

We have attempted to suggest that functional programming uses a *descriptive* programming formula where imperative programming is more *prescriptive*. This suggests that the functional style should be an ideal way of specifying data structures and we shall see that this is indeed one of the areas of application where this method of programming excels. Because of its very nature, functional programming should also be good at describing functions on data structures such as searches which extract information from them and functions (called *maps*) which copy whole structures, applying a function to every sub-structure to specify a new data structure.

Of course the applicative style of programming is not a palliative for all the ills of the programming world any more than any other programming paradigm such as object oriented programming or relational database programming. Clearly each style of programming has its own adherents and is better for certain tasks than others. Perhaps functional programming is less successful at dealing with situations where selective updating of structures is required, because this ordinarily requires overwriting store. What *can* be done in such instances with applicative tools is to make an updated *copy* of the part of the structure which needs changing, leaving other parts to be shared, unchanged, by both the old data structure and the new one. This preserves the referential transparency properties and provides an approximation to updating which may be sufficient in many cases. But we should emphasise that, especially where two or more 'processes' need to share the effects of a common update, difficulties may arise which cannot easily be solved in this way.

It has often been said that we are living with a continuous *software crisis*. It is realised in many quarters that it is not enough to spend money on increasingly powerful hardware without making considerable simultaneous investment in software. This is still a labour intensive section of the computing industry, and with a cheaper and cheaper unit cost for hardware, it becomes clear that anything we can do to alleviate the problems encountered by programmers must be cost effective. One way in which functional programming can help is in the field of *prototyping* where quick initial working solutions to problems can provide a rapid interaction between programmer and customer. There is growing evidence, as mentioned in section 1.7, to show that functional programming provides a good workbench upon which to fashion quick model solutions and that these may then be refashioned into more efficient ones once the applicability of the solutions to the problem in hand have been demonstrated. In chapter 10 we talk about such transformation techniques.

1.11 SUMMARY

In this introductory chapter we have identified a basic problem with the majority of modern computing systems and languages — that of the von Neumann bottleneck. We have suggested that a different style of programming, the applicative style, using a referentially transparent framework, may be more conducive to operation on possible new parallel hardware and that it will be easier to argue with mathematical rigour about static programs. We have pointed out that Church's λ-calculus is a good foundation upon which to build such a rigourous framework because it deals particularly well with the functional style that manifests itself in applicative programming.

Chapter 2

Introduction to Functional Programs

2.1 GETTING STARTED

The best way of learning about functional programming is probably to do some of it. Let the reader therefore imagine that he or she is sitting at a computer terminal interacting with a system which runs functional programs. Haskell is an internationally designed functional programming language which was designed with several aims in view among which were that "It should be suitable for teaching, research, and applications, including building large systems" [huda91]. In this chapter we shall be concerned with the first of these properties and our main aim is to introduce readers to the basic properties of Haskell while using the language to illustrate the fundamental ideas of functional programming.

The interaction presented here consists of a number of *expressions* written by the user, which the Haskell system[1] is to evaluate. The system prompts the user with the symbol >. Lines in the following dialogue (shown in teletype font) which start with this symbol are therefore to be imagined as being typed by the user whereas the others represent Haskell's response to them.

```
hello from Haskell
>1+2?

3
what next?
```

---

[1] Several such systems exist. There are current developments of Haskell known to the author at Glasgow, Göteborg, Oxford, St.Andrews and Yale and no doubt others exist. The dialogue shown here most nearly resembles a simplification of the output from the system at Yale University.

The work that we gave Haskell to do was in the form of an *expression to evaluate*. Note in particular that we did not write a *command* like we might have done in a conventional programming environment, for instance `print(1+2)`. We merely assumed that the computer would automatically give us the value of the single expression we gave it. In fact the `1+2` is a *whole Haskell program*. Each such program is merely *an expression* which *denotes* a value which the system has to print in a canonical form. Each program is therefore a *description* of a value (or group of values) which gets printed as the answer. Programs must be followed by a question-mark to signal to the system that the end of the expression has been reached.

Thus we can think of the entire Haskell system as a kind of sophisticated *desk calculator*. As with such machines the usual arithmetic facilities are available — addition(+), subtraction(-), multiplication(*) and division(/). For example:

```
>216 * 34?

7344
what next?

>7344 / 34?

216.0000000000000
what next?

>7 / 3?

2.333333333333333
what next?
```

Note that Haskell has floating point numbers as well as integers and that division using / gives a floating result. Floating point numbers are distinguished from integers by having a decimal point. If integer division is wanted, there is an operator `div` which throws away the remainder and leaves an integral result:

```
>7 `div` 3?

2
what next?
```

Similarly there is a `rem` operation which leaves the remainder throwing away the quotient[2]:

----

[2]In fact the operators supplied as standard with Haskell include *two* remainder operators. The other is `mod` and the difference between it and `rem` is only apparent if the dividend and divisor have different signs. Remainder always has the same sign as the dividend and modulo has the same sign as the divisor. Moreover   x `div` y   always has the same sign as   x * y   and is truncated towards zero. The following rule always applies:

(x `div` y)*y + (x `rem` y) has the same value as x.

```
>7 `rem` 3?

1
what next?
```

and we can even request both quotient and remainder at once using the operator `divRem`:

```
>7 `divRem` 3?

(2,1)
what next?
```

Notice how a pair of results can be returned as the result of an operation.

The operators `div`, `rem` and `divRem` only apply to integral numbers, but +, -, * and / are *overloaded* and can also be applied to floating point numbers.

```
>9.87654321 / 1.23456789?

8.000000072900001
what next?
```

When an integral number appears in a place where a floating number is expected, it is allowable to leave off the decimal point.

```
>7.0 / 3?

2.33333333333333
what next?
```

More complicated expressions are allowed (using bracketing if necessary) with the usual conventions; for instance multiplication and division take precedence over addition and subtraction.

```
>(3 + 4) * 5 - 2?

33
what next?
```

2.2 NAMES

It is sometimes convenient to be able to give a name to a subexpression which may be long and complicated or which may occur more than once in the main expression. Consider for example:

```
>let u = 5
>    v = 2
>in
>(u + v) / (u - v)?

2.333333333333333
what next?
```

or, for calculating the surface area of a sphere,

```
>let pi = 3.141592653589793
>    r = 5.76
>in
>4 * pi * r * r?

416.9220176949629
what next?
```

The general rule is that any expression can be qualified by a preceding let-clause which gives a list of definitions of certain constants in the form of equations[3].

It is extremely important to note that these equations are not assignments but *declarations* or *bindings*. They are similar to a mathematician's statement of fact (for instance 'let *x* be *3*') and are completely static. The names whose definitions are given are not variables but *constants*. They can never be changed. Because of the fact that functional programs introduce names in this fashion — namely to describe constants — and that such names are only declared, never assigned to, functional programming has also been called *descriptive*, *static* or *declarative* programming.

2.3 FUNCTIONS

Consider the following example of a Haskell interaction:

```
>sqrt 2?

1.414213562373095
what next?
```

Here `sqrt` is a (predeclared) *function* for calculating square roots. We apply functions to their arguments in Haskell by juxtaposition. Note that we don't need brackets around the argument. We could just as easily have written `sqrt(2)`, `sqrt((2))` or even `(sqrt)2`. Round brackets in Haskell are exclusively used for grouping subexpressions together to break the precedences of operators; but programmers are at liberty to use them elsewhere if desired. If a proper sub-expression is enclosed in them the value of the whole expression will not change. In general we try to do without brackets wherever possible as they tend to clutter up the programming text. We shall find that, in the functional discipline, great use is made of functions and application.

Users can define their own functions by writing functional equations in a similar fashion to those for constants. For example a function called `area` for the area of a circle can be defined and used with

```
>let area r = pi * r * r in
>area(5.0 + 0.7)?

102.070345315132
what next?
```

---

[3]In fact we need not have defined π as it is predeclared in Haskell. It is a user's right however to supply their own local definitions of whatever they like.

Note the need for the brackets in this case. Otherwise the expression would be interpreted syntactically as `(area 5.0) + 0.7`. Functional application is syntactically very strongly binding in Haskell. Where we write `f x` we can think of an invisible *application* operator sitting between the `f` and the `x`. This operator has the highest of all binding powers in Haskell.

2.4 SCOPE

Consider the following variation of the above definition

```
>let area r = let pi = 3.141592653589793
                 in pi * r * r
>in
>area(5.0 + 0.7)?

102.0703453151324
what next?
```

Note the subsidiary or *local* let-clause giving our own version of π. It only applies to the right hand side of the definition of *area*. Those readers who are familiar with any block structured imperative language will realise that this is a manifestation of the idea of *scope*. The scope of a name or identifier in such languages and in similarly block structured functional languages is that part of the program in which the name can be legally used to have the given, defined meaning.

The scope rules of Haskell dictate that if an expression of the form shown in Figure 2.1 occurs, the scope of the identifier `vi` is the whole of `e` and all of the right hand sides of all the definitions after the `let`. (This applies to definitions of functions as well as to definitions of ordinary names. As we shall see there is very little syntactic difference between a functional name and one of another kind, say floating point or integer.)

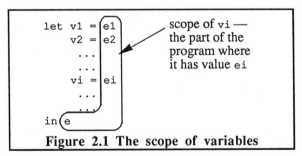

Figure 2.1 The scope of variables

This definition of scope has an additional consequence. Since each new variable is available to all the others, including the ones that have gone before, the order in which the definitions are written down cannot matter. For instance:

```
let x = u+v
    y = u-v
    z = x/y
    u = f 3
    v = u-2
    f a = a*a in z + 1/z
```

is a perfectly acceptable program. This order-independence emphasises the fact that definitions are not assignments.

By introducing function definitions, we have allowed another way of specifying new identifiers. A function's variable (a in the example above) also has a scope which, in Haskell is the right hand side of the definition of the function[4].

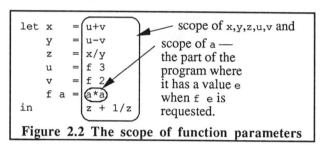

Figure 2.2 The scope of function parameters

There is a proviso about what are called "holes in the scope" of an identifier. A hole is created when a subsidiary definition is made of an identifier with the same name as one in an outer scope. Thus, for instance, in

```
let x = 2
in x +
        ( let x = 1
          in x )
```

the scope of the outer x is the whole expression *except for* the "hole" created by the inner definition whose scope is the expression in brackets. Thus the x on the last line is in the scope of the *inner* definition and the value in this case is 2+1=3, not 2+2.

Haskell allows another form of local definition called a *where clause*. Here is yet another example of the definition of area with a subsidiary definition of π.

```
>let area r = pi * r * r where pi = 3.141592653589793
>in
>area(5.0 + 0.7)?

102.0703453151324
what next?
```

In this example, we can see that it is possible to qualify one definition with another. Definitions are qualified with where-definitions while expressions are qualified with let-definitions. The scope of variables defined in subsidiary where-definitions is their right hand sides and that of the definition being qualified. For example:

---

[4]We shall extend this definition of scope of variables later — see this section below and section 3.11

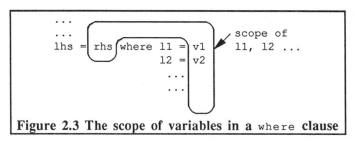

Figure 2.3 The scope of variables in a `where` clause

In many languages, and this is the case here, the scope of all names can be determined *statically*, i.e., merely by looking at the program's lexicographic layout and, in particular, without having to execute the program. Consider for instance the following example (which has been invented to illustrate the point rather than to be an example of the way to program!):

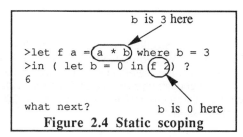

Figure 2.4 Static scoping

Here we can work out from the textual position of the definition b = 3 that it applies to the expression a * b and that the definition b = 0 is irrelevant. This is in stark contrast to *dynamic* scoping which is what happens in such internationally known languages as LISP [mcca62] (though a number of more modern dialects of LISP such as SCHEME [stee87] have adopted static scoping). With dynamic scoping the definition which had been made *most recently in time* during the dynamic execution of the program would have been the one determining the value of the variable involved. Static scoping follows mathematical convention since mathematics has no concept of dynamic execution of expressions. In particular dynamic scoping destroys referential transparency in a program as it is no longer possible to say statically what values are bound to the various names used in the program.

The reader will notice that in fact there is no real difference between, on the one hand, binding an argument name to its value when applying a function and, on the other, binding a name to an expression in an equation. In both cases the name is called a *formal parameter* and the expression it is bound to is called an *actual parameter*. There is very little difference in the binding of x to e1 in

    let f x = e2 in f e1

and in

    e2 where x = e1

2.5 DEFINITION BY CASES

What is a function? We can think of it as a mapping from an argument set to a value set which assigns one value in the latter corresponding to any given member in the former. In computing this mapping is often specified by giving an *algorithm* for calculating it. But there is no reason, at least for finite sets, why we should not merely elaborate the mapping by writing out the correspondence as a sequence of cases, for example:

```
>let f 1 = 0
>    f 2 = 1
>    f 4 = 6
>    f 5 = 5
>    f 0 = 3
in f(2 + 3)?

5
what next?
```

One might reasonably ask what would have been the result if we had asked for `f(1 + 2)` instead of `f(2 + 3)`. We would have been told that `f` was undefined for that argument since 3 was not in the argument set. The above may seem like rather a trivial example, but its concept can be extended to functions with infinite argument sets if we allow 'catch-all' default cases. The ubiquitous *factorial* function can then be defined by the pair of equations:

```
fac 0 = 1
fac n = n * fac(n - 1)
```

with the convention that the second one only holds if n is not 0, i.e., if the first equation isn't applicable. The reader should note that, although this defines `fac` over an infinite argument set, this set is not the set of integers. Although this algorithm allows an attempt to be made to evaluate `fac` for arguments less than zero or with fractional parts, the function is undefined for these arguments (because the algorithm 'goes into a loop'). The distinction between an algorithm and the function it implements is discussed in the next section. We can still however regard `fac` as a *partial* function over the integers.

2.6 ALGORITHMS

It may be tempting to think of equations such as the above as a mathematical statement of the function (total or partial) rather than as a piece of programming or indeed as anything to do with a computer at all. That is in a certain sense true, and when we come to consider correctness in chapter 9 we will use equations in that manner: but it should also be remembered that the equations also represent *an algorithm* for computing the function as well as the function itself and it is important to keep a clear distinction between functions and algorithms. An algorithm is merely a set of rules for computing a function while a function is a mapping between values which is not necessarily specified as a set of rules. This is not mere hair-splitting: there may be several algorithms for one function. That is where the skill in computer programming comes in, allowing us to choose an appropriate one — for example one that is fast or one that is space saving or one that is easy to understand.

Another point worth making about the equations viewed from a computational point of view is that the defining = sign has a *direction*. It would be no good to write

```
n * fac(n - 1) = fac n
```

although this would still be a mathematical truth; because the equations can also be thought of as a series of *rewriting rules* where the left hand side is to be replaced by the right hand side with the appropriate substitution being made for the argument.

Such rewriting rules are purely algorithmic rather than functional. They merely manipulate symbols formally and have nothing to do with the *meaning* of the function except in so far as the transformations are supposed to *preserve* the meaning of the expressions being manipulated — this is an aspect of *referential transparency*. To reiterate what we said in the introduction — referential transparency is the property which allows a proper subexpression of an expression being evaluated to be replaced by another with the same value (usually a simpler one when the evaluation is by computer) without altering the meaning of the whole.

Algorithms tell us how to calculate functions — not what they are. This all suggests that the only basic operation we should be able to perform on a function is *apply* it to an argument. In particular we should not be allowed to *look inside* a function to find out how it works. Functions are essentially not decomposable. To analyse a function would be similar to looking inside a number, 5 say, and finding the bit pattern that represents its implementation. That *might* be the way it's implemented but really that's irrelevant to the programmer and programmers should not rely on a particular implementation to get their results.

2.7 DATA TYPES AND OPERATORS

Every expression in Haskell has a value, ideally thought of as being an abstract entity (like a number) but in practice a value representable in some way inside a computer. Every such value has a *type* and in most cases the value can be *printed*.

We shall see in chapter 4 that Haskell supports an unlimited number of user defined data types but we are only going to consider a few simple (predefined) types at this early stage. We have met some of these already. They are *integral* numbers whose type is written Int, *floating point* numbers whose type is written Float[5], and *functions*. We will consider functions in greater detail in the next chapter.

Some other fundamental data types of object are those of *truth values* whose type is written Bool (sometimes these are called *Booleans* or *logicals*) and *characters,* of type Char. All of these are *simple* (atomic) data types; We shall soon explore the facilities of *lists* and *tuples* which are *compound* data types — that is objects of these types can be built from components of other types and can be broken down in a number of ways as we shall see in a later section of this chapter.

Each data type is characterised by a set or *domain* of values and by some operations. We may sometimes be a little lax and identify the type itself with the set

---

[5]In Haskell there are several kinds of integral and floating point numbers and users can even add their own. But we are only considering simple cases here. Later, in section 4.8 we shall talk about overloading in greater detail.

of values of that type. The simple data types `Int` and `Float` are computer models of ideal infinite sets and we have seen that some of the operations on them are +, −, * and so on. The domain of functions is another infinite one and as we have argued, its only associated basic operation is that of application[6]; but the `Bool` and `Char` types are finite domains. There are only two truth values and they are written `True` and `False`. Instead of using Haskell as a numerical desk calculator we could use it to question the truth or falsity of propositions. Thus for instance:

```
>2 == 3?

False
what next?

>let fac 0 = 1
>    fac n = n * fac(n - 1)
>in
>fac 3 == 6?

True
what next?
```

Note the use of == as an operator for testing the equality of objects and which yields `True` or `False` and that = is reserved for making definitions. Other relational operators which can be used for the comparison of numbers (both integral and floating) but which yield truth values as a result are the well known <, >, ≤, ≥ and ≠. The latter three are written <=, >= and /= in Haskell. The operators == and /= are applicable to values which are of a range of types, not just numbers. Thus we can ask:

```
>2 < 3?

True
what next?

>x >= y
>where x = 3
>      y = 3?

True
what next?

>(2 > 3) == (3 > 4)

True
what next?
```

It makes no sense to compare certain types of object, however. For instance we cannot compare two functions (or strictly two algorithms) as it is not computable whether they both represent the same function.

---

[6]Functions are further restricted to be applicable only to the right type of argument. It is not permitted, for instance, to apply a function taking an `Int` argument to a `Char`.

Besides the comparison operators which produce truth values there are operators which act on truth values themselves. These are the well known *logical* operations not, 'and' (written &&) and 'or' (written ||), also known as *negation, conjunction* and *disjunction*. So we can ask, for instance:

```
>2 < 3   &&   not (4 < 5)?

False
what next?
```

Note that the relational arithmetic operators are more binding than && and ||. A complete table of precedences of predefined operators is given in appendix A.

2.7.1 Guards

With the aid of truth values, we can now extend our method of function definition by using so called *guards*. Recall that the definition of fac that we gave above

```
fac 0 = 1
fac n = n * fac(n - 1)
```

went into a loop if given a negative argument. It would clearly be preferable for an error message to be issued in such a case. We can arrange for this to happen by limiting the default case to positive n with a Bool guard written after a vertical bar in the appropriate definition:

```
fac 0         = 1
fac n | n > 0 = n * fac(n - 1)
```

With this version, an attempt to calculate fac (-3), say, will find that there isn't an appropriate case to deal with n = -3 and a message to that effect will be issued when the function is called. Another way of writing this function would be:

```
fac n | n == 0 = 1
      | n >  0 = n * fac(n - 1)
```

Note that two cases with different guards can be written with only one occurrence of the function name and argument name.

Here's another example:

```
incomeTax lsd | lsd < 3200     = 0.0
              | residue <= 20000 = residue*0.25
              | otherwise       = 20000*0.25 +
                                  (residue-20000)*0.4
                                  where residue = lsd-3200
```

There are two points to be noted here. The identifier otherwise acts as a catch-all default. It is predeclared to have value True. Secondly the where clause qualifies all three cases so that the scope of the identifier residue (and any others that might have been declared in the local definition) is as shown in the following figure.

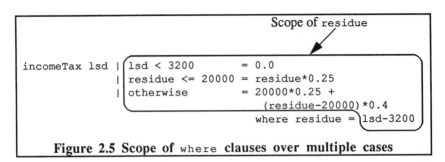

Figure 2.5 Scope of `where` clauses over multiple cases

2.7.2 Characters

Let us turn next to the type `Char`. There are 256 different characters, the first 128 of which constitute the ASCII character set. Individual characters are represented in Haskell by using surrounding them with single quotation marks. Thus here is a rather boring calculation:

```
>'A'?
'A'

what next?
```

Certain invisible characters are not usually written in this direct way. If it is desired to insert a tab, for instance, into some result, it is encoded by placing the special character \ before the letter t thus: '\t'. In a similar fashion '\a' stands for an 'alert' (a bell or beep on some terminals), '\b' stands for a backspace, '\f' for a form-feed, '\n' for a new line, '\r' for a carriage return and '\v' for a vertical tab. In addition, if you want to quote a quote sign you can escape it so that '\'' and '\"' are single and double quotes respectively.

Clearly we need some way of putting characters together to make *strings*. That subject will be discussed under the next section where lists are considered.

There are two predeclared functions `ord` and `chr` which translate characters into unique integers in the range [0,255] and vice-versa on a 1-1 basis. Because the `ord` values of the lower case letters in ASCII are a fixed distance away from those of the uppercase letters (and are consecutive), we can write the following useful function to convert from one to the other:

```
toUpper c | isLower c  =   chr (ord c - (ord 'a' - ord 'A'))
          | otherwise  =   c

isLower c              =   'a' <= c && c <= 'z'
```

In a similar fashion we can write a function to convert to lower case and one which converts a digit into the corresponding integer by:

```
digitVal c | isDigit c =   ord c - ord '0'

isDigit c              =   '0' <= c && c <= '9'
```

Characters may be compared using the relational operators. If x and y are of type Char, x < y if and only if ord x < ord y and so on for the other operators.

2.8 LISTS

A *list* is an ordered set of objects called its *component elements*. Such a list may be specified by writing the components separated by commas and enclosed in square brackets.

```
>[1,4-2,3]?

[1,2,3]
what next?

>[toUpper 'a','B',toUpper 'c']?

"ABC"
what next?
```

We can see that a list is evaluated by evaluating its elements and then displaying the results in list form. As can be seen from the second example there is a special way of displaying a list of characters. It shows up as a string of characters between *string quotes* " . In fact, as the next example shows, the user is allowed to write lists of characters, which are known as *strings*, in this more convenient way though it is not obligatory to do so:

```
>"Hello from Haskell"?

"Hello from Haskell"
what next?

>[ [1,3,5] , [2,4,6] ]?

[[1,3,5],[2,4,6]]
what next?

>[ "Hello" , ['t','h','e','r','e'] ]?

["Hello","there"]
what next?
```

The components of lists must all be of the same type. Such lists are said to be *homogeneous*. As the second and third examples above show, however, the components may be (homogeneous) lists themselves. If the component elements of a list are of type t, then we write [t] for the type of the list itself. Thus "Hello" is of type [Char] and [[True,False],[False]] is of type [[Bool]][7].

---

[7]We have not yet seen a need to be able to write down the type of any Haskell object. We will discuss types in greater detail later.

Lists can have any number of components, including just 1 or even none at all. There are no special notations for these. A list with one member is not the same as the member itself.

```
>[1]?

[1]
what next?

>(1)?

1
what next?

>[[1,2,3],[1,2],[]]?

[[1,2,3],[1,2],[]]
what next?
```

2.8.1 Constructing Lists

The examples above are particularly simple because they involve very little calculation. As well as describing lists merely by writing down their elements separated by commas and surrounded by square brackets, it is possible to construct them by lengthening previously created ones using the operator : (sometimes called *cons* for 'construct') which is such that h:t is a list with the element h added at the front (left hand end) of the list t. The element h and the list t are called the *head* and *tail* of the newly constructed list.

```
>let list = [2,3,4]
>in 1:list?

[1,2,3,4]
what next?
```

The reader may have noticed that the notation using square brackets and commas only is in fact redundant because [a0,a1,a2,…,an] is equivalent to a0:a1:a2:…an:[]. The more compact comma notation is, however, more convenient and is always preferred when Haskell is displaying structure. In addition, strings are shown with the usual quotation marks round them

```
>let list = [3]
>in 1:2:list

[1,2,3]
what next?

>'h':"ello"

"hello"
what next?
```

Note from the above example that the operator : is right associative, i.e. a:b:c means a:(b:c) and not (a:b):c.

There is another operator ++ which, instead of adding to the front of a list, *appends* one list to another:

```
>let l = [1,2,3]
>    m = [4,5]
>in l ++ m?

[1,2,3,4,5]
what next?

>let l = [1,2,3]
>    m = [[4,5]]
>in l : m?

[[1,2,3],[4,5]]
what next?
```

It would be illegal to try to evaluate [1,2,3]:[4,5] as this would try to create an inhomogeneous list with head a list and other elements integers.

2.8.2 Selection

Above we have seen various ways of constructing lists. It is also possible, of course, to find out what is in a list. This is done by *subscripting* the list using the !! operator. The subscript of the first element of all such lists is 0.

Thus for instance we can say the following:

```
>let primes = [2,3,5,7,11]
>in primes !! 3?

7
what next?

>let x = [[1],[2,3],[4,5,6],[7,8]]
>in x !! 2?

[4,5,6]
what next?

>let x = [[1],[2,3],[4,5,6],[7,8]]
>in (x !! 2) !! 0

4
what next?
```

It should be noted that we could have written x !! 2 !! 0 instead of (x !! 2) !! 0 in the last example as !! is left associative. All the various notations and operators can of course be mixed provided the rule of homogeneity is observed at all times:

```
>let x = ["ab","cde"]
>in '(' : ( x!!1!!2 : x!!1 ++ x!!0 ) ++ ")."

"(ecdeab)."
what next?
```

2.9 PATTERN MATCHING

The method we have given for specifying functions by cases is really one that can be thought of as *matching* the actual argument to which the function is applied to the correct formal argument in the list of cases specified in the definition. This matching process can be extended to ask whether an argument is a list or not; and if so to give names to the list's constituent parts. For instance:

```
>let f [x , y] = (x + y)/(x - y)
>in f [1 , 2]?

-3
what next?

let sum []      = 0
>    sum [x]     = x
>    sum [x,y]   = x + y
>    sum [x,y,z] = x + y + z
>    list        = [2 , 3]
>in sum list * sum(1 : list)?

30
what next?

>let sum []       = 0
>    sum (a : b) = a + sum b
>in
>sum [1 , 2 , 3 , 4]?

10
what next?
```

Several interesting points should be noted here. First this gives us a mechanism for passing more than one parameter to a function. To do this we wrap up the arguments we want to pass into a list and pass the list. It can therefore be seen that in theory functions need never have more than one argument. In fact, in Haskell, no function is *allowed* more (or less) than one argument. This method of passing several arguments in one list is often attributed to Landin [land65]. We will see another method of simulating functions of more than one argument later in this chapter (see the section on tuples) and yet another in the next chapter. In fact this mechanism of passing arguments also allows *polyadic* functions (functions which take different numbers of arguments on different occasions) to be defined — as the second and third examples above show. The second is only defined on lists of fewer than four arguments but the third works on lists of *any* length and adds up the elements it finds there. It is still a function of one argument like any other in Haskell but calls may *appear* to have more than one; for instance:

```
sum [1,3,5]
```

is a call of sum on a list with three components. The operators : and the [,] notation which are used for list *synthesis* when on the right hand side of definitional = signs can be seen being used for list *analysis* when used on the left. They form part of what are known as *patterns*. What other operators are allowed here? Could we write f(x ++ y) = ...? The answer is no because there is no unique way of analysing a list into two concatenated parts. The list could be split in two (providing it had at least one member) in any of a number of places. In fact : and [,] notation are the *only* list operators allowed on the left of definitions involving lists though we shall see later that other constructing operators are allowed for different compound data types. However patterns may be of any complexity. For instance if it was known that a given argument was a list with two elements, which were lists themselves, one could write such functions as:

```
f [(a:b),(c:d)] = a+c : (b ++ d)
```

Corresponding to the pattern operators which are called *constructors* when used on the right hand side of definitions for list synthesis, there are some others for list analysis called *selectors*. They are represented by the same operators (: and [,]) but are used on the left of the definitional = sign. If one wants to have *explicit* selector functions for taking lists apart one can define:

```
hd (a : b) = a
tl (a : b) = b
```

to take the head and tail of a list and these can then be used on the right. Because of the extended matching mechanism however, hd and tl are hardly ever needed. They are defined nevertheless in the modules of standard functions which are predefined in preludes to Haskell executions (see Appendix B).

A further point to be remarked upon is that this addition of patterns to the matching process is in the spirit of writing equational definitions. We can still think of the equations as *facts* that can be used when trying to prove things about functions being specified. To maintain this equational view, patterns can appear in definitions of non-functional objects. For example:

```
>let [a,b] = [3,4] in a+b?

7
what next?

>let (p:q:r) = "Hello" in (p:'\'':r)?

"H'llo"
what next?
```

2.10 TUPLES

Lists are homogeneous structures. Tuples (pairs, triples, quadruples, quintuples, ...) can be inhomogeneous. Tuples are written with round brackets instead of square ones. In fact we have already met a tuple near the start of this chapter when we used the `divRem` operator.

```
>7 `divRem` 3?

(2,1)
what next?
```

The answer here is a tuple with two components — a pair.

Tuples can take part in pattern matching. For instance:

```
>let avge (a,b) = (a+b)/2
>in avge (7 `divRem` 3)?

1.5
what next?
```

Because tuples can be inhomogeneous, this gives us a way of passing several arguments of different types to a function. For instance:

```
>let addToEnd (element,list) = list ++ [element]
>in addToEnd (3,[1,2])
```

Here we see the use of a pair whose first element is an integer and whose second is a list of integers. Although this kind of inhomogeneity is allowed, it does mean that functions with such arguments can no longer be polyadic. They must always be applied to arguments of the same type. If the components of a tuple are of types t1, t2,...tn, we write the type of the tuple as (t1,t2, ...tn). In the above, the type of the argument is (Int,[Int]).

2.11 SHOW

Most objects in Haskell can be displayed and Haskell, usually automatically, provides a way of displaying objects of any suitable type. Thus, in these instances, Haskell detects that an integer or a list or a tuple or whatever is to be displayed and adds any brackets and commas or the string quotes depending on the type of the object being displayed. In fact Haskell is applying a function called show to each displayable object which converts them from their internal form into characters for display. show is an overloaded function and can be applied to any printable type of object. Nearly everything can be shown in this way, but it is clear that it is not sensible to show everything. For instance a function cannot be shown as users are not supposed to be able to discern its internal structure.

Users can, if they wish, invoke show directly if they wish to convert objects to string form ([Char]), for example to add formatting and layout characters to an output, or even to strip off characters from the output.

Users are allowed to provide their own way of showing objects which over-ride the automatically provided show function but we will not discuss that subject here. Details may be found in the Haskell report [huda91].

2.12 CONDITIONALS AND CASES

The mechanism for pattern matching discussed earlier in the chapter is powerful. It allows us to restrict arguments in a given case to be of a given 'shape'. In combination with guards it gives us nearly everything we need in order to define functions of any complexity. There is another perhaps more conventional way of restricting the applicability of a function and that is by the use of a *conditional*. The value of

```
if e1 then e2 else e3
```

is that of e2 or of e3 depending upon whether e1 evaluates to True or False. Conditionals allow us to define, for instance, the absolute value function by:

```
abs x = if x < 0 then -x else x
```

The reader will see that certain of the functions defined earlier in the chapter could be written using conditionals instead of by matching:

```
>let fac x = if x==0 then 1
>                    else x * fac(x-1)
>in fac 3?

6
what next?

>let f x  =  if x==1 then 0 else
>            if x==2 then 1 else
>            if x==4 then 6 else
>            if x==5 then 5 else
>            if x==0 then 3 else
>            1 `div` 0
>in f(2+3)?

5
what next?
```

The division by zero in the last line of the definition of f is merely an inelegant way of forcing an undefined object to be generated. It will produce an error (though a different one from that which is generated by the previous definition of f in section 2.5).

Some people prefer the guards method of programming but others prefer to use an explicit conditional. It's all a matter of style. Conditionals make guards more explicit. In a similar manner, Haskell provides a *case expression* which makes the pattern matching we have seen in function definitions more explicit and provides a kind of conditional based on the success or failure of pattern matching. Here is yet another version of the definition of factorial:

```
fac n = case n of
          0         -> 1
          m | m>0 -> m * fac(m-1)
```

Here we see that an explicit list of two patterns, 0 and m (the second with a guard) are matched against n and, if one of the matches succeeds, a corresponding expression after the -> is chosen as the value. If no match does succeed, the value is undefined. The scope of any variables appearing in a case pattern is the guards (if any) following it and the corresponding expression after the arrow. Such an expression may be qualified with a where clause allowing further locally defined objects to be available in the guards and expression.

This example also shows the use of a *literal* value (the 'constant' 0) as a pattern. The function f above could be defined by:

```
f x  =   case x of
            1 -> 0
            2 -> 1
            4 -> 6
            5 -> 5
            0 -> 3
```

2.13   MODULES   AND   THE   INTERACTIVE ENVIRONMENT

We have presented, in this introduction to programming in Haskell, an interactive desk-calculator-like system which allows users to evaluate expressions of a quite complex nature, however the definitions we have made have all been local ones using let or where to restrict the scope of the things we define. In particular none of the identifiers in patterns used in one interactive evaluation is available for use in any of the later ones.

To preserve definitions, they can be organised into groups called *modules* and then evaluations can be made in an environment consisting of the things defined in one or more of the modules. In particular, we have seen that certain predeclared functions and operators are available, such as pi, sqrt, !! and even such basic operators as +, -, *, :, ++, ... These can be used because evaluation is taking place in the presence of a module called Main which has *imported* the definitions of all these items from another module, the *standard prelude*, called Prelude.

Strictly speaking, the evaluation a Haskell program consists *solely* of an evaluation of a variable called main in the module called Main. A useful system may, however, provide for an interactive facility such as the one described in this chapter. The present system also allows definitions to be added to Main in an interactive fashion so that they may be used in subsequent interactions. If a set of definitions is preceded by :def, they are used to extend the definitions already in module Main and can then be used in subsequent interactions. As with expressions to be evaluated, the definitions must be terminated with a question-mark. Thus for instance:

```
>:def pythag (x,y) = sqrt ( x*x + y*y )?

what next?
>
>pythag (3,4)?

5.000000000000000
what next?
```

and pythag can be used in all subsequent evaluations.

Most systems should also allow users to edit the text of whole modules of their own, compile them and import them into Main. That, however, is system dependent and beyond the scope of this book.

2.14 MISCELLANEOUS POINTS

Various final points that we will mention in this chapter are connected with comments, the rules for writing identifiers, layout of programs and a short section on a few of the predeclared operators and functions in the Haskell `Prelude` module.

2.14.1 Comments

Comments can be put on any line of Haskell by placing them after two consecutive minus signs. Everything from then on up to the end of the line will be ignored. For example:

```
x=pi*r*r        -- the area of the circle - radius r
```

A second style is useful for 'commenting out' whole areas of code. Such a comment can stretch over several lines and are surrounded with comment brackets: they start with {- and end with -}. Comments of this style can contain other comments (of either style) within them, so that comment brackets have to match properly.

2.14.2 Identifiers and Operators

We have used identifiers (like `pythag`, `fac`, `x`, `y` ...) and operators (like +, -, ! !, : ...) quite freely throughout the examples in this chapter. But there are rules as to how you can write them.

Identifiers can consist of letters, digits, primes (') and underlines (_) but must start with a letter. In fact, until we consider user defined constructor functions and types in chapter 4, the first letter must be lower case. Certain identifiers are *reserved* for special purposes. We have met only some of them. They include `case`, `of`, `if`, `then`, `else`, `let`, `in`, `where`... For a complete list, consult appendix C or the Haskell report.

Operators consists of collections of symbols from the set ! #$%&*+./<=>?@\^| :. In addition - and ~ can be used to start an operator but cannot appear after the start. Furthermore addition if an operator starts with : it is a constructor (see chapter 4). As with identifiers there are some reserved ones including =, | and ->. Users can define their own operators. Here's an example:

```
x %% y = 2*x*y/(x+y)
```

Identifiers can be used as (infix) operators if enclosed in back-quotes `, for instance `` `div` ``. In a similar fashion, operators can be used where an identifier is normally placed by enclosing it in round brackets (see section 3.10.2).

2.14.3 Layout

Lists of declarations are always preceded by one of `where` (to qualify definitions or `case` alternatives) or `let` (to qualify expressions). Lists of `case` alternatives are similarly preceded by `of`. In all of these constructions, the layout of the program is used to delimit the list of declarations (or alternatives). It is allowable to delimit these lists explicitly with the brackets { and } before and after so long as semicolons are also explicitly used as separators between the declarations. Thus, for instance:

```
x*y where { x = 2 ; y = x-1 }

case m-1 of { 0 -> 1 ; 1 -> 2 ; n -> n*(n-1) }
```

We will not give the exact rules for using implicit layout here except to say that a semicolon is inserted and a new definition started when a new line starts in the same column as the first such definition and the list finishes (a } is inserted) when a new line starts further left than the first definition. Complete rules can be found in the Haskell report.

2.14.4 A few useful predeclared functions and operators

The following is a list of some useful additional functions and operators which can be used with the basic kinds of values we have described here.

```
exp, log -- Napierian exponent and logarithm
sin, cos, tan, asin, acos, atan,
            sinh, cosh, tanh, asinh, acosh, atanh
abs        -- the absolute value of x
signum     -- abs x * signum x == x
x ^ n      -- raises any number x to a positive integral power n
x ^^ n     -- n may be negative. The result will be floating
x ** y          = exp (log x * y)
x `logBase` y = log y / log x
even x          = x `rem` 2 == 0
odd x           = x `rem` 2 /= 0
```

2.15 SUMMARY

In this chapter we have seen how to use some of the basic facilities of Haskell. We shall introduce many other details of the language in later chapters.

The main points covered were the interactive calculation of expressions, names and their scope, functions and their definition by cases; also contrasting them with algorithms which say *how* to calculate them rather than *what* they are; some of the types of values which can be manipulated in Haskell and many of the predeclared operators available to do such manipulation; lists, sublists and pattern matching; and finally conditionals and some odds and ends.

This chapter has introduced you to the tools of the trade. In the next we shall examine some of the tricks of the trade, the methods and styles used in programming more serious problems.

2.16 EXERCISES

1. Write Haskell dialogue to calculate the following 'sums' :

   a) The area of a square of side 1.532m

   b) The average of 1.23, 2.45, -6.50 and 9.76

c) The value of the polynomial $a + bx + cx^2$ if x is given by $p - 2q$ and the values of a, b, c, p, q are $1.2, 3.4, 5.6, 7.8$ and 9.0 respectively

d) The surface area of a closed cylinder of height h and radius r for various values as follows:

h	r
1.234	5.678
0.864	9.765
9.364	5.371

2. Define a function f such that $f(x) = x+3 \ (mod \ 5)$. Use methods which elaborate cases as well as a more straightforward method.

3. Define a function to evaluate

$$\binom{m}{n} = \frac{m!}{n! \ (m-n)!}$$

which is a formula for the number of ways of picking out n things from a collection of m of them.

a) Using the factorial function fac as a subsidiary.

b) Using the recurrence relation:

$$\binom{m}{n} = \frac{m}{n}\binom{m-1}{n-1} \qquad \text{for } n > 0$$
$$\binom{m}{0} = 1$$

c) Using the recurrence relation:

$$\binom{m}{n} = \binom{m-1}{n} + \binom{m-1}{n-1} \qquad \text{for } n > 0$$
$$\binom{m}{0} = 1$$

Comment on the different algorithms used. Can the fact that

$$\binom{m}{n} = \binom{m}{m-n}$$

be of any use?

4. What are the values, if any, of the following Haskell expressions:

a) `[1,3,4,6] !! 2`

b) `"ABC" == ['A','B','C']`

c) "ABC" == ('A':'B':'C')

d) "ABC" == ('A':'B':'C':[])

e) "ABC" == ("AB" ++ "C")

f) "ABC" == ('A' ++ "BC")

g) "ABC" == ('A' : "BC")

h) "ABC" == 'A' : "BC"

i) let x = "CDE" in ("AB" ++ x) !! 2

j) let x = "CDE" in ("AB"++[x]) !! 2

k) let x = "CDE" in ["AB",x] !! 1

Now two harder questions which may become easier when you've read the next chapter. Nevertheless try them now.

4. Assume that a √ function is not available. Define one using the Newton-Raphson method which replaces a guess x at $\sqrt{a}$ by

$$\frac{1}{2}\left(x + \frac{a}{x}\right)$$

which, if $a>0$, is guaranteed to be a better guess.

5. Using the above function write a Haskell program that writes out :

```
The square root of 1 is 1.000000000000
The square root of 2 is .............
. . .
. . .
. . .
The square root of 10 is ............
```

Hint: Use show.

Chapter 3

Techniques and Methods

3.1 INTRODUCTION

In this chapter we shall look at some more advanced examples which enter into the spirit of applicative programming. The last chapter introduced the syntax of applicative programs written in Haskell and most of the semantics (meanings) associated with the expressions of the language. Most of that was probably familiar to a greater or lesser extent to imperative programmers though it may not be immediately obvious how to translate algorithms into a purely descriptive form. We shall discuss how to do this kind of translation below but some of the tools and techniques needed for general applicative programming will be described first.

3.2 RECURSIVE FUNCTIONS AND INDUCTION

In the last chapter we introduced two examples of recursive functions (*fac* and *sum*). We shall see many such examples in this chapter (and in the rest of the book: it is central to this style of applicative programming) and we hope that readers feel that this is an easy and natural way to program.

This method usually resolves itself into a way of defining functions by cases and is one heavily used in mathematics and logic. Cases are of two kinds:

a)   *Recursive cases* where we use some *recurrence relation* to calculate the value in terms of applications of the function to other simpler values.

b)   *Base cases* (often only one) which define the function using a more direct definition.

For instance, in the case of factorial, we used the recurrence relation:

$$n! = n \times (n\text{-}1)! \text{ for } n>0$$

35

and the base case:

$$0! = 1$$

A resemblance to *The Principle of Induction* (see for instance [klee52]) can be seen here[1]. Using that principle we *prove* properties (rather than *calculating values*) by their relation to their truth for simpler cases. For a further discussion see chapter 9. The resemblance is not accidental and we shall see later that there is often a duality between proofs of properties of programs and their methods of specification.

As some further examples of this method of programming let us consider some functions for manipulating sets. First we need to think of a way of *representing* (or modelling) sets in Haskell. An obvious method is to use a list to collect the elements together. Of course sets are more than just lists. They have other properties; for instance they don't contain any duplicate members. So, in order that duplicates can be detected, we will need a function which tests for set membership. Using the inductive method we isolate three cases, two of them base cases. First we can say that nothing is a member of the null set.

```
member (x,[]) = False
```

The first argument x is the item we are testing for membership and the second [] the set being searched. The second base case is when we have a non-empty list whose first element is the member we are searching for.

```
member (x,s:ss) | x==s      = True
```

And the last case is the recursive case. Here we also have a non-empty list but the first element isn't equal to the element being tested for. What we do is call the member function recursively to ask if x matches some other member of the set:

```
member (x,s:ss) | otherwise = member (x,ss)
```

and Haskell allows us a shortened form of putting the latter two cases together without repetition of the pattern:

```
member (x,[])               = False
member (x,s:ss) | x==s      = True
                | otherwise = member (x,ss)
```

Once we have membership we can define the functions union and intersection, again using the inductive method:

```
union (s,[])                = s  -- base case
union (s,t:ts) | member (t,s) = union (s,ts)
                     -- 1st recursive case. Ignore duplicates
               | otherwise  = t:union (s,ts)
                     -- 2nd recursive case
```

---

[1]Those not familiar with this basic principle should refer to sections 9.2 *et seq.*.

Now `intersection` is very similar:

```
intersect (s,[])                     = []
intersect (s,t:ts) | member (t,s) = t:intersect (s,ts)
                   | otherwise    = intersect (s,ts)
```

Finally set difference completes our package of useful functions to operate on sets.

```
diff ([],t)                       = []
diff (s:ss,t) | member (s,t)   = diff (ss,t)
              | otherwise      = s:diff (ss,t)
```

Notice how the induction is in this case on the first argument because there is not a good recurrence relationship on the second (but this is of course arbitrary due to choice of argument order).

3.3 COMPLETENESS

We will shortly be introducing what is probably a radically new concept to most newcomers to functional programming — that of a function as an object in its own right, a 'first class citizen'. To motivate these ideas, we first discuss two principles of *completeness* which are applicable to Haskell and many other declarative languages.

The first principle is one of *syntactic completeness*. Its basic idea is that there are no 'special cases' in the syntax of the language. If an expression is syntactically correct then it may be replaced by another (possibly enclosed in parentheses to keep operator priorities correct) and the whole program will still be syntactically correct. Note that this says nothing about the meaning of the program (whether it still computes the same value or not), only about whether it is grammatically correct or not. More formally if e and e' are grammatical Haskell expressions and e'' is a properly formed sub-expression of e, then the expression obtained by replacing e'' by (e') in e is grammatically correct. One might think that this principle was self-evident. Be that as it may many programming languages do not adhere to it as a matter of course. For instance in the Pascal case statement:

```
case <expression> of
<case label list>: <statement>;
<case label list>: <statement>;
.
.
.
end
```

the principle can be seen to be broken in two ways. Firstly the case label lists have to be *constant expressions* rather than general expressions and secondly the statements after the colons cannot be expressions at all, only statements. There really should be no objection to being able to write, for instance,

```
numberoflegs := case animal of
                spider,octopus :8
                horse,cat,dog  :4
                human          :2
                triffid        :3
                end
```

instead of

```
if (animal = spider) or
   (animal = octopus) then numberoflegs := 8 else
if (animal = horse) or
   (animal = cat) or
   (animal = dog) then numberoflegs := 4 else
if (animal = human) then numberoflegs := 2 else
if (animal = triffid) then numberoflegs := 3 else error
```

or

```
sign := case true of
        x<0 : -1
        x=0 :  0
        x>0 :  1
        end
```

instead of

```
if x<0 then sign := -1 else
if x=0 then sign := 0 else
if x>0 then sign := 1 else error
```

All that is needed here is to allow conditional expressions as well as conditional statements and to generalise case tests to allow expressions to be tested against expressions rather than merely against constants.

The objection is sometimes made that this kind of thing makes programs more inefficient; but any good compiler should be able to optimise such things without much difficulty. (The intention here is not to criticise Pascal. It is merely one language among many and was felt to be more likely to be familiar to more readers). The principles of completeness used in Haskell are not applied cleanly in many imperative language designs.

A second (related) completeness principle deals with the meanings or semantics of Haskell expressions and is concerned with what *types* of object may be manipulated in various contexts. There are an infinite number of types of objects in Haskell's data space but they may be grouped into — basic types (integers, floating, truth values, characters), lists, tuples and functions[1]. What *semantic completeness* says is that all these objects have the same *civil rights*. They are all *first class citizens* and their civil rights are (extending those in [turn76]) :

- All objects can be named
- All objects can be the value of some expression.
- All objects can be members of a list.
- All objects can be elements of a tuple.
- All objects can be passed to a function as a parameter.
- All objects can be returned from a function as its result.

Two kinds of object which are second class citizens in Haskell are types and modules. The interested reader should consult [tenn81] and [morr79] for more discussion on the topic of completeness.

---

[1]and, as we shall see later, users may define their own types.

3.4 HIGHER ORDER FUNCTIONS

Probably most readers of this book will be familiar with semantic completeness in terms of the idea of lists of lists, giving names to lists and even functions that take a list as their parameter. What may be less familiar is the idea of lists of functions and functions which return other functions as their result. Note that both completeness principles require these ideas to be allowed. First class citizenship, in particular for functions, is quite central to the ideas of applicative programming presented here. Functions which accept other ones as parameters or which produce a function as their result are called *higher order* functions.

As a first example consider the following Haskell definition:

```
>let succ  = add 1
>    add x = xadder
>              where xadder y = x+y
>in succ 3?

4
what next?
```

In this example the effect of `add x` is to create a function, called locally `xadder`, which adds x to things (i.e. to its parameter y). Thus `succ` is a function which adds 1 to things.

As a slightly less trivial example, consider:

```
>let squadd       = compose (square,successor)
>    square x     = x*x
>    successor x  = x+1
>    compose (f,g) = h where h x = f(g(x))
>in
>squadd 3?

16
what next?
```

The definition of central interest here is that of `compose`. It takes a pair of parameters, `f` and `g`, both of which are functions and returns a third, `h`, whose effect is that of composing the functions. The definition of the function `squadd` gives an example of its use.

Note that what we now have is:

a) A new mechanism for passing two or more parameters to a function. We could write, with the above definition of `add`, for instance, `add(3)(4)` which would give 7 as its result. The `add(3)` produces a function which is then applied to 4. As has been pointed out before we usually prefer to do without brackets wherever we can and write `add 3 4`. This method is sometimes called 'Currying' after the logician Haskell B. Curry who uses it extensively in combinator theory [curr58, curr72]. It first appeared in work by Schönfinkel [scho24].

b) A mechanism for *partially applying* functions. The curried[1] functions
really only take one variable (as with all Haskell functions) and so we
need only mention one variable when calling them. This is clear in the
calls used to define squadd and succ above.

3.5 SYNTAX OF FUNCTION DEFINITIONS

In fact the form of definition used to define compose and add above is so common
in applicative programming, namely

```
f x = g where g y = exp
```

that a special notation is used, consistent with our principle of writing equations
which can be regarded as stated truths. We can write instead:

```
f x y = exp
```

Note that the function g does not appear any more. It was, after all, a kind of
dummy name just as the variable of integration is a dummy in calculus. The
compose and add functions can now be written:

```
compose (f,g) x = f(g(x))
add x y = x+y
```

Note that we are using a mixture of methods of passing more than one parameter in
the compose case — both the Landin and the Curry method. There is no reason
why we shouldn't use the Curry method for both cases and write:

```
compose f g x = f(g(x))
```

The author in fact prefers the curried method as a matter of style and also because it
is slightly more flexible in its ability to allow partial parameterisation. A further
point to note is that the above arguments are somewhat academic since composition
is actually predefined in the Haskell prelude as the operator . (in imitation of ∘). Its
definition is:

```
(f . g) x = f(g x)
```

Thus we could define:

```
compose f g = f.g
```

if we really wanted a function, rather than an operator, to do composition.

----

[1]Perhaps we should say 'Curry'd'.

3.6 SIMULATION OF A STACK

As a further slightly more ambitious example let us consider the simulation of a calculating machine which uses a stack for working storage for its intermediate results. It would seem reasonable to use lists to implement stacks so that we could, for instance represent the stack:

```
   |                 |
   |                 |
   |-----------------|
   |      7.0        |
   |-----------------|
   |     -3.2        |
   |-----------------|
   |      2.1        |
   |_____|
```

by using the list [7.0 , -3.2 , 2.1]. It is convenient to use the left hand end of the list as the top of the stack because it is easy to add and delete elements there using the operator : .

Some operations that we want to perform on stacks are:

1. Push a number onto a stack.

2. Pop two elements, add them, and push the result back again.

3. As 2. but subtract.

4. As 2. but multiply.

5. As 2. but divide.

6. Create an empty stack.

7. Pop an element off a stack.

In a functional environment these operations will be framed as functions and we need to determine what kinds of arguments each takes and what it returns as results. The push operation takes a number to be pushed as its argument and it will also have to know which stack to push it onto. This will be provided by a second argument. The function will return as its result the stack as modified by the push operation. We can write the function in one of two ways, either using a tuple for the arguments:

```
push (x,stk) = x:stk
```

or, using currying:

```
push x stk = x:stk
```

These demonstrate the two methods of passing more than one parameter to a function; the first by wrapping up x and stk in a pair of elements and passing that single argument to push; and the second by arranging that push returns a function which is then to be applied to stk to return a stack as its result. For reasons which will become apparent below we will use the curried version.

It can be shown that the types of the two versions of push have isomorphic domains. Given *any* function f :: (A,B) -> C[1] there is a corresponding function g :: A -> (B -> C) such that f(a,b)=g(a)(b) and *vice-versa*. In fact we can, in Haskell, write a function curry which transforms f into g and another landin that transforms g into f.

```
curry f  = g where g a b = f(a,b)
landin g = f where f(a,b) = g a b
```

or

```
curry f a b   = f(a,b)
landin g(a,b) = g a b
```

The types of add, subtract, multiply and divide are Stack -> Stack and those of emptystack and pop are Stack and Stack -> Float respectively.

The arithmetic functions are just as easy to define. Each of them is a stack manipulating function and needs no extra information:

```
add       (x:y:stk) = y+x:stk
subtract  (x:y:stk) = y-x:stk
multiply  (x:y:stk) = y*x:stk
divide    (x:y:stk) = y/x:stk
```

Note how we use the pattern matching x:y:stk to identify the top two members of the stack x and y and the remainder stk (as well as checking that the stack has at least two elements on it) and then use : again on the right to put the result back on the stack.

We need a way of creating an empty stack and a method of getting an element off a stack when the calculation has been finished. These are easily defined by:

```
emptystack = []
pop [single] = single
```

The second of these is a special case of a more general function that we could have defined for taking elements off the stack when it has more than one member. In such a case we would want to return not only the top element but the state of the remaining stack:

```
pop (top:rest) = (top,rest)
```

However we will use the simpler version as this stack simulation *always* leaves a single element on the stack after a calculation has been done.

---

[1]If a function f maps objects of type T1 to objects of type T2, we can write this in Haskell as f::T1 -> T2

Having defined these functions we can now use them to do simple sums. For instance:

$$12.2 * (7.1 / 6.7 - 4.3) + 2.2$$

has as its reverse Polish [rand64]

$$12.2 \ 7.1 \ 6.7 \ / \ 4.3 \ - \ * \ 2.2 \ +$$

and we could translate that into a series of stack operations, naively naming every intermediate result, by using the Haskell program:

```
let s0 = emptystack
    s1 = push 12.2 s0
    s2 = push 7.1 s1
    s3 = push 6.7 s2
    s4 = divide s3
    s5 = push 4.3 s4
    s6 = subtract s5
    s7 = multiply s6
    s8 = push 2.2 s7
    stack = add s8

in pop stack
```

Each of the names `si` shows a *state* of the stack being modelled as each manipulation is done on it. It is as well to note that this series of definitions is still static and timeless even though we are modelling a dynamic situation. In particular the definitions could be made in any order (although that would of course make the program much more difficult to understand). They do *not* logically take place one after another but are simultaneous though it is open to us to conceive of them as being execution steps.

A more acceptable way of doing this would be to miss out the intermediate states in their explicitly named form — the `si` — and just write:

```
pop(add(push 2.2(multiply(subtract(
    push 4.3(divide(push 6.7(
        push 7.1(push 12.2 emptystack))))))))))
```

which is more compact but suffers from the fact that it must be read from right to left.

Remembering that each of `push 12.2`, `push 7.1` etc. is a function and that we have the possibility of combining functions by composition, we see that what we want to do is:

```
let f % g    = g . f
    actionson = push 12.2 %
                push 7.1 %
                push 6.7 %
                divide %
                push 4.3 %
                subtract %
                multiply %
                push 2.2 %
                add
in pop (actionson emptystack)
```

3.7 MODELLING CONVENTIONAL PROGRAMMING

The preceding example — modelling the states of a stack — should give us a clue as to how to set about 'translating' programs expressed in a procedural language such as Pascal say into applicative ones. The element which is missing in applicative programming is in general a *store* which can be changed. However, in dire circumstances the store can always be *modelled*. That is what we did above with the dynamic element, the stack, which is after all a particular kind of store. We wrote several stack transforming functions and simulated the stack's changing nature by applying these functions to get *new* stacks.

It is not our aim to teach users to write functional programs by straight translation of procedural programs. It is to be expected that users will gain a technique for expressing algorithms applicatively *from scratch* without first writing them in a procedural language or even thinking of them in procedural terms. Nevertheless users of Pascal, C and other store based languages may, at first, be mystified as to how to express algorithms which may seem fundamentally store based.

Perhaps the archetypical construct of procedural languages is the `while` loop.

```
while <test> do <command>
```

Here the `<command>` is specifically designed to have a *side effect* which is carried out repeatedly until the `<test>` is no longer satisfied. This construct is so geared to the traditional imperative style of programming that one wonders at first where to start in chosing an applicative equivalent. What building block could we possibly replace it with? The answer is that, instead of changing things, we can repeatedly describe new things in terms of old ones by applying functions. Consider then a general function:

```
while test f x
```

The `test` parameter will be a predicate function which is applied to `x`, `f x`, `f (f x)`, `f (f (f x))` .... The first of these $f^n x$ which gives the value `False` when `test` is applied to it (i.e. the first that fails the test) will be the value of the whole loop. We can define this in Haskell by:

```
while test f x | test x    = while test f (f x)
               | otherwise = x
```

As an example of the use of `while` let us take a simple procedural algorithm and see how it can be written in applicative form. The Pascal function

```
function quot(i,j:integer):integer;
var q:integer;
begin   q := 0;
        while (i >= j) do
        begin   q := q + 1;
                i := i - j
        end;
        quot := q
end;
```

calculates the quotient of two integers by repeated subtraction. We first give a directly produced Haskell function which expresses the same algorithm:

```
quot (i,j) | i >= j    = quot (i-j,j) + 1
           | otherwise = 0
```

But we can also use our `while` function to code the algorithm in the following way. Two things are changing as the Pascal version of the algorithm proceeds, i and q. In Haskell we can model this small piece of store by wrapping them up together as a pair of elements — (i, q) — and it is this that must be transformed and tested. The loop is then embedded in the function as a whole:

```
quot (i,j) = lastq
          where (lasti,lastq)     =
                    (while notfinished transform (i,0))
                notfinished (i,q) = i >= j
                transform   (i,q) = (i-j,q+1)
```

The use of the pair (i, 0) initialises our small piece of simulated store and the `transform` function carries out the storage changes represented by the two assignments in the Pascal loop. Note the use of the pattern (lasti,lastq) to extract the answer once all the necessary transformation has been done. Another thing to notice is that j is used in the two functions `notfinished` and `transform` even though it is not a parameter of either of them. We could have made it a parameter but it is not necessary to do so as it is not part of the state vector which we are modelling.

It should be clear from this example that the use of `while` is only needed as a last resort or possibly to make clear models of processes involving stored quantities and imperatives. Its use *will* cope with all kinds of loops (even ones with non-local variables being assigned to — this requires a little thought) but there is often a more straightforward method which is much simpler.

3.8 NON-LOCAL VARIABLES

If we look at the more direct first solution we gave to the quotient problem, we see that one of the parameters, j, doesn't change as the recursion proceeds. This suggests that we could make j non-local to the central loop and cut down on the amount of parameter passing going on:

```
quot (i,j) = quot' i where
          quot' x | x >= j    = quot' (x-j)
                  | otherwise = 0
```

This technique of factoring common subexpressions out of loops will be familiar to many imperative programmers. We give a word of warning however. Some implementations of functional programming languages use a program transformation technique called λ-lifting to optimise performance for particular hardware by putting non-local parameters back into parameter lists behind the backs of programmers. We shall see this technique and the reasons for using it in section 7.7 but suffice it to say that 'obvious' optimisation techniques by users may not be so clearly advantageous as they at first seem.

3.9 ACCUMULATING RESULTS

A common method of functional programming involves the idea that an answer can
be accumulated piece by piece as a calculation progresses. In the above example,
for example, the answer is accumulated by adding 1 to it every time round the loop
(whether we use a direct method or use the `while` function).

There is a common technique which allows the accumulation of results in one of the
parameters. Here is an alternative version of the division routine which first passes
the calculation on to a subsidiary function `quot'` whose second parameter starts at 0
and gets 1 added to it each time the function is called:

```
quot(i,j) = quot'(i,0)
            where quot'(x,y) | x >= j    = quot'(x-j,y+1)
                             | otherwise = y
```

When $x < j$, the second parameter contains the answer which is returned.

Here is a version of the union function which accumulates its result:

```
union s []                    = s
union s (t:tt) | member t s = union s t
               | otherwise  = union (t:s) tt
```

As another example, here is the factorial function written using an accumulating
parameter:

```
fact n = fact'(n,1)
         where fact'(0,ans) = ans
               fact'(n,ans) = fact'(n-1,n*ans)
```

If it is not immediately clear how these functions are working, a little hand-
simulation may add light. For example:

```
fact 4 = fact'(4,1)
       = fact'(3,4)
       = fact'(2,12)
       = fact'(1,24)
       = fact'(0,24)
       = 24
```

In the examples above, it may be commented that both the `quot` and the `fact`
functions seem more contrived than their original versions. However accumulation
sometimes offers substantial improvements in performance as is demonstrated by
the following example. Consider how we might write a function for reversing the
elements in a list. Perhaps the most obvious way would be to reverse the tail of the
list recursively and then buckle the head onto the end of the result:

```
reverse [] = []
reverse (h:t) = reverse t ++ [h]
```

This method, though expressive, is inefficient because the ++ operation is invoked
and appending is itself an operation which is defined recursively, for instance by:

```
[]      ++ y = y
(h:t)   ++ y = h:(t ++ y)
```

and this means that each of the reversed sub-lists will be traversed (twice) to add a single element to its end:

```
reverse [1,2,3] = reverse [2,3] ++ [1]         -- traverse [1.2.3]
                = (reverse [3] ++ [2]) ++ [1]
                = ((reverse [] ++ [3]) ++ [2]) ++ [1]
                = (([] ++ [3]) ++ [2]) ++ [1]
                = ([3] ++ [2]) ++ [1]          -- traverse [3]
                = (3:([] ++ [2])) ++ [1]
                = (3:[2]) ++ [1]               -- and back
                = [3,2] ++ [1]                 -- traverse [3,2]
                = 3:([2] ++ [1])
                = 3:(2:([] ++ [1]))
                = 3:2:[1]                      -- and back
                = 3:[2,1]
                = [3,2,1]
```

But, by using an accumulating parameter, we can improve this considerably:

```
reverse x = pour x []
            where pour []     ans = ans
                  pour (h:t)  ans = pour t (h:ans)
```

We have called the subsidiary function `pour` as it can be imagined that we are pouring list elements from one parameter to the other:

```
reverse [1,2,3] = pour [1,2,3] []
                = pour [2,3] [1]
                = pour [3] [2,1]
                = pour [] [3,2,1]
                = [3,2,1]
```

A further comment about this style of parameters being used as accumulators is that the functions written this way tend to be *tail recursive*. That is to say, the last thing that they do is to call another function (often themselves). Many implementations of functional languages make use of this property to optimise the code generated by their compilers. Instead of *calling* the second function and then returning from two functions in quick succession, the first function *jumps* directly to the second and one return at the end returns from both functions at the same time. Note however that, like the non-local variable factorisation technique described in the last section, the efficacy of tail recursion relies on the implementation. Moral: Functional programming languages are meant to be tools for rapid prototyping. Users should not spend too much time 'improving' their programs by hand while probably making them more obscure and possibly less efficient. Many such improvements can be made automatically or semi-automatically by the compiling system which knows which ones really are improvements. We shall talk about program transformation in chapter 10.

3.10 MAPS, FILTERS AND FOLDS

The next group of techniques of applicative programming that we explore is connected with the kind of iteration done by `while` but in these cases the iteration is specifically over given data structures.

3.10.1 Maps

A common requirement in computing is to do something to every element of an `array` or other data structure. This is called *iteration* over the structure and manifests itself in functional programming as a function which, given one structure, describes another, each of the elements of the resultant bearing some functional relationship to the corresponding elements of the original.

For a one dimensional array modelled by a Haskell list this is not hard. We call the function which abstracts this idea `map`. It takes a function, `f` say, which transforms individual elements and produces as its result another function `map f` which transforms a whole list element by element. Thus for instance `map square` would transform `[1,3,5,7]` into `[1,9,25,49]` if `square` were to be defined by:

```
square x = x*x
```

The definition of `map` is by induction on the lists it has to work with. The base case is the empty list. Otherwise an obvious induction applies `f`, its subject function, to the head of the list and `map f` to the tail:

```
map f []    = []
map f (h:t) = f h : map f t
```

With this definition we can now indeed say:

```
let squareall = map square
    square x = x*x
in
squareall [1,3,5,7]
```

and get `[1,9,25,49]` as the result.

As a slightly more ambitious example let us see how we might write a matrix transposition function. If we are to represent a vector as a list of elements then a matrix can naturally be represented by a list of vectors. When faced with such a matrix, `transpose` sees a list of rows. To construct the first row of the result it needs the first element of each of those rows and it can get them by using `map` to do selection. The base case is encountered when none of the rows have anything in them:

```
transpose ([]:rest) = []
transpose x         = map hd x : transpose (map tl x)
```

where `hd` and `tl` are functions predefined as:

```
hd (p:_) = p    -- note that Haskell allows _ as a 'don't care'
tl (_:q) = q    -- pattern. No binding is made to _
```

It is perhaps easier to see what is happening here with an example:

```
transpose [[1,2],[3,4],[5,6]]
         = [1,3,5]:transpose[[2],[4],[6]]
         = [1,3,5]:[2,4,6]:transpose[[],[],[]]
         = [1,3,5]:[2,4,6]:[]
         = [[1,3,5],[2,4,6]]
```

The function transpose is sometimes called zip because if it is applied to a list of two rows it zips the rows together producing a single list each member of which consists of two elements joined together in a 2-list.

We can now use transpose to write a vector addition function. The two vectors to be added are joined together to make a matrix with two rows. This is transposed using the function developed above to get a vector of 2-lists each of which represents a pair of objects to be added together. This list of additions can itself be done using map.

```
vectoradd xs ys = map add (transpose [xs,ys])
                  where add[x,y] = x+y
```

This is a slightly convoluted way of doing vector addition designed principally to show off the properties of map. A more sensible way would be to use a version of map which takes more than one argument:

```
map2 f []      []      = []
map2 f (h1:t1) (h2:t2) = f h1 h2 : map2 f t1 t2
```

and then define:

```
vectoradd = map2 add
            where add x y = x+y
```

3.10.2 Filters

Filters are another way of traversing lists but instead of carrying out a function on each member of the list they pick out of the list all those elements which satisfy a particular property. Such a property is represented by a function which yields True or False depending on whether its argument has the property or not. For instance we would like

```
filter negative [1, -5, -6, 3, 4, 0]
```

to yield [-5, -6] in the presence of the definition

```
negative x = x<0
```

The definition of filter is very similar to that of map, but instead of applying its subject function to each element of a list to generate a new list element, it is applied to see if that element should be included in the new list:

```
filter pred [] = []
filter pred (h:t) | pred h     = h:rest
                  | otherwise = rest
                              where rest = filter pred t
```

Sometimes it is desirable to filter out all the elements that satisfy the property instead of keeping them in. We can do this with `filter` itself:

```
remove p = filter (not.p)
```

though we could, of course, make a separate definition:

```
remove p [] = []
remove p (h:t) | p h       = rest
               | otherwise = h:rest
                           where rest = remove p t
```

Sometimes we want to use `filter` and `remove` simultaneously so that we get two lists returned, one of elements with a property and the other of elements without it. One way of defining a function to do this is:

```
partition p []    = ([],[])
partition p (h:t) | p h       = (h:yesses , nos)
                  | otherwise = (yesses , h:nos)
                  where
                  (yesses , nos) = partition p t
```

For example let us use `partition` to sort a list into order using Hoare's method known as *quicksort* [hoar62]. This method partitions the elements to be sorted into two lists, those less than and those greater than or equal to a particular element. Often the first element is chosen as this *pivot* element. The two partitions are then sorted recursively by quicksort itself and the resulting parts stuck together again in the right order:

```
quicksort [] = []
quicksort (h:t) =
     quicksort left ++
     h : quicksort right
     where (left,right) = partition (< h) t
```

This solution exhibits a new feature of Haskell — the use of a *section*. If · is an infix operator, then (· x) is a function which puts its argument before the ·, in other words, it is as if we had made the definition:

```
(· x) y = y · x
```

Thus (< h) in quicksort is a function which tests if its argument is less than h and it is this function that `quicksort` partitions with respect to.

In a similar fashion, we can write (x ·) with the 'definition'

```
(x ·) y = x · y
```

We are even allowed to abstract operators from both their arguments and write (·) x y instead of x · y. In a similar manner, functions of two arguments may be used as infix operators if placed inside back-quotes. We saw this in use when we introduced `div`, `rem`, ... in chapter 2. Instead of x `div` y we can say div x y because `div` is just a (curried) function of two variables.

The function `quicksort` will sort a list of type [t] so long as type t has an ordering relation < defined on it. It is an *overloaded* function. We shall discuss overloading more fully in chapter 4.

3.10.3 Folds

A final pair of list traversing functions are `foldl` and `foldr`. Consider the following definitions:

```
addup      []     = 0
addup      (h:t)  = h+addup t
multiply   []     = 1
multiply   (h:t)  = h*multiply t
unite      []     = []
unite      (h:t)  = union h (unite t)
     -- union is a curried form of the one
     -- given near the beginning of the chapter
```

In each case we want to collapse a list by placing an operator between the elements of the list.

$$l_1 + l_2 + \ldots + l_n$$
$$l_1 \times l_2 \times \ldots \times l_n$$
$$l_1 \cup l_2 \cup \ldots \cup l_n$$

In the first two cases the operator was a standard Haskell infixed binary operator and in the third it was a curried function, `union`, of two variables but there is no essential difference between the two: infixed operations can always be represented by curried functions of two variables as we saw above.

Since this action of operator embedding is a commonly used one, we can provide it as a tool by abstracting the concept and writing a function `foldr` which takes a general binary operator and inserts it between the elements of the list. We have to be a little careful about what we do when we operate on an empty list and when the inserted operator is not associative. The first of these problems can be dealt with by considering what the logical *identity* of the binary operator is. Since 0 is the identity of addition (adding 0 has no effect — it is like the identity function) it is the initial value for adding up numbers. When we multiply the starting value will be 1 and when we unite the initial value will be the empty set. These identities provide the answers in the base cases when we are considering empty lists. The general `foldr` function must be supplied with the identity and can be defined as follows:

```
foldr infix id []    = id
foldr infix id (h:t) = h `infix` (foldr infix id t)
```

and we can now define

```
addup = foldr (+) 0
multiply = foldr (*) 1
unite = foldr union []
```

This folding function is called `foldr` because it folds up lists from the right. i.e., we are calculating:

$$l_1 + (l_2 + (\ldots + (l_n + 0)\ldots))$$
$$l_1 \times (l_2 \times (\ldots \times (l_n \times 1)\ldots))$$
$$l_1 \cup (l_2 \cup (\ldots \cup (l_n \cup \varnothing)\ldots))$$

Because addition, multiplication and union are associative operations, this is of no great importance here, but it might be in the general case. If a left associative version is required we define:

```
foldl infix id []    = id
foldl infix id (h:t) = foldl infix (h `infix` id) t
```

Note how `id` is being used as an accumulating parameter here.

Burge [burg75a, burg75b] defines a slightly more ambitious kind of fold which he calls `list1`. (A left associative version called `list2` is also discussed). This function not only applies an infixed operator between all the elements but also applies a prefixed operator to all the elements of the list first:

```
list1 id infix prefix [] = id
list1 id infix prefix (h:t) =
        (prefix h) `infix` (list1 id infix prefix t)
```

With this function a number of other functions (some of which we have already seen) can be defined. In the following `i` is the identity function (defined by `i x = x` and `k` is defined by `k x y = x` — that is `k x` is the function which returns the constant `x` whatever it is applied to.

```
sum        = list1 0  (+)   i
product    = list1 1  (*)   i
x (++) y   = list1 y  (:)   i      x
concat     = list1 [] (++)  i
map        = list1 [] (:)
length     = list1 0  (+)   (k 1)
```

3.11 LIST COMPREHENSIONS

Maps and filters constitute such an important concept that they merit a notation of their own. The notation is that of Zermello-Fränkel set abstraction [frae53], which allows mathematicians to define sets based on the members of other already existing sets. It was originally introduced into KRC [turn81a, turn82a], a functional language developed by Turner and he called expressions in the notation *set expressions*. They are now more often known now as *list comprehensions*. The notation is based on the idea that one is allowed to write expressions of the form:

```
[ f x | x <- s , p x ]
```

which means 'The list of all `f x` where `x` is drawn from the list `s` and condition `p x` is satisfied'. As can be seen, a list comprehension can incorporate both a map from all members, `x` of `s` to `f x`, but also a filter (called a *guard*) to ensure that `p x` is satisfied for each element that is included in the constructed list. These are both optional so that, for instance, we could filter out all the odd elements from a list by:

```
[ x | x <- s , even x ]
```

and we could square every element in a list with

```
[ x * x | x <- s ]
```

In fact we can *define* the functions map and filter by

```
map f s    = [ f y | y <- s ]
filter p s = [ y | y <- s , p y ]
```

and so we can either think of list comprehensions being defined in terms of maps and filters or *vice versa*.

We can use several *generators* (<-) and guards separated by , in a list comprehension so that, for instance:

```
[ (n*n-m*m,2*n*m,n*n+m*m) | n <- [2 .. 100] ,
                            m <- [1 .. n-1] ]
```

makes a list of some of the Pythagorean triples (x,y,z) such that $x^2+y^2==z^2$. ([a .. b] is a shorthand allowed in Haskell for the list [a, a+1, … ,b]). If gcd is a function which finds the greatest common divisor of two integers, then by adding two guards, we can eliminate triples which have common divisors:

```
[ (n*n-m*m,2*n*m,n*n+m*m) | n <- [2 .. 100] ,
                            m <- [1 .. n-1] ,
                            gcd n m = 1 ,
                            odd (m+n) ]
```

This mechanism represents a new kind of *abstraction*. Note that lists of this kind contain *dummy variables* (x, y, z, m and n in the above examples) and that these variables have a *scope* which is the expression before the | and after the , which appears after the appropriate generator. In other words, the generators come into play from left to right.

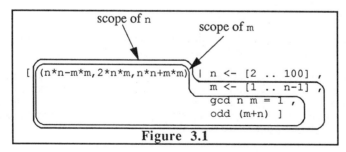

Figure 3.1

In fact the variables defined in the generators can be generalised to pattern matches so that, for instance:

```
[ x+y | [x,y] <- s ]
```

takes all the elements of list s which are pairs of elements and adds their components. Any members of s which are not 2-lists are ignored (filtered out).

As a slightly more ambitious example let us take the `quicksort` function given above and rewrite it making use of comprehensions

```
quicksort [] = []
quicksort (h:t) = quicksort [ x | x <- t , x <= h ] ++
           h : quicksort [ x | x <- t , x > h ]
```

We shall return to comprehensions in section 7.4 where lazy evaluation is considered.

3.11.1 Translation to simpler Haskell

The list comprehension notation can be considered, of course, as a further sugaring of Haskell (which can itself be viewed as a sugaring of λ-Calculus); and it is easy to see, at least informally, how to translate comprehensions into simpler Haskell. The expression:

```
[ e | p <- s ]
```

where p is a pattern and e is an expression involving the variables in p and s is any expression, can roughly[1] be translated into

```
let fn p = e in map fn s
```

using a suitably chosen name `fn` which does not interfere with those already present in the original expression. Similarly, guards can be coped with by using the `filter` function.

```
[ e | p <- s , g ]
```

translates approximately into

```
let fn p   = e
    pred p = g
in map fn (filter pred s)
```

The translation of expressions which involve more than one generator or guard is only a little harder and we leave this as an exercise for the reader.

Another more accurate way of looking at the semantics of list comprehensions is to think of the rules which could be used to rewrite them to simpler expressions. Such rules are not difficult to give and are similar to writing definitions of functions. Let us consider guards first. If a guard evaluates to `True`, then computation can proceed but if it is `False` the resulting list is empty:

```
[exp | False , gs]  ⇒ []
[exp | True  , gs]  ⇒ [exp | gs]
```

---

[1]This is not an exact translation and does not capture the idea that only elements of s which match the pattern are selected. For an accurate version, see below.

where further guards and/or generators are represented by `gs`. For generators again there are two cases. Either (the base case) we have run out of elements to draw from or (inductive case) there are still elements to be used for generation of the new list. The former case is like having a `False` guard — it terminates the computation. The latter is slightly more complicated as it is where the hard work takes place:

```
[exp | pat <- []  , gs] ⇒ []
[exp | pat <- h:t , gs] ⇒ ([exp | gs] where pat = h) ++
                           [exp | pat <- t , gs]
```

Finally, if there are no more guards or generators, computation terminates:

```
[exp | ] ⇒ [exp]
```

3.12 SUMMARY

In this chapter we have examined some of the chief stylistic techniques used in applicative programming. These are dominated by the method of inductive case analysis which makes heavy use of recurrence relations. Another technique heavily used is that of curried functions. This springs quite naturally from the fact that Haskell satisfies completeness principles.

We saw that a number of *ad hoc* techniques can be used to implement programs in various ways. In particular tail recursion and accumulating parameters were discussed. We also discussed in basic terms the methods that could be used for translating imperative programs into applicative ones by modelling store.

A number of functions for iterating along lists were described. These did mapping, folding and filtering. Finally we presented the list comprehension notation based on ZF set expressions which is a natural way to express maps and filters and showed how simple examples can be transformed to more conventional Haskell.

3.13. EXERCISES

Many of the following exercises use functions which have been described in the text and others that are given in Appendix B which lists the Haskell prelude. This contains many useful functions which are usually preloaded when the system is entered. Some of the answers to the exercises will be found among the functions given there.

1.   What are the values of:

a) `map (+ 1) [1,0,-1,3]`

b) `map reverse ["ABLE","WAS","I","ERE","I","SAW","ELBA"]`

c)
```
let sum = fold (+) 0
    in
    map sum (transpose [[1,2,3],
                        [4,5,6],
```

```
                            [7,8,9]] )
```

d)
```
   let transform [a]     = [a]
       transform (a:b:c) = a+b : c
       x = [1,2,3]
       ok [x]    = False
       ok (h:t) = True
   in while ok transform x
```

e)
```
   let double = w (+)
          w f x = f x x
   in double 3
```

2.   a)   Write a function which makes a copy of a list.

   b) Is there ever any need to use a function which makes a copy of a list?

3.   Write a function which makes a copy of a list of numbers except that all negative ones are replaced by zero.

4.   Write a curried function `take` such that `take` n is a function which, applied to a list, returns the first n elements of the list, or the whole list if it's not long enough. Similarly, write `drop` which throws away the first n elements, returning the remainder.

5.   Write a function which finds the greatest common divisor (g.c.d. — sometimes known as the highest common factor or h.c.f.) of its two arguments. Write another which takes a list of numbers and finds the g.c.d. of all its members.

6.   Write a function `length` that computes the length of a list (without using `listl` as in the text of the chapter).

7.   Write a function `for` which takes three arguments m , n and f and returns the list `[f(m), f(m+1), ... ,f(n)]`

8.   Define a function which selects the sub-list of a list starting at the m'th element and ending at the n'th. You can use `for` to do this. Try with and without it.

9.   a) Write a function `merge` which takes a list of sorted sequences and merges them into a single sorted sequence.

   b) Hence write a function to sort a sequence of values.

10.   Use a filter to write a function which calculates the difference between two sets a different way from that given near the start of the chapter.

11.   Review your answers to other questions in this set of exercises in the light of the ZF notation.

12.   Write a function which removes the nth member of a list. Could a filter be used here?

13. Write a function to find the last element of a list.

14. Write an operator ! ! ! which has the same effect as ! ! but also indexes from the right hand end of the list if given a negative argument. Thus [1,3,5,6] !!! 0 = 1 and [1,3,5,6] !!! (-1) = 6.

15. Write a function which converts an integer to a string of digits which represent it in number base n.

16. Write a function format which takes two arguments — a format control string and a list of strings to be formatted. The result should be a string which is basically a copy of the control string but with the following replacements:

    %% ⇒ %
    %n ⇒ a new line
    %p ⇒ a new page
    %s ⇒ a space
    %x ⇒ an object from the list to be formatted
    %ln ⇒ an object left justified in a field of length n
    %cn ⇒ an object centred in a field of length n
    %rn ⇒ an object right justified in a field of length n

    For instance

    ```
    let out = format "[1]%s%x%s|%l5|%c5|%r5%n%n[2]"
    in out ["3","33","33","33"]
    ```

    would produce

    ```
    [1].3.|33...|.33..|...33

    [2]
    ```

    where . has been used here to make spaces visible.

17. An association list is a model of an associative store and connects values with names (or addresses). It can be represented by a list of pairs each being a name and its associated value. Invent functions lookup and update which interrogate and change the store (the latter by producing a new store — remember that we can't really change anything when programming applicatively).

18. Write a function that justifies text (given as a string) in a given column width by inserting or deleting spaces or new lines to make left and right margins align properly. You should initially assume that each character in text will occupy the same amount of space. Add any bells and whistles you can think of.

19. Write a package of functions which does multi-length integer arithmetic by holding numbers as strings of digits in some convenient number base.

20.   Write a package (using that in the above example) to do rational arithmetic.
        Numbers could be held as numerator-denominator pairs.

Chapter 4

Types

4.1 INTRODUCTION

Up till now, we have been working with a rather restricted view of Haskell's types. We shall now look at some of the more sophisticated features of the language's type system which add considerable power and facility to the Haskell user's toolset.

Many modern programming languages (functional and otherwise) have rich type systems and the types in a program are usually checked statically; that is, at compile time the types of objects are checked or even inferred and this ensures that little or no type checking need be done at run time. There is one particular feature of many functional programming languages, Haskell included, which interacts strongly with a static typing regime and that is pattern matching. We have used the pattern matching facilities available in Haskell for distinguishing cells constructed with a : from [] cells (see for instance section 3.2 and the definitions of set operators) and for separating out equations dealing with particular constants as base cases (e.g. section 2.5). A generalisation of this pattern matching facility is however available together with inductive methods of definition by pattern matching and, as we shall see (in chapter 9), on proving correctness. This generalisation is discussed below in some detail.

In addition, this is the correct time to talk about types in greater generality and also about the idea of *type inference* in functional languages. These concepts are also pertinent to many imperative languages. The ideas of static typing are an important pedagogical tool in *any* programming language as they allow the detection of many programmer errors at compile time. A further reason for their importance is that it is possible to compile much more efficient code for evaluating objects whose types are known early, because information of this kind may be used to optimise the code produced. As a simple example the addition of two numbers need not have any safeguards compiled in to make sure that they *are* numbers as this will already have been checked at compile time.

59

4.2 TYPE OPERATORS

Let us start by recapitulating what we know already about the Haskell type system. The base types include integers (`Int`), booleans (`Bool`), floating point numbers (`Float`) and characters (`Char`).

If a function f maps arguments of type A to results of type B, we write the type of f as $A \rightarrow B$ and we write

$$f \in A \rightarrow B \quad \text{or} f : A \rightarrow B$$

Haskell normally deduces the types of objects and there is often no need for users to write their types, but if they wish to, the symbol `::` is used to assert type membership (because `:` is already reserved for list construction).

```
f :: A -> B
```

The operator `->` is being used to *construct* a new type from two old ones. Clearly type expressions of an arbitrary complexity can be made in this way. It has become conventional to specify the type of a curried function without the use of brackets whenever possible so that we might write:

```
plus :: Float -> Float -> Float
```

meaning

```
plus :: Float -> (Float -> Float)
```

Another Haskell type operator in Haskell is that of Cartesian product. Given two types `A` and `B` we can talk about pairs whose first element is an `A` and whose second is a `B`. Clearly this can be extended to triples, quadruples, and so on and we want to be able to mention the types of such tuples. For the Cartesian product of types `A1`, `A2`, ... `An` we write `(A1,A2, ... An)` (some languages use the concrete syntax `A1*A2* ...*An` and mathematics uses $A_1 \times A_2 \times ... \times A_n$. Haskell tries to use a similar concrete syntax for types as it does for the objects that belong to these types).

We shall see in section 4.4 on algebraic types that we can think of lists of objects as being constructed using Cartesian product types and function types. Nevertheless we often find it useful to have a built-in type constructor for making list types. We have seen that we write `[T]` for the type of a homogeneous list whose elements are all of type `T`. Heterogeneous lists, where different elements can have different types, are not allowed in Haskell[1]. Fixed format structures or records which contain objects of different types can be implemented as Cartesian tuples as shown in the last paragraph or by using algebraic types as we shall see in section 4.4.

---

[1]These can be dealt with by users explicitly specifying the different kinds of object allowed in a list and then making their union into an algebraic type.

4.3 POLYMORPHIC TYPES

Consider a function `and` which takes a list of booleans and returns the fold of the operation `(&&)` on them. Clearly according to the scheme described above it has type

```
[Bool] -> Bool
```

But some functions have a more general type than this. What is the type of the function `length` which finds the length of a list? Clearly the result obtained when the function is applied (the range) is an integer, but the original list can be a (homogeneous) list of objects of any kind, α say. We therefore say that it has type

```
[alpha] -> Int
```

We say that the type is *polymorphic* (many shaped) as opposed to *monomorphic* (uniquely shaped) as `and` is. There are two possible ways of regarding a polymorphic function such as `length`. We can either think of it as having an infinite number of types of which `[Int] -> Int`, `[Bool] -> Int` and `[Float -> Float] -> Int` are just three examples. We say that, for all α, `length` has type `[α] -> Int`. Alternatively, we can build the polymorphism into the syntactic form of the type and say that `length` has one type written:

```
∀ α . [α] -> Int
```

The difference between the two approaches is a philosophical one and we shall gloss over it though we will incline to the former way of thinking in this text and the ∀ is certainly not written explicitly in Haskell.

As another example, the `map` function is doubly polymorphic in that it applies a function of type `alpha -> beta` to a list of `alpha`'s getting a list of `beta`'s as result and consequently `map` has type:

```
(alpha -> beta) -> [alpha] -> [beta]
```

The exercises given at the end of this chapter invite you to work out the types of some other common functions and we shall see how such types can be inferred in section 4.7.

The above kind of polymorphism is often called *parametric polymorphism* [stra67] and it is only one of a number of different kinds of polymorphism. We shall also be concerned here with a kind known as *ad-hoc polymorphism*. This is used when a function (or more commonly an infixed operator) is used in a number of different ways with different types. For instance it is common practice in many different programming languages to *overload* the arithmetic operators so that they apply equally well to integers and floating point numbers (and sometimes to other arithmetic types such as complex numbers). On the other hand we cannot parameterise this kind of polymorphism as easily since the functions involved apply to a finite number of types. We can say that + is of type `Int -> Int -> Int` *and* of type `Float -> Float -> Float` *and* of type `Complex -> Complex -> Complex`. We shall see how this type of polymorphism can be handled in a regular way in section 4.7.

4.3.1 New Type Names

Using the operations we have discussed above, users of Haskell are allowed to give
new names to types by writing a definition such as the following:

```
type String = [ Char ]
```

Such *type synonyms* may be parametrised to allow the definition of new type
constructors. For instance, in section 3.6 we described the modelling of a stack by
using lists. Our programs for stack manipulation would be better described in terms
of stacks rather than lists:

```
type Stack alpha = [ alpha ]
```

Here `alpha` is a *type variable* which can be substituted by a type expression,
allowing, for instance:

```
type Workstack = Stack Float
```

and we can then describe a function such as `push`, which we encountered in section
3.6 for pushing a floating point value onto a stack, as having type:

```
push :: Float -> Workstack -> Workstack
```

4.4 ALGEBRAIC TYPES

The above example suggests that users can have a different conceptual idea of the
type of objects they were using from the actual types being used to build their
model solution. Above we merely gave a new name to an old type. *Algebraic types*
allow a user to express a larger range of ideas *directly*, instead of having to write a
solution which uses a perhaps unnatural implicit mapping between reality and
model.

It is possible to model many kinds of data structures using simple Haskell head-tail
(cons) lists. For instance, we can implement arrays as lists of cells joined through
their tails. But it is difficult if not impossible, for example, to implement labelled
binary trees by using lists or tuples. The limitation arises because lists are
constrained to be homogeneous and therefore cannot be used to model structures
with arbitrary depth.

Let us look again at the ideas we use for constructing functions inductively. These
have mainly fallen into two classes, those using mathematical induction and those
using induction on lists. An example of the former kind is the function `factorial`
defined as a base case equation:

```
factorial 0 = 1
```

and an inductive or recursive case equation:

```
factorial n = n * factorial(n-1)
```

where `n/=0` is implied.

An example of the second kind is the `length` function defined with a base case:

```
length [] = 0
```

and an inductive case:

```
length (h:t) = 1 + length t
```

Thus we can do induction on at least two different data types, `Int` and `[alpha]`.

Both of the kinds of inductive definition given above are, it turns out, special cases of a more general kind of induction called *structural induction*. In just the same way as we define functions by induction over all the integers and over all lists, we can define functions over all structures of a given kind by looking at the simple structures as base cases and by looking at more complicated structures, built from simpler ones by using *constructor functions*, as inductive cases. With lists the constructor function is the infixed operator : which constructs a new list from an old one and another object by sticking the latter on the front of the former — it is a binary constructor; and there is also a constructor for the base case, written [] in Haskell which constructs a null list from nothing at all — it is a 'zero-ary' (or nullary) constructor also known as a constant! A constructor function which needs *n* arguments is called an *n-ary constructor*.

We could formalise this by giving a definition of the type of all lists as follows:

```
data List = Nil | Object : List
```

"An object of type `List` is either constructed out of nothing and is `Nil` or it is constructed using : from an `Object` and another `List`". We use `Nil` rather than [] because constructors defined by users have to be names starting with a capital letter or operators starting with : — the predefined syntactical notation [, , ,] is an addition to Haskell which is not strictly needed but has been added for the purely pragmatic reason that lists constitute a very common data structure.

It is a little more difficult to see how this can be done with the integers but if we refer to the classical axioms for the natural numbers, all becomes clear and we can use the type definition:

```
data Nat = Zero | Succ Nat
```

which says that natural numbers are either constructed as the constant `Zero` (more often written 0) or by using the prefixed constructor `Succ` on another number. Again we have shorthand ways of writing positive natural numbers, so that we write, for instance, 3 rather than Succ(Succ(Succ Zero)).

Our definition of factorial could then be written in the long hand:

```
factorial Zero     = Succ Zero
factorial (Succ n) = (Succ n) * factorial n
```

Notice how we have re-drafted the second equation to calculate *(n+1)!* in terms of *n!* rather than, as in the original, *n!* in terms of *(n-1)!*. This is more logical because we now have two *mutually exclusive* (and comprehensive) equations as the definition of the function. Before, we had to add the (implicit) rider n \= 0 to the second equation but this is now not needed as `zero` is not the successor of any natural number.

The point here is to show that these definitions are really of the same kind. We supply type definitions by enumerating construction methods for the objects we are interested in. For functions on these objects, we then supply a set of equations giving the algorithm as rewrite rules for each of the construction cases.

How could we extend this sort of idea to, say, labelled binary trees? Such trees are of two kinds: They either have a label and two sub-trees (an inductive case) or else they are empty (a base) so a Haskell definition of this algebraic data type could be:

```
data Tree = Tip | Node Object Tree Tree
```

The `Tip` constant represents the empty tree and the `Node` constructor allows us to construct new trees from an `Object` and two other trees. `Object` is another type. We can make this definition parametric by adding a type parameter:

```
data Tree t = Tip | Node t (Tree t) (Tree t)
```

and this now describes trees with labels of type `t`.

The rules about capitalisation in Haskell are that type variables are not capitalised while constant types (nullary type constructors) and type constructors are capitalised. The same applies to value variables, constants and constructors.

This algebraic type mechanism allows the definition of what in Pascal are called *enumerated types*. For instance one could define the days of the week as follows:

```
data Day = Sunday | Monday | Tuesday | Wednesday |
           Thursday | Friday | Saturday
```

and then write such functions as:

```
tomorrow Sunday    = Monday
tomorrow Monday    = Tuesday
tomorrow Tuesday   = Wednesday
tomorrow Wednesday = Thursday
tomorrow Thursday  = Friday
tomorrow Friday    = Saturday
tomorrow Saturday  = Sunday
```

This type has seven nullary constructors or constants. A very well known type which appears predeclared in Haskell has two:

```
data Bool = False | True
```

with appropriate familiar operations. Note the capital letters on the truth values because they are (nullary) constructors.

One can also use the algebraic type mechanism to provide traditional structure creating functions.

For instance one might write:

```
type Name = [ Char ]
type Age = Int
data Sex = Male | Female
data Person = Makeperson Name Age Sex
```

This method of programming really gives us no new facilities but permits an explicit use of a constructor function and allows an extra level of type checking to be imposed on programs which use it. It provides a style of programming which may be pleasant to some users.

Although the Haskell philosophy of algebraic types is that they consist of a number of constructors each of which produce a member of the type, it is possible to think of them in a slightly different way. Each constructor can be thought of as producing a separate type and the whole type being defined is then a *union* of the constructed types. Then, when we write a function over this union type and provide a case analysis, what we are doing is projecting out of this union at run time.

4.4.1 Pattern Matching in Haskell

A `data` definition not only describes a new type but implicitly defines constructor functions to allow creation of objects of that type. For instance in the case of non-parametric trees as given above `Tip` and `Node` are manufactured with types:

```
Tip :: Tree

Node :: Object -> Tree -> Tree -> Tree
```

When we parameterise the `Tree` type, these become:

```
Tip :: Tree alpha

Node:: alpha -> Tree alpha -> Tree alpha -> Tree alpha
```

In addition to being usable as constructors on the right hand side of definitions, these functions can be used in patterns in inductive definitions of functions. For instance, here is a function to find how many tips a tree has:

```
tips Tip                 = 1
tips (Node val left right) = tips left + tips right
```

and here is another which makes a list of the labels on a tree in one particular order:

```
labels Tip                 = []
labels (Node val left right) =
        labels left ++ [val] ++ labels right
```

Of course patterns can be used in other contexts where they are relevant. Here is a list comprehension which selects the values found at the roots of all appropriate trees in a forest represented as a list of trees:

```
roots forest = [ val | (Node val left right) <- forest ]
```

4.5 ABSTRACT TYPES AND MODULES

We have already emphasised the point in this chapter that one of the main reasons for providing user defined types is to allow a problem to be approached directly rather than using an inappropriate model with types of its own, ill-suited to the level of abstraction the users want to use. Algebraic types provide some relief from this problem. But their use has its limitations. One view of a type is that it is not just a collection of data but that it should incorporate, in some sense, all the operations that can be carried out on that data. Thus, for instance, if one were to introduce a type `Stack` (nearly as classic an example in types as `factorial` is for functions) one might well want to supply the operations `push`, `pop`, `add`, ... which we discussed in section 3.6 *as part of the type*. In addition, it may be advantageous for users to be restricted in what they can do to objects of a particular type. By wrapping up the allowable operations on a type as part of the type, we provide just this sort of protection and privacy. Users will not see the details of the implementation method and will only be able to manipulate objects of the type using the tools provided by the systems programmer who implemented it. The kind of type we obtain by using this method of abstracting the important features of a type into a restricted *interface* is called an *abstract type*. Algebraic type definitions in themselves provide a restricted form of abstract type with the implicitly defined constructor functions as interface; but users are not allowed to add their own items to the interface.

Many languages, and Haskell is no exception, allow users to describe abstract data types. Haskell has a construct which is called a module, which can be used to describe abstract types. Here is one implementation of the `Stack` type:

```
module Stack(Stack, push, pop, empty, isempty,
             add, subtract, multiply, divide)
    where
        abstype Stack a = EmptyStk | Stk a (Stack a)
        push x s        = Stk x s
        pop (Stk h s)   = (h, s)
        empty           = EmptyStk
        isempty EmptyStk = True
        isempty (Stk h t) = False
        add (Stk top (Stk next rest))      = Stk (next+top) rest
        subtract (Stk top (Stk next rest)) = Stk (next-top) rest
        multiply (Stk top (Stk next rest)) = Stk (next*top) rest
        divide (Stk top (Stk next rest))   = Stk (next/top) rest
```

Only the items given after the module name (`Stack`) are made visible to users of the type. In particular `EmptyStk` and `Stk` cannot be used outside the definition of the abstract type so the algebraic type used to implement the stack is not made public (not *exported* from the module). In a more complicated example, there might well have been other functions used in the implementation which were however not exported for general use. The exported items together with information about them such as their types constitute what is called the *interface* to the module or abstract data type.

In Haskell, abstract types of this kind are included as a subset of the larger kind of entity, the *module*. The idea of a module, in most computer languages which have them, is to provide a unit of separate compilation. But it is evident that when a group of logically connected entities are grouped together in the way that happens with a module they are doing nearly the same job as abstract types. Modules may import some or all the facilities provided exported other modules. For details we refer the reader to the Haskell report.

In Haskell, a program is a module, and there are several modules of standard pre-declared objects which can be automatically invoked called *preludes*. There is a prelude, `PreludeList`, for example, which contains a large number of list manipulating functions and operators. Another is called `PreludeIO` and contains functions for use in input/output such as the functions `show` and `read`. In particular there is the standard prelude, called simply `Prelude`, which includes all the others by importing their facilities. Some of the functions available in the various preludes are given in Appendix B.

4.6 ARRAYS

As well as algebraic types and tuples, Haskell has a structured data type of *arrays*. Theoretically arrays do not give us more expressive power as they may be modelled by lists or some other more complicated data-type associating an index type (acting as a subscript) with a value type for the values of the array elements. But a properly implemented array type (operationally thought of as having elements of the array in contiguous storage) has the advantage of allowing constant access time to all the elements. An association list allows access to an element with time proportional to the distance of the element from the head of the list. This can be improved by implementing hashing schemes and/or using sorted trees for storing associations but it is extremely difficult (probably impossible) to match the performance of a conventional array because arrays are so well matched to the stores of conventional von Neumann machines.

Arrays in Haskell are created with the built-in function `array` which takes a pair of bounds and an association list (which we discuss in greater detail below) and produces an array as result. Here are two examples:

```
primes = array (1,5) [ 1 := 2,
                 2 := 3, 3 := 5  4 := 7, 5 := 11]
dinners = array (Sunday,Saturday) [ Sunday  := "roast beef",
                                    Monday  := "skirlie",
                                    Tuesday:= "haggis",
                                    Friday  := "trout",
                                    Wednesday:="stovies",
                                    Saturday:="ham",
                                    Thursday:="collops"]
          -- a perverse order, but that is immaterial
```

The associations `index := value` are of type `Assoc a b` where a is the index type[1] and b that of the associated values. The type of the resulting array is `Array a b`. Thus the types of the two examples are `Array Int Int` and `Array Day [Char]` respectively and the type of `array` itself is:

---

[1]Any type which has ordering relations and equality defined on it can be an index type, including integral types, characters and enumerated types such as `Day`. Tuples of these types can be used to subscript multi-demensional arrays.

```
    (a,a) -> [Assoc a b] -> Array a b
```

The operator := is (pre)-defined by

```
data Assoc a b = a := b
```

Arrays are indexed using the operator !. Thus, in the above example
dinners ! Friday is "trout". The bounds function returns the bounds of an
array expression to which it is applied.

Here are some further examples, some taken from the Haskell report:

```
powersof2 =
   array (1,max) ((1 := 1) : [i := 2*powersof2(i-1)
                                 | i <-[2..max]] )

-- scale an array by a given number
scale x a = array b [i := a!i * x | i <- range b]
            where b = bounds a
      {- range takes a bound pair and returns a list of indices
in that range -}

-- inner product of two vectors
inner v w | bw == bv  = foldl (+) 0 [v!i * w!i | i <- range bv]
          | otherwise = error "inconformable arrays for inner"
            where bv = bounds v
                  bw = bounds w

-- slices of a matrix
row i m = array b [m!(i,j) | j <- range b]
          where ((1,1'),(u,u')) = bounds m
                b              = (1,u)
col j m = array b [m!(i,j) | i <- range b']
          where ((1,1'),(u,u')) = bounds m
                b'             = (1',u')
```

4.7 TYPE INFERENCE

One of the most important ideas of functional programming languages is that of
automatic type inference. It has become known as ML-style or Hindley-Milner type
inference because it was first implemented for the language ML about 1976
[miln78].

The idea of having a static type system is that it should be possible to glean details
of the types of objects early in the life cycle of programs and factor this information
out for use by compilers and people who want to prove properties of programs (see
chapter 9). In addition, if a program turns out to be ill-typed, it would be useful to
know about it as early as possible and a static type system allows type checking at
compile time to issue appropriate error messages. Type *inference* as distinct from
type *checking* allows, in addition, for a compiler to find the types of objects in a
program *automatically* without users having to give information about them.

It is becoming clear (see for instance [stem89]) that type systems can be a trap for the unwary, a black hole into which programming language designers can fall if they are not careful to stay above the event horizon. The real trouble is that a too powerful type system is not amenable to type checking, far less inference, in the sense that it may not be decidable whether an object has a given type or not. The type system of ML and a number of applicative languages following its lead, in particular Haskell in the present case, was specifically chosen for striking a good balance between power and amenability to automatic inference.

We now give an example of the inference of the type of a function giving an idea of how a general inference algorithm might work.Consider the `foldr` function defined in Haskell as follows:

```
foldr f zero []    = zero
foldr f zero (h:t) = f h (foldr f zero t)
```

From external sources, we already know the types of certain functions used in the definitions. In particular we know that : has type `alpha -> [alpha] -> [alpha]` and we know that the null list `[]` has type `[alpha]` — it's a list of anything at all. Type inference proceeds by examining each equation separately and then looking at its parts in a top-down approach. At each stage we will have some, but possibly not all, of the information about various identifiers in the equations.

At the start, all we know is the information about the external functions (like : and `[]`). Looking at the first equation, we see several things. First `foldr` is a function of three curried variables, so we can tentatively give it type `beta -> gamma -> delta -> epsilon`. From this we can assign type `beta` to `f`, `gamma` to `zero` and we can see that `delta` must be `[alpha]` from our knowledge about `[]`. Proceeding to the right hand side of the equation we see that `epsilon` must be the same as `gamma`, the type of `zero`. Thus, from the first equation, we have found out that `foldr` has the type `beta -> gamma -> [alpha] -> gamma`.

From the left hand side of the second equation and our information about `:`, we gain the additional knowledge that `h` must have type `alpha` and `t` the type `[alpha]`. Looking now at the right hand side, we see that `f` must itself be a function of two curried arguments and have type, say, `zeta -> eta -> theta` which we therefore have to equate to `beta`. Moreover `zeta` must be `alpha` (the type of `h`) and `eta` and `theta` must both be `gamma` as this is the result type when `foldr` is applied to all its arguments. Putting all of this together, we see that the type of `foldr` is

```
(alpha -> gamma -> gamma) -> gamma -> [alpha] -> gamma
```

and we can glean no more information. This then is the fully polymorphic type of `foldr`, called its *principal type scheme* and we can use it in equations defining other functions or objects to check that they too are type correct and to infer their types.

In several places in the above analysis, we equated types. We gained information about them from different sources and were able to add to it as we went along. This equating of types is not a completely trivial matter and is called type *unification*. When one complicated type is equated with another, it is possible that neither is a variable and unification will then involve equating their sub parts, and their sub-sub-parts and so on; and this must be seen to happen in a consistent manner. For example suppose we were trying to equate

```
alpha -> beta -> alpha
```

with

```
gamma -> [delta -> gamma] -> delta
```

we have to be able to find out that the most general type which matches these two is

```
alpha -> [alpha -> alpha] -> alpha
```

The process is easy to automate as another recursive information gathering top-down algorithm.

As a point of interest, unification was first applied in a completely different context, to automatic theorem proving. Here a matching process needs to spot if terms in the steps of proving a theorem have the same form and an exactly similar unification algorithm is invoked to find out [robi65].

The reader interested in type inference should refer to [miln78] or [card85] for further details of automatic type checking. The former is where Robin Milner first formally presented the algorithm for type checking which we have presented here informally. The latter presents a more detailed but very readable view of how automatic inference is carried out in practice. Chapters 8 and 9 of [peyt87] by Peter Hancock also give a good overview of this whole subject.

4.8 OVERLOADING

We mentioned in section 4.3 that polymorphism was of two main kinds — parametric and *ad-hoc*. The latter is called *ad-hoc* because it is usually applied to a small set of types chosen in an *ad-hoc* way. For instance it is traditional to use the operator + to stand for addition both of integers and floating point numbers. FORTRAN programmers may, in addition, use it for complex numbers. Another name for this kind of polymorphism is *overloading* because the operator in question, + in this case, is being used to mean two different operations, and on the computer they will probably be carried out in different ways — most machines have different hardware for integer and real arithmetic and complex addition is usually performed by a small subroutine which does two floating point additions. We might write the type of + as

```
Int->Int->Int  ∩  Float->Float->Float  ∩ ...
```

where the intersection sign is meant to signify that the operator has all the types at once. This is in contradistinction to the case of parametric polymorphism where, again, the same name can have many types at once, but there are an infinite number of them (*any* type can be substituted for a type variable). *Ad-hoc* typing usually allows a preset finite number of types to be attached to names. In addition, with parametric polymorphism, the implementation of the name is usually the same, whichever actual type is meant on any given application of the name. For instance the function `tl` which finds the tail of a list has the parametric type

```
[alpha] -> [alpha]
```

but it is implemented in a way which is independent of what `alpha` is.

The situation is even worse than this when one considers functions like show (for converting objects to string form for display) which has an infinite number of types

```
alpha -> [Char]
```

but still has to be implemented in an *ad-hoc* way, with different code needed for showing integers, floating point numbers, lists .... In fact *some* types of object shouldn't be shown at all. How do you print a function (not its algorithm) or an object of an abstract type, where the user is not supposed to see how the implementation works? The equality function is like this as well. There are some types of object that it makes no sense to test for equality, for instance functions.

There are further problems attached to *ad-hoc* types. Going hand in hand with overloading is the problem of automatic *coercion*. It is common practice in mathematics and imperative programming to allow mixed mode arithmetic where, for instance, one might want to add an integer to a floating point number or a floating to a complex. Since most machines do not have hardware which can cope directly with these situations, we usually find that the types are organised into a hierarchy so that, in this instance, the floating point numbers are a subset of the complexes and the integers of the floating point. An automatic type conversion of an object to a 'higher' type is inserted and this is called a coercion. For instance, if x is floating point and i is an integer then x+i might be compiled as x+intToFloat i. In Haskell, no such *automatic* coercion is done, but a number of type conversion functions are supplied so that users may insert explicit calls to these as needed.

A final problem with overloading is due to the fact that users sometimes want to overload operators in ways which are not built in, *ad-hoc*, to the language they are using. For instance suppose that an implementation of formula manipulation is required. If a and b are two formulae, users would probably prefer to be able to write a+b than formula_add a b, so that what is required here is overloading of + to a new type, that of formulae.

Solutions to these problems have, themselves tended to be *ad-hoc* ones. ML admits overloading of the equality operator just to types which allow equality. An early functional language, SASL [turn76], fully overloaded equality in the knowledge that it is impossible to implement, say, functional equality properly — it returns False if you try to equate two functions, unless they are the same object in the implementation (i.e. pointers to the same place in store) when True is returned. As far as arithmetic is concerned, the language Miranda[1] [turn85b] conflates integers and floating point numbers into one type called num. ML has both integers and floating point but does not allow users to define overloaded functions of their own.

A uniformly regular solution to some of these problems has recently been developed [wadl88] and has been incorporated into Haskell. This method abstracts the idea that ML uses, which groups together those types which admit equality. Here one can group types together into *classes*, each of which is required to have certain operations defined on it. Thus Haskell does have a (predefined) class called Eq and any type defined to be in this class must have associated with it the equality operation (==) and the inequality operation (/=); but Haskell also has a number of other classes. Ord is a class comprising types which must have the relations < and

---

[1] 'Miranda' is a trademark of Research Software Ltd.

<= defined on them as well as the equality operators. It is a *sub-class* of Eq. These classes are specified by the Haskell statements:

```
class Eq a  where                        -- simplified definitions
      (==), (/=) :: a -> a -> Bool
class Eq a => Ord a
      where (<), (<=), (>), (>=) :: a -> a -> Bool
```

We can read the first of these as saying that "Type a is in class Eq if it has an equality operator and a not equals of type a -> a -> Bool defined". The second equation says that if a is of class Eq then it can be of class Ord if it has the following additional operators. In other words the Ord class is a sub-class of Eq and in addition to equality, types in Eq must have < and <= ... defined on them.

It is perfectly proper for users to add types they have invented to these classes, so long as they provide at least the specified operations for the class. To do this, one has to define an *instance* of the appropriate class. Here is an example:

```
data Person = Makep [Char] [Char]
                             -- Name and Insurance code
   instance Eq Person where
       Makep name1 no1 == Makep name2 no2 = no1==no2
```

This is saying that two Persons are defined to be equal if their insurance codes are the same. Notice that we throw back the equality of two persons onto the string equality of their Insurance codes. We assume that [Char] also belongs to the Eq class and that *its* equality function is defined elsewhere.

Haskell has quite a number of predefined classes, many of them numerical. For instance there is an Integral class and Haskell provides two instances of it one of which we have used extensively in previous chapters, Int. The other is Integer. The former is a fixed precision integer (possibly a 32 bit word implementation) and the latter is an arbitrary precision integer with an unspecified method of implementation. And of course there is no objection to users providing their own integral types provided they have the proper operations operators defined on them. The Integral class is a subclass of 5 other classes (see appendix D) including Eq and Ord so it has the relational operations defined. It is a subclass of a class called Num which has (+), (-), (*), negate, abs and signum defined. The Integral class adds operators of its own including div, rem, mod, divRem.

Users are also allowed to define overloaded functions of variables with types in such classes. For instance squaring might be defined simultaneously for all types in class Integral by

```
square :: Integral a => a -> a
square b = b * b
```

The first line specifies the type[1] of the function and can be read as "square has type a -> a provided a is an Integral type". The second line describes how to square for each Integral type by invoking the correct multiplication for that type — every

---

[1] This type can be inferred automatically.

Integral type is constrained to have such an operator. Thus overloading of square is achieved in terms of overloading of *.

Wadler, in his paper on *ad-hoc* polymorphism, shows that the introduction of classes of types does not mean that automatic type inference has to be thrown away. Only a fairly simple modification needs to be made to Milner's classical methods for inferring types.

The ideas of classes and sub-classes in this solution bears a strong resemblance to the class concept found in Object Oriented programming languages [stro86]. Sub-classing really constitutes another type of polymorphism which has been called *inclusion* polymorphism. Haskell classes provide a particular inclusion polymorphism solution to the problem of overloading.

4.9 LAWS

The algebraic types which were introduced in section 4.4 are what are known as *free* algebraic types. This means two things:

* that *any* value manufactured using the constructor functions implicitly supplied when the type was specified is a legal value of the type.

* that a value manufactured in this way is *independent* of all other values of the type.

But this may not always be what is wanted. For instance, we might want to allow the construction of lists of objects only if the objects are in ascending order of magnitude. Again, one might want to say that two different constructed objects were really the same. For instance if one wanted to simulate the ordinary formulae of arithmetic by overloading the arithmetic operators +, -, ... to construct formulae from others, one might want to equate e+f with f+e and so on.

In the first of these cases one is preventing the manufacture of some of the objects of the type and in the second one equating several of the values. In both cases, we no longer have a free algebra.

The first version of the programming language Miranda [thom85] allowed non-free algebras[1] by overcoming the above difficulties in the following way. When a user attempts to create a value with the type concerned, a set of rules called *laws* are invoked to check whether the value is a legal one. The laws consist of a set of rewrite rules which transform illegal values into legal ones. Thus the two problems are dealt with in the same way by reducing values in the type to a canonical form. The laws are specified by the Miranda programmer by writing the rewrite rules as if they were extra function definitions for the constructor functions (but using => instead of = in the definitions).

---

[1]Later versions withdrew this feature as there are semantic difficulties associated with it. Haskell does not have the laws feature but the rest of this section shows how their effect can be achieved.

For example, suppose that one wants to create an algebraic data type of values which represent rational numbers. One way of doing this would be to specify each value as a structure with two fields for the numerator and denominator[1]:

```
rational ::= Pair num num
```

so that the rational ¾ is represented, for instance, by `Pair 3 4`. But there must be a proviso that the numerator and denominator have no common factor and that they are not both zero. We may also insist that the numerator be positive. So the following laws may be added to the definition immediately after a slightly modified version of the abstract type definition:

```
rational ::= Pair num num | Indeterminate
Pair 0 0 => Indeterminate                  || 0/0 is meaningless
Pair 0 d => Pair 0 1          ,d/=1        || Zero
Pair n 0 => Pair 1 0          ,n/=1        || Infinity
Pair n d => Pair (-n) (-d)    ,n<0         || Make numerator +ve
Pair n d => Pair (n/g) (d/g)  ,g/=1        || Divide out
              where g = gcd n d
```

As another example, consider an implementation of arithmetic expressions with constants, variables and unary and binary operations. We make the laws carry out some elementary algebraic simplifications:

```
expr ::= Const num | Var string | Minus expr |
            Sum expr expr | Difference expr expr

Minus (Const n) => Const (-n)

Sum (Const m) (Const n) => Const (m+n)
Sum (Const 0) e         => e
Sum e         (Const 0) => e

Difference (Const m) (Const n) => Const (m-n)
Difference (Const 0) e         => Minus e
Difference e         (Const 0) => e
```

and it is clear that this definition can be expanded to deal with other operators (see Exercise 7).

Before leaving laws, it is interesting to note that they, like many of the functional concepts we have discussed in this book, can be regarded as 'sugaring' of something simpler. In later versions of Miranda and in Haskell, there is no facility for expressing laws. However it is possible achieve their effect by calling functions which evaluate to values in a free algebraic type. Users have fo discipline

---

[1]The concrete syntax of Miranda is here trivially different from that of Haskell. The key-word `data` is used by Haskell to introduce an algebraic type but Miranda indicates such a type by using `::=` as a separator in the definition. Types don't start with a capital letter in Miranda. Of more semantic interest is the fact that Miranda makes no distinction between integers and floating point, lumping them all together in the type `num` to avoid problems of overloading.

themselves always to call the reducing functions when constructing new objects of the types concerned so that only lawful objects are ever retained. A hint of this is perhaps given in the previous example where it should be obvious that we are making the formula constructors do the work of functions as well. This can be made more formal by replacing all calls to the constructor functions by calls to some extra functions (which we can imagine might be added by a compiler for Miranda during the desugaring process).

Let us give these functions (this time written in Haskell) the same names as the constructors, but with lower case letters at the start. These functions deal with the rewriting where necessary and eventually call the real constructors when no further rewrites are needed:

```
data expr = Const num | Var string | Minus expr |
            Sum expr expr | Difference expr expr

const n = Const n
var s = Var s

minus (Const n) = const (-n)
minus e         = Minus e

sum (Const m) (Const n) = const (m+n)
sum (Const 0) e         = e
sum e         (Const 0) = e
sum e1        e2        = Sum e1 e2

difference (Const m) (Const n) = const (m-n)
difference (Const 0) e         = minus e
difference e         (Const 0) = e
difference e1 e2               = Difference e1 e2
```

In this definition expr is a free algebraic type, but calls to the auxiliary functions will have the same effect as if constructors in a non-free type had been invoked. The auxiliary functions cannot, however, be used on the left hand side of definitions. Only constructors can appear in patterns.

We cannot complete this chapter without mentioning an encyclopædic, but nonetheless very readable, article by Cardelli and Wegner [card86]. Many of the concepts discussed in this chapter, and others besides, are examined in depth there.

4.10 SUMMARY

In this chapter we have discussed a number of different concepts related to types. We have investigated type expressions and the operators used to build new types. We have defined the concept of monomorphic type and three kinds of type polymorphism have been investigated, parametric, *ad-hoc* and inclusion. We have seen that algebraic types add considerable expressiveness to a language allowing enumerated types and structures to be used as well as the more general union of a number of Cartesian products, each one labelled or tagged by a constructor function. The use of such functions as discriminators in pattern matching has been investigated. We have also considered abstract types and modules. We have outlined a method of type inference used in a number of languages. *Ad hoc* types

and overloading have led to a more general solution by grouping types into classes.
Finally we have seen that non-free type algebras can be made available by the
disciplined use of rewriting functions in place of constructors.

4.11 EXERCISES

1.   Infer the polymorphic types of the following functions abstracted from the
     Haskell reference manual:

```
last [x]        = x
last (x:y:zs)   = last (y:zs)

length []       = 0
length (x:xs)   = length (xs) + 1

foldl f z []       = z
foldl f z (x:xs) = foldl f (f z x) xs

sum             = foldl (+) 0
```

2.   Construct an algebraic data type for binary trees with labels at each node.
     Write functions which constructs such trees from items of the label type such
     that the trees are sorted so that all labels to the left of a given node come
     before those at that node and all to the right come after it. Write a function
     which flattens such a tree into a sorted list of labels.

3.   Construct an abstract data type for a queue. Attempt to supply an
     implementation (hidden from the user of the type) which allows access to the
     head of the queue and the construction of a new queue by adding elements to
     the end of an existing one. Both these interface functions should operate in
     time independent of the length of the queue. What implications does this
     exercise suggest for searching and 'updating' (by copying all unchanged
     nodes) a general graph?

4.   Use Miranda laws to extend the natural numbers defined in section 4.4 to the
     positive and negative integers by introducing a predecessor function in
     addition to the existing successor function. How may this datatype be
     implemented in Haskell?

5.   Use laws to implement a data type of lists constrained to be in sorted order.
     Realise this datatype in Haskell.

6.   Use the laws discipline to allow the building in Haskell of binary search trees
     which are constrained to be balanced.

7.   Expand the lawful algebraic type given in section 4.8 for simplifying
     expressions to include other operators such as multiplication, division and
     exponentiation. How can such algebraic rules as commutativity (e+f=f+e),
     distributivity (e*(f+g) = e*f+e*g) and associativity (e+(f+g)=(e+f)+g) be
     incorporated into such a simplification system?

8.   We saw in question 17 of the exercises of chapter 3 that a store could be
     modelled as a list of pairs representing names and their values. An alternate
     model of a store keeps the names and values on a binary sorted tree.

Implement `lookup` and `update` in this alternative way. Write modules which represent the two versions of this abstract data type showing how the implementation can be kept private to the module.

9. Suppose an arithmetic expression (AE) is represented (for simplicity) by either

    a) A number (which requires no further computation) or

    b) A construction consisting of one of the operators :+, :-, :* or :/ applied to a left operand and a right operand which are themselves AEs. e.g. the expression (1+2)*(3-4) might be represented by:

        ```
        (Number 1 :+ Number 2) :* (Number 3 :- Number 4)
        ```

        Write a function that evaluates such AEs.

10. Using a similar representation to that in the example above but allowing the use of variables as well as constants, write a function that will differentiate an AE with respect to a given variable. What steps are needed to simplify expressions to make them readable?

11. Write a function which translates a string representation of AEs (see examples above) e.g. "a*(b+c)" into the data structure representation for AEs and another to translate back again.

12. Write a function which evaluates AEs given in the string form of the above exercise in an environment given by an association list which pairs variables with their values (see question 8). Note that full arithmetic evaluation may be impossible in the absence of values for some of the variables and that simplification and symbolic evaluation may be needed instead.

Chapter 5

Lambda Calculus

5.1 INTRODUCTION

In this chapter we make a start on studying the theory lying behind applicative programming and in it we shall concentrate on what might be called the essence of applicative programming. We shall see how Haskell expressions can be regarded as convenient sugarings of expressions in a simpler and more fundamental language. Sugaring is used to make programming easier (or sweeter). It adds nothing new to the system except syntactic convenience.

One of the principal ideas in applicative programming is that of referential transparency — that we may take an expression and substitute in it, for any proper subexpression, another with the same value. Or to put it another way — the value of an expression depends only on the values of its subexpressions. Thus we see that the idea of *substitution* is very central. One of the important ideas behind λ-calculus is that of substitution. Another important issue which is fundamental to the λ-calculus is that of *abstraction* and this allows a consistent model of function definition and application.

We shall approach the λ-calculus informally and give a more formal definition later. Part of the informal approach will involve writing Haskell programs to illustrate some of the ideas central to the λ-calculus, substitution and abstraction. The use of Haskell is purely for convenience.

5.2 ABSTRACTION

The idea of *naming* something is a process of *abstraction*. When we calculate $2+1$, $3+1, 5+1, 16+1$ we detect a pattern and feel that it might be useful to calculate $x+1$ for any x — or at any rate for any numerical x. This concept is of course central to mathematics and to computing where it is of the essence that we should try to develop programs not just to do one job but to be as general as possible. The replacing of a whole class of objects by a name representative of an element of the class is roughly what we mean by abstraction and it allows us to approach functions naturally. We can now say

$$f x = x+1$$

and thereafter talk about the function f. However we could just as easily have said

$$f y = y+1$$

and we would have described the same function. The name of the argument doesn't matter — it is a dummy variable. In fact the function we have described here is the one which maps its argument (whatever its name is) into the number one greater than that argument. Note that this English language description does not mention the name f at all and we can see that we could equally have written

$$succ\ x = x+1$$

The name f or $succ$ is of course useful to refer to the function but we should not really have any obligation to give it a name at all — just in the same way that it is convenient but not strictly necessary to give the name π to 3.1415926....

In fact, as Curry has pointed out, the way mathematicians name functions is not systematic. Consider for example the 'definition' of P:

$$P[f(x)] = \begin{cases} f'(0) & \text{if } x = 0 \\[2ex] \dfrac{f(x)-f(0)}{x} & \text{if } x \neq 0 \end{cases}$$

where $f'(0)$ means the differential coefficient of $f(x)$ at $x=0$. What does $P[f(x+1)]$ mean if for example $f(x)$ is x^2? One possibility is first to form $g(x)=f(x+1)=(x+1)^2$ and then $P[g(x)]=P[x^2+2x+1]=x+2$. Alternatively we can form $h(x)=P[f(x)]=x$ and then $h(x+1)=x+1$ which gives a different answer to $P[g(x)]$. This is no mere splitting of hairs as examples of this ambiguity leading to a mathematical error are known to exist.

How then are we to divorce the name of a function from its value (and will this solve the particular problem above)? We shall use the notation of λ-expressions invented by Church [chur41]. The function that we have called f and $succ$ above will be written:

$$\lambda x\,.\,x+1$$

In general if E is an expression which contains zero or more occurrences of the variable x then $\lambda x.E$ denotes the function which maps x to (the value of) E.

So now instead of writing $succ\ x=x+1$ we can write $succ = \lambda x.\,x+1$ instead.

Haskell has a way of writing anonymous functions. It uses \ for a λ and, because . is more commonly reserved for function composition, this is replaced by ->. Thus the definition

```
succ  x  =  x+1
```

can be replaced by

```
succ = \ x -> x+1
```

The operation which forms λx . E from x and E is called *functional abstraction*. It is clear that this may be extended to more than one variable provided that we abstract only one such variable at a time. For instance starting from $x+y^2$ we can form first of all λx. $x+y^2$ which is a function which adds y^2 to things (whatever y is) and then we can make $\lambda y.(\lambda x$. $x+y^2)$ by abstracting y and this function is a mapping from its argument to another function which itself maps *its* argument to the final numerical value.

This notation has an additional advantage with respect to functions of more than one variable. In loose parlance if we were to say 'Take the function $x+y^2$ and apply it to 2 and 3' we would not know whether the x were to be 2 and the y to be 3 or *vice versa*. But using λ-expressions we can now either say 'Take the function $\lambda x.(\lambda y.$ $x+y^2)$, apply it to 2 (giving the function $\lambda y.2+y^2)$ and then apply that to 3 (giving 11)' or we can say 'Take the function $\lambda y.(\lambda x$. $x+y^2)$, apply that to 2 (giving λx. $x+4)$ and apply that to 3 (giving 7)'. A function which is created by abstracting one variable after another is commonly called a *curried function*.

5.3 REDUCTION

Our example above demonstrated the process called *reduction* which loosely speaking (we shall tighten the concept up later) is as follows. Suppose E is an expression which we abstract to λx.E. Then the operation of applying this function to an argument F is as usual written by juxtaposing the function to the argument though we shall leave out the brackets round the argument whenever this is not ambiguous. Thus we get $(\lambda x$.E)F and this can be reduced to a value obtained by substituting F for x wherever it appears in E. We write this E[x := F] following Barendregt who has written one of the standard works on the λ-calculus [bare84]. Other ways of writing this are found, the most common being [F / x] E and E[F / x]. We shall see below that this intuitive idea of reduction must be tightened up because the idea of substitution is fraught with difficulties concerned with name clashes.

Returning to the example of ambiguity presented above, it is now possible to see what made it confusing. First when we said $P[f(x+1)]$ we were misusing the terminology by thinking of $f(x+1)$ as a function where actually it is a number. The operator P is applicable to functions like f, not to numbers like $f(x+1)$, and can be defined by:

$$P=\lambda F.\lambda x.\left(if\ x=0\ then\ D(F)(0)\ else\ \frac{F(x)-F(0)}{x} \right)$$

where D is a differentiating operator which we assume defined on functions of one variable by some numerical process. Thus we see that λ-notation allows the two possible interpretations of $P[f(x+1)]$ to be distinguished unambiguously as one of:

$$P[\lambda x.f(x+1)]$$

or

$$\lambda x.\ P(f)(x+1)$$

5.4 λ-EXPRESSIONS

We are now ready to try to give a more rigorous definition of what we mean by λ-expressions.

DEFN 5.1:   Let V_0, V_1,... be a set of *variables* or *identifiers*. The following are λ-expressions:

a)   Any V_i is a λ-expression.

b)   If L is a λ-expression and X is a variable then $(\lambda X.L)$ is a λ-expression called an *abstraction*. An abstraction is a model of a function. X is called the *bound variable* and L the *body* of the abstraction.

c)   If L_1 and L_2 are λ-expressions then $(L_1\ L_2)$ is a λ-expression called a *combination*. L_1 is called the *rator* and L_2 the *rand* of the combination. This construct models a function (the ope*rator*) being applied to an argument (the ope*rand*).

We should note certain points at this stage. Firstly the syntax given above is very rigid. For instance, every abstraction and combination must sctrictly have the brackets shown in the definition. However there are some conventions which allow the use of shortened forms which will cut down the amount we have to write. The conventions are as follows.

We will use $x, y, z,...$ for variables. We will omit parentheses wherever possible with the understanding that groups of λ's coming together in abstractions associate to the right and that groups of terms combined with one another associate to the left. Thus:

$$(\lambda\ x.(\lambda\ y.(...(\lambda\ z.(E))...)))$$

may be written

$$\lambda\ x\ y\ ...\ z.E$$

and

$$(...((E_1\ E_2)\ E_3)...\ E_n)$$

is more easily understood by writing

$$E_1\ E_2\ E_3...E_n$$

A further convention to note is that we shall take the body of an abstraction to be the largest possible λ-expression after its dot. Thus: $\lambda\ x.A\ B$ means $(\lambda\ x.A\ B)$ and not $(\lambda\ x.A)\ B$.

One point which may seem puzzling at first is that variables are amongst the allowable λ-expressions but *constants* are not. Church [chur41] has shown how certain λ-expressions can be made to mimic integers, truth values and other commonly used constants so it is really possible to do without them. Nevertheless we will allow constants to be added to our set of allowable λ-expressions. This convention allows us to write such things as $1+2$ and consider it to be a λ-expression because it is the application of a rator (+, a constant function) to a pair of constants *1* and *2*. As well as dealing with constants, the operation of pairing can be coped with in *pure* λ-calculus. The conditional expression *if* E_1 *then* E_2 *else* E_3 will also be allowed as it may be considered to be short for an expression such as *cond* E_1 E_2 E_3 for a suitably defined function *cond*. In other words we will allow ourselves the luxury of writing expressions for which we have an already familiar notation.

5.5 THE DANGERS OF SUBSTITUTION

Let us examine the statement we made above when we said that *(λ x.E)* F reduces to E[x := F], and that this was meant to model functional application. Unfortunately the idea of substitution is, although perhaps intuitively obvious, rather fraught with pitfalls when it comes to rigorous definition as the following example given by Stoy [stoy77] shows. (Stoy points out that a number of famous mathematicians have given incorrect definitions of substitution including Hilbert, Gödel and Quine). The example is based on the fact that in integral calculus we are allowed to change a variable of integration without affecting the result:

$$\int_a^b f(x)\, dx = \int_a^b f(y)\, dy$$

But suppose $f(x) = x^2 + \int_c^d xy\, dy$. Now we *cannot* substitute y for x and say

$$\int_a^b [x^2 + \int_c^d xy\, dy]\, dx = \int_a^b [y^2 + \int_c^d yy\, dy]\, dy$$

because the two *y*s are not the same. What is wrong is that x is a *free variable* of the formula $\int_c^d xy\, dy$.

and such a free variable becomes *bound* if changed to *y* as *y* is already bound. We will define the terms *free* and *bound* rigourously below.

This fallacious example occurs in integral calculus but very similar difficulties arise in any system in which bound and free variables occur together with substitution. Examples abound and some are:

a) Predicate Calculus where ∀ x and ∃ x are quantifiers which bind the variable x.

b) Computer languages with procedures and functions where the identifiers are organised using a block structure. Here the formal parameters are bound variables.

c)   Tensor Calculus where the summation convention [lawd62] is used. This is
a convention that a formula in which a variable appears twice is to be
summed over all possible values of that variable. For example

$$\delta_i^i$$

is taken to mean

$$\delta_1^1 + \delta_2^2 + \delta_3^3 + \delta_4^4.$$

d)   The λ-calculus where the variable in an abstraction is a bound variable.

We can therefore see that we are going to have to take some care about the
definition of substitution and its associated concepts. Let us start with free and
bound variables. In what follows we use the symbol $\Leftrightarrow$ to mean 'if and only if'.

DEFN 5.2:   The variable X is *free in the expression* E in the following cases:

a)   If E is a variable then X is free in E $\Leftrightarrow$ X $\equiv$ E

b)   If E is a combination $E_1 E_2$ then X is free in E $\Leftrightarrow$ X is free in E_1 or X is
free in E_2.

c)   If E is an abstraction λ Y.E_1 then X is free in E $\Leftrightarrow$ X $\not\equiv$ Y and X is free in
E_1.

We use the operator $\equiv$ to mean 'is the same syntactic entity as'.

Note that freedom is a relative term. A variable can be free in an expression but not
free in some of its sub-expressions and vice-versa. For instance x is not free in the
expression $\lambda x \cdot xy$ but it is in the sub-expression xy.

A simple definition of a bound variable is just to say that it is one that is not free but
that is slightly simplistic. It would mean, for instance, that x is bound in y (because
it's not free!). We again use an inductive definition.

DEFN 5.3:   The variable X *is bound in* E as decided by the following cases:

a)   If E is a variable then X is not bound in it.

b)   If E is a combination $E_1 E_2$ then X is bound in E $\Leftrightarrow$ X is bound in E_1 or
bound in E_2.

c)   If E is an abstraction λ Y.E_1 then X is bound in E $\Leftrightarrow$ X $\equiv$ Y or X is bound
in E_1.

Note that a variable can be both bound and free in an expression. For example: x
occurs both bound and free in $(\lambda x \cdot x) x$.

It is interesting and important to note that the concept *bound* is different from
(though related to) the concept *bound to* which is a binary relation often used in
computing circles and usually meaning the correspondence between a formal

parameter in a procedure and an actual parameter which the procedure is being applied to. This is of course the mechanism that reduction is trying to model. When we reduce $(\lambda X.E)$ F we say informally that X (the formal parameter) gets bound to F (the actual parameter) so that during the substitution (execution of the procedure) all the free occurrences of X get replaced by F.

Another concept which is related to one in computing circles is that of *scope*. It will be useful to give a definition of what we mean by it in the context of λ-expressions.

DEFN 5.4: The scope of a bound variable is the entire λ-expression in which it occurs bound except for the text of any included abstractions whose bound variable is the same identifier.

5.6 MODEL OF A TEST FOR FREEDOM

At this stage, to provide some extra practice in Haskell programming, let us define a Haskell function that tests for freedom. First we must design a representation for λ-expressions. We could do this in a number of ways but perhaps the simplest is to define an algebraic data type:

```
data Lam = Var Int | Comb Lam Lam | Abstr Int Lam
```

This states that a λ-expression (Lam) can be constructed by using Var to make a variable (by supplying the variable number as an Int) or by using Comb to make a combination from two other λ-expressions or by using Abstr to construct an abstraction from a variable whose number is supplied and another λ-expression which will be the body. Thus, for instance the λ-expression $\lambda x\,y\,.\,x\,y$ (a shorthand way of writing $\lambda x\,.\,\lambda y\,.\,x\,y$) might be represented by

```
Abstr 1 (Abstr 2 (Comb 1 2))
```

We shall see presently why we are representing variables by integers.

We are now ready to write our function for testing whether a variable X is free in an expression E. The Haskell code is as follows:

```
isfree x (Var y)         = x == y
isfree x (Comb rator rand) = isfree x rator || isfree x rand
isfree x (Abstr bndvar body)  = x \= bndvar && isfree x body
```

A similar function can be written for testing if a variable is bound. This is left as an exercise for the reader.

We can now come to a proper definition of what we mean by substitution. We will define, using cases as usual, what we mean by E' = E[X := F]. We can think of [X := F] as an operator which transforms one λ-expression, E, into another, E'.

DEFN 5.5: E' $\equiv$ E[X := F] is defined by the following three cases:

1. If E is a variable

    a) If E $\equiv$ X then E' $\equiv$ F

    b) If E $\not\equiv$ X then E' $\equiv$ E

2.   If E is a combination E ≡ A B then E' ≡ (A[X := F]) (B[X := F])

3.   If E is an abstraction E ≡ λ Y.A

    a)   If X is not free in E then E' ≡ E

    b)   If X is free in E but Y is not free in F then E' ≡ λ Y.(A[X := F])

    c)   If X is free in E and Y is free in F then E' ≡ λ Z.(A[Y := Z] [X := F])
          where Z is any variable which is not X and not free in F or E

This definition is quite complicated, especially in the abstraction case, and perhaps needs some explanation.

Variables are relatively simple. If a variable is the variable of substitution, X, then we merely replace it by the expression F but otherwise it does not get substituted at all. Thus for example:

$$x [x := y] ≡ y$$

$$z [x := y] ≡ z$$

The combination case is also simple. We merely do the substitution in the rator and the rand and make a new combination by sticking the two results back together again. So:

$$(x (y x)) [x := z] ≡ (z (y z))$$

Finally in the case of an abstraction the problems arise; but these are not as difficult as they at first seem. If X is not free in E, no substitutions have to be made at all. For example:

$$λ x . (x y) [x := y] ≡ λ x . (x y)$$

If however it is free in E (and hence in A the body of E) then a substitution could possibly introduce a name clash. There's no problem if Y, the bound variable of E, is not free in F because no name clash can then be introduced. For example:

$$λ x . (x y) [y := z] ≡ λ x . (x z)$$

Otherwise however we have to *change the variable* to something safe. So the [Y := Z] merely represents this change of variable. The new variable Z must be chosen so that it is not free in F because that would cause the same problems that Y caused; it must not be free in A either because if so it would suddenly become bound in λ Z.(A[Y := Z]). So, for example:

$$λ x . (x y) [y := x] ≡ λ z . (z y)$$

Again we may clarify this by writing a program to implement a function to calculate a substitution. We first write two auxiliary functions. The first is needed by clause 3 (c) to select new variables for us. In first we suppose s to be a set of variables (integers in our implementation). The function delivers a variable not in the set s. In fact it delivers the first such variable in the ordering 1,2,3....

```
first s = find 1 s
         where find x s | x `elem` s = find (x+1) s
                        | otherwise  = x
```

Here `elem` is a version of the `member` function given in section 3.2. Similarly the definition given next uses standard prelude functions rather than the un-curried ones given in chapter 3.

Our second ancillary function is for finding all the free variables in an expression so that we can choose another which is not free:

```
frees (Var v)          = [v]
frees (Comb rator rand) = union (frees rator) (frees rand)
frees (Abstr var body)  = difference (frees body) [var]
```

We can then write our function which substitutes F for X in E:

```
subst x f e@(Var v)
    | x==v       = f
    | otherwise = e
subst x f (Comb rator rand)
              = Comb (subst x f rator) (subst x f rand)
subst x f e@(Abstr var body)
    | not(frees e `contains` x)
                  = e
    | not(frees f `contains` var)
                  = Abstr var (subst x f body)
    | otherwise = Abstr z (subst x f (subst var z body))
                  where z = first (union (frees e)(frees f))
```

This definition uses a feature of Haskell which we have not met before. The pattern `e@(Abstr var body)` is called an *as-pattern*. It allows us to use e as a name for the value being matched by `(Abstr var body)` and thus to give names simultaneously to the whole value and to its parts. Strictly speaking it is not needed. As-patterns are just extra syntactic sugar. We could have written:

```
subst x f e
    | not(frees e `contains` x)
                  = e
    | not(frees f `contains` var)
                  = Abstr var (subst x f body)
    | otherwise = Abstr z (subst x f (subst var z body))
                  where z = first (union (frees e)(frees f))
                        (Abstr var body) = e
```

but this is arguably less readable. A similar pattern is used in the first case of `subst`.

5.7 CONVERSION

Having made some rigorous definitions of such concepts as *free* (definition 5.2) and *substitution* (definition 5.5) we come to the central section of the chapter, the definition of our model of functional abstraction as embodied in *reduction* and *conversion*. Reduction is the process whereby we substitute an actual parameter for a formal one (or bound variable) when applying an abstraction to another λ-expression. This is pure symbolic manipulation in that we *convert* one λ-expression into another. We shall see that in fact there are several different kinds of convertibility, but the fact that one λ-expression can be converted to another is meant to model some sort of *equality* between λ-expressions in the sense that they denote the same value. So far our formal discussion of λ-expressions has been restricted to their syntactic properties but we shall have to square up to the fact that they are meant to have some meaning sooner or later. We shall see that there are some grave but fortunately solvable problems associated with giving meaning or semantics to λ-expressions.

Let us meanwhile continue our syntactic exposition by giving a definition of what we mean by *reduction*:

DEFN 5.6:   We define three ways in which a λ-expression is related to another by *reduction*:

α λ X.E reduces to λ Y.E [X := Y] if Y is not free in E

β $(\lambda$ X.E$)$ F reduces to E [X := F]

η λ X.$($ F X $)$ reduces to F if X is not free in F

These three, α-reduction, β-reduction, and η-reduction correspond to *change of variable, functional application* and *extensionality* respectively. We have discussed the former two at some length but we need to say something about the latter. Two functions (strictly λ-expressions) are equal by extension if they always give the same result when applied to the same argument. What we are saying in admitting η-reduction is that the function of X which gives F X when applied to X is the same as F itself.

Now we have to extend the meaning of *reduces to* (by any of the three rules given above) so that we can reduce sub-expressions inside larger expressions. This is very easy. We add to the above definition the following clauses.

DEFN 5.7:   If a λ-expression, X, reduces to another, Y, then

1)   X Z reduces to Y Z for any λ-expression, Z

2)   Z X reduces to Z Y for any λ-expression, Z

3) λ Z.X reduces to λ Z.Y for any variable, Z

and a final set of extensions is designed to allow us to carry out arbitrarily many reductions one after the other (including 0) and to reverse the direction of reductions.

When we allow reductions to go in either direction we call them *conversions*. To do this we form what mathematicians call the *reflexive symmetric transitive closure* of the *reduces to* relation and make it into an equivalence relation.

DEFN 5.8:   Conversion. If X, Y and Z are arbitrary λ-expressions:

1)   If X reduces to Y then X converts to Y

2) If X converts to Y and Y converts to Z then X converts to Z

3) X converts to X

4) If X converts to Y then Y converts to X

The above means is that conversion is the same as reduction except that any number of basic reduction steps are allowed (including zero) and the reductions are allowed to run backwards.

At this point we break off to give some examples which will we hope help to illustrate some of the points made above. We can use the relations $\overset{\alpha}{\Rightarrow}$, $\overset{\beta}{\Rightarrow}$ and $\overset{\eta}{\Rightarrow}$ to illustrate particular single step reductions (using definitions 5.6 and 5.7 and $\overset{*}{\Rightarrow}$ to mean any of the reductions used any number of times (definition 5.8 (2)). The more general concept of conversion (in any number of steps) is symbolised by $\simeq$.

Examples of reductions:

$$(\lambda x . x) y \overset{\beta}{\Rightarrow} y$$

$$(\lambda x . y x) y \overset{\eta}{\Rightarrow} y y$$

$$(\lambda x . y x) y \overset{\beta}{\Rightarrow} y y$$

If $S \equiv \lambda x y z . x z (y z)$ then

$$S S S S \overset{\beta}{\Rightarrow} ((\lambda y z . S z (y z)) S S \overset{\beta}{\Rightarrow} (\lambda z . S z (S z)) S \overset{\beta}{\Rightarrow} S S (S S)$$

but we would probably do these last three β-reductions all at once and say

$$S S S S \overset{*}{\Rightarrow} S S (S S)$$

We can also say

$$S S S S \simeq S S (S S)$$

and indeed

$$S S (S S) \simeq S S S S$$

Continuing:

$$
\begin{aligned}
S S S S &\overset{*}{\Rightarrow} S S (S S) \\
&\overset{*}{\Rightarrow} \lambda z . S z (S S z) \\
&\overset{*}{\Rightarrow} \lambda z . S z (\lambda z' . S z' (z z')) \\
&\overset{\beta}{\Rightarrow} \lambda z . S z (\lambda z' z'' . z' z'' (z z' z'')) \\
&\overset{\beta}{\Rightarrow} \lambda z z''' . z z''' ((\lambda z' z'' . z' z'' (z z' z'')) z''') \\
&\overset{\beta}{\Rightarrow} \lambda z z''' . z z''' (\lambda z'' . z''' z'' (z z''' z''))
\end{aligned}
$$

This can not be reduced further except by using α-reduction.

5.8 NORMAL FORMS

It can now be shown by rather tedious but simple arguments that we can do away with α-conversion in the following fashion:

First of all we can place all expressions which are α-convertible (convertible using any number of α-reduction steps) to each other in an equivalence class. This partitions the space of all λ-expressions L into subsets which we can write L/α. Then we can work using these equivalence classes instead of the λ-expressions themselves. However it is still expedient to use representative λ-expressions from the sets to represent the sets themselves. Thus instead of $(\lambda x. x)/\alpha$ we will merely write $\lambda x. x$ (or $\lambda y.y$ or $\lambda q.q$ ...) and now instead of writing $\lambda x. x \overset{\alpha}{=} \lambda y.y$ we can instead write $\lambda x. x = \lambda y.y$. Often we will give names to these functions. For instance the set $\lambda x. x$ is called I — the identity function and $\lambda x y. x$ is called K. These functions without free variables are called *combinators* and we we shall meet others later.

To non-mathematicians all the above may seem like splitting hairs. On the other hand mathematically inclined readers may be disturbed by the informality. We have tried to steer a middle course retaining the *meaning* or *semantics* of conversion and reduction without getting overpowered by its technicalities. The main thing to note is that the introduction of the symbol = is quite significant. Equality is a difficult philosophical concept and usually indicates that some meaning is being invested in the expressions being discussed. Two expressions are equal if and only if they mean the same thing. In the example above $\lambda x. x$ and $\lambda y.y$ both mean the identity function. Note that the attribution of meaning takes us away from the strictly syntactic view of expressions as collections of characters obeying certain rules allowing them to be combined together. We now have to include a semantic view as well — a mapping onto something outside the language of expressions. In this case it is a mapping from λ-expressions to functions (or strictly speaking to L/α).

We have seen that it is possible in the case of α-conversion to place λ-expressions into equivalence classes and choose a representative of the class to denote the class itself. It is easy to choose the representative because they are all the same bar renaming and any will do. We will probably choose one with a bound variable which is different from others with which we are working because that will reduce the risk of having to change variables at a later stage. Suppose however that we try to do the same with β-conversion. Place all the λ-expressions which are equal to one another (i.e. β-convertible) in one equivalence class. Now, however, we have a problem. What shall we do to pick a representative of the class?

Consider the expression 2+3. The Haskell system will tell us that 2+3=5, because 5 is in *canonical form*. We always try to get rid of operators like + by *applying* them to arguments. In the λ-calculus the equivalent idea is called *normal form*. To get to normal form we simplify (using β-reduction) whenever we can.

DEFN 5.9: A *redex* (*red*ucible *ex*pression) is one of the form $((\lambda X.E) F)$ for some variable X and λ-expressions E and F.

A redex is therefore an expression on which a β-reduction may be carried out.

DEFN 5.10: A λ-expression which does not contain any redexes as subexpressions is in *normal form*.

In the same way as we allowed all α-convertible expressions to be equal, we would like to extend equality to β-convertible expressions; that is, expressions convertible by a number of β-reduction steps. Thus we should place all the λ-expressions in equivalence classes and choose a representative element of the class as the *value* of the expressions in the class. We have seen that, in Haskell, the value of an expression is that obtained by evaluating it. Thus it would seem natural to choose as the representative of a group of λ-expressions modulo β-reduction some element which is in normal form (because it cannot be reduced to anything smaller).

There is however a difficulty. There are λ-expressions which are not only not in normal form but never β-reduce to such a form. The most commonly quoted example is given by:

$$(\lambda x. x\ x)\ (\lambda x. x\ x)$$

This expression is a redex and a β-reduction on it produces the same expression we started from. While we have technically carried out a reduction no real reduction in the size or complexity of the expression occurs at all. The situation is worse with some expressions actually growing in size:

$$(\lambda x. x\ x\ x)\ (\lambda x. x\ x\ x) \overset{\beta}{\Rightarrow} (\lambda x. x\ x\ x)\ (\lambda x. x\ x\ x)\ (\lambda x. x\ x\ x)$$

An objection may be raised that $(\lambda x. x\ x)$ represents a function that applies its argument to itself and that this is pathological. Several answers can be given to this. First that the λ-expression exists without reference to any meaning that may be imposed on it. We are therefore bound if we study λ-expressions at all to study their syntactic properties at the very least. Secondly any mathematician will tell you that it is often the pathological cases that point the way to deep and interesting problems in a theory. Thirdly, perhaps self-application is not really all that strange after all. It can even be useful. If we are allowed to use self-application we can, for instance, do away with recursion. As an example of how to do this we can define the factorial function[1] as follows:

```
selfapply x = x x
fact x = selfapply fact' x
         where fact' f 0 = 1
               fact' f n = n * selfapply f (n-1)
```

Note that none of the functions is (even mutually) recursive. But for instance

---

[1] Haskell will not allow this definition as x x cannot be given a type in the Haskell type system. The dynamically typed language SASL [turn79a] allows this definition.

```
fact 2 = selfapply fact' 2
       = fact' fact' 2
       = 2 * selfapply fact' 1
       = 2 * fact' fact' 1
       = 2 * 1 * selfapply fact' 0
       = 2 * 1 * fact' fact' 0
       = 2 * 1 * 1
       = 2
```

We will see below how $\lambda x.\, x\, x$ can be used to build a λ-expression which models a fixed-point finding function which allows the reduction of *any* recursive function to a non-recursive form.

Perhaps we should not be surprised that there are λ-expressions which do not converge to a normal form under β-reduction. We are, after all, modelling computational processes and there are plenty of those which do not converge (i.e. terminate).

5.9 ORDER OF REDUCTION

Careful readers will have noticed that certain λ-expressions have more than one redex. Does it matter which one is chosen to reduce first? Might we get to different normal forms depending on which order we carry out reductions? If this were the case then it would make nonsense of our decision to choose a normal form as representative of the whole equivalence class, because one would be as good as another out of the possibly many normal forms; and they would *not* be the same (in the sense of α-conversion).

We must also determine whether some orders of evaluation terminate while others do not. Luckily there are two fundamental theorems of the λ-calculus called the *Church-Rosser Theorems* which can help us with such questions. The first of these guarantees that if a normal form exists then it is unique (up to α-conversion). The second gives us an order of evaluation that guarantees to find the normal form if it exists.

THEOREM: The First Church-Rosser Theorem

If $A \simeq B$ then there is a C such that $A \overset{*}{\Rightarrow} C$ and $B \overset{*}{\Rightarrow} C$

We will not prove this rigourously as most proofs are long-winded [chur41, bare84, klop80] (although recent developments have cut down its length [hind86]). However we can give an outline of what happens. Suppose that an arrow in the following diagrams represents a single β-reduction step. Then suppose the following represents a λ-expression P undergoing β-reduction using two different redexes and giving Q and R:

Then it is not difficult to believe that we can complete the diamond to obtain:

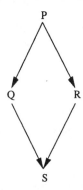

This *parallel moves* lemma is the starting point of the proof. (In fact it may take more than a single reduction step to complete one of the sides of the diamond.) Suppose now that A and B are interconvertible. This means that there is a conversion path of single steps, some along forward and some along backward arrows, of reduction steps leading from A to B. For example:

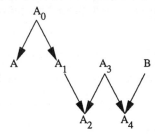

What we do now is to complete the diamonds to get:

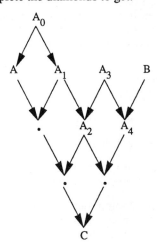

and the item at the bottom, C, is then such that $A \overset{*}{\Rightarrow} C$ and $B \overset{*}{\Rightarrow} C$.

For a detailed proof of the theorem, the reader is referred to Barendregt [bare84] or Hindley et al. [hind86]. Now why does the theorem guarantee that a normal form of N, if any, is unique? Suppose there were two, N_1 and N_2. Then we would know that $N \overset{*}{\Rightarrow} N_1$ and that $N \overset{*}{\Rightarrow} N_2$ and so $N_1 \simeq N_2$. Hence by the first Church-Rosser theorem there is an N' such that $N_1 \overset{*}{\Rightarrow} N'$ and $N_2 \overset{*}{\Rightarrow} N'$. But N_1 and N_2 were themselves normal forms so that the only expressions they can reduce to are α-equivalent forms. Hence N' is α-equivalent (=) to N_1 and N_2. They are therefore α-equivalent to each other.

Thus there is always a representative which we can use as the value of a group of β-equivalent λ-expressions which have a normal form, *viz.* that normal form itself. But if a λ-expression has a normal form this does not necessarily mean that every reduction sequence will reach it. For instance consider the λ-expression:

$$(\lambda \, y.z)((\lambda \, x. \, x \, x) \, (\lambda \, x. \, x \, x))$$

and remember that we are modelling functional application. The usual way of applying a function to an argument (in procedural terms) involves evaluating the argument first and then calling the function. This is the essence of the method of procedure call used in many languages which is known as *call by value*; its technical name as an order of evaluation is *applicative order*. Unfortunately however this order does not always converge to the normal form (if any). The argument (rand) of the application in the above example has no normal form (as has been pointed out earlier in the chapter) and so any attempt to reduce it before applying the rator $\lambda \, y.z$ is doomed to failure by going into a loop.

Another order of evaluation is *normal order*. This involves calling the function *before* evaluating the argument and it is roughly equivalent to the old Algol60 concept of *call by name* (see [seth89] for further details). More technically when there is more than one redex in a λ-expression a normal order reduction always chooses the leftmost one. This *does* work in the example above because the rator $\lambda \, y.z$ ignores its rand altogether and never tries to evaluate it. Such a function is called a *non-strict* function.

DEFN 5.11:   A *strict* function is one that yields no normal form (under any order of evaluation) if applied to an argument that has no normal form.

Luckily the second Church-Rosser theorem provides us with some assistance.

THEOREM: The Second Church-Rosser Theorem

> If A has a normal form, then reducing A in normal order is guaranteed to converge onto that normal form.

Again we will not prove this theorem but will appeal to intuition in the following manner: only non-strict functions or abstractions need be considered because it is only by *ignoring* their arguments that functions can converge when applied to divergent arguments; and in that case they had better not evaluate those divergent arguments before application. Thus evaluation in such cases had better be done outside in. This means that functions will have to be called before their arguments are evaluated and this is exactly what we mean by normal order.

We shall see later (in chapter 7) that this method of application has profound significance to what is called *lazy evaluation* and allows the programming in certain applicative languages of infinite objects (e.g. the set of non-negative integers $\{1,2,3,... \}$). It has in general more expressive power than applicative order, the method favoured by many imperative programming languages.

Let us however point out that normal order evaluation has some disadvantages. The first of these is efficiency. Consider the λ-expression *(λ x. x+x)(3+2)*. In applicative order we will get the following sequence of reductions (regarding the + as an abstraction which adds its arguments):

$$(\lambda x.\ x+x)(3+2) \overset{\beta}{\Rightarrow} (\lambda x.\ x+x)5 \overset{\beta}{\Rightarrow} 5+5 \overset{\beta}{\Rightarrow} 10$$

But with normal order we will get:

$$(\lambda x.\ x+x)(3+2) \overset{\beta}{\Rightarrow} (3+2)+(3+2) \overset{\beta}{\Rightarrow} 5+(3+2) \overset{\beta}{\Rightarrow} 5+5 \overset{\beta}{\Rightarrow} 10$$

and an extra evaluation of the argument has to take place because it appears twice in *(λ x. x+x)*. This would of course be much more serious in cases where the actual argument *(3+2)* was more expensive to compute. Luckily we shall see a way round this when we come to consider methods of implementation both of applicative and of normal order in chapters 6 and 8.

There is another main reason why this order of evaluation has not been considered worthy of use in imperative languages since the disappearance of Algol 60's call by name. To programmers who use this method of calling parameters execution seem to happen in a rather counterintuitive order; and in imperative programming *order matters* because imperative programming is fundamentally side effect driven and the order in which such effects appear is absolutely crucial. However there are *no side effects* in applicative programming and so there is no corresponding worry that things will be done in the right order[1]. We *will* be concerned about whether the order is normal or applicative because, as we saw above, one is possibly more efficient and the other able to find normal forms of more expressions but we will specifically not be worried that we might get the *wrong answer* (because there is only one normal form).

5.10 CONVERTING HASKELL TO λ-EXPRESSIONS

We have tried to demonstrate that the use of λ-expressions can act as an effective model of static expressions such as those which can be written in Haskell. One of our aims will be to show that any Haskell expression can be translated into an equivalent λ-expression and that indeed Haskell is merely a sugaring of the λ-calculus to make it palatable as a useful programming language. We shall see that one way of implementing applicative languages is to implement instead the evaluation (or reduction) of the equivalent λ-expressions. This presupposes that we

---

[1]In practical terms, this may not be so cut and dried. Debugging a functional program may be made harder when normal order is used as, once again, users are suddenly interested in order of evaluation.

can indeed translate (or compile) Haskell expressions to λ-expressions. For very simple expressions this is easy. Take for instance the Haskell expression 1+2. This may be thought of as the application of a rator *primPlusInt*[1] to the rand *1* and the result being applied (in curried fashion) to a second rand *2*. If we use the sign ⇒ to mean *compiles to* (connecting a Haskell expression in Courier font on the left to a λ-expression in Times italic font on the right) then

$$1+2 \Rightarrow ((primPlusInt\ 1)\ 2)$$

and in general if E and F are two Haskell expressions that compile to λ-expressions E' and F' and • is some Haskell infixed operator then:

$$E \bullet F \Rightarrow ((\bullet\ E')\ F')$$

with the brackets (which are only missed out by convention anyway) put in for safety to ensure the correct associativity of the applications.

We have assumed in the above that the simplest expressions of all (constants and variables) compile into themselves. Expressions with the only Haskell unary operator, -, such as -3 and applications of functions to arguments, are already in suitable applicative form and need no further modification except to say that we convert the operator to the appropriate primitive function, *primNegInt* during the compilation process, so as to distinguish unary and binary:

$$E-F \Rightarrow ((primMinusInt\ E')\ F')$$

$$-E \Rightarrow (primNegInt\ E')$$

5.10.1 Expressions with definitions

We now go on to see how to translate expressions with names in them. First of all consider a simple example:

```
let x=2 in x+1
```

We note that a binding is present here. The formal x is bound to the actual 2. This mechanism is, we have seen, modelled by application of an abstraction to an operand which gives rise to similar binding when the abstraction undergoes β-reduction. Thus the above translates to:

$$(\lambda x.((primPlusInt\ x)\ 1))\ 2$$

and in general[2] when V is a variable and E and F are expressions translating to E' and F':

$$\texttt{let}\ V=F\ \texttt{in}\ E \Rightarrow (\lambda\ V.E')\ F'$$

---

[1]Assuming, for the moment, that we are working with Ints, this is a primitive machine coded function for adding integers. We deal with overloading below in section 5.10.7.

[2]We use times italic font for those parts of a Haskell expression which have already been converted to λ-expression form and courier font for Haskell expressions themselves.

We say something later about the translation of `let` expressions involving more complicated patterns than simple variables.

Definitions of functions are also easy — we are after all modelling functions. For example:

```
let f x = x * x in f 3 + f 2
```

first of all compiles to:

```
let f = λ x. x*x in f 3 + f 2
```

and then, using the previous rule, to:

$$(\lambda f. (f\ 3\ +\ f\ 2))(\lambda x.\ x*x)$$

which binds the f to the $(\lambda x.\ x*x)$. Finally, translating the bodies which are operator expressions we get, showing full bracketing:

$$((\lambda f.((primPlusInt\ (f\ 3))\ (f\ 2)))\ (\lambda x.(((primMulInt\ x)\ x))))$$

the general rule being:

$$\texttt{let}\ FN\ V = F\ \texttt{in}\ E \Rightarrow (\lambda\ FN.E')(\lambda\ V.F')$$

5.10.2 Definitions within definitions

Cascaded definitions will now be no more difficult except in scale. Suppose for instance that E is the Haskell expression:

```
let y=2 in let f x = x+y in f 3
```

then

$$E \Rightarrow (\lambda y .(\lambda f.(f\ 3))\ (\lambda x.(primPlusInt\ x)\ y))\ 2$$

5.10.3 Simultaneous definitions and patterns

Let us now turn to *simultaneous* definitions such as:

```
let x = 3
    y = 1 + x
in (x + y) * (x + 2)
```

We are tempted at first to consider this in the same way as a cascade by rewriting it as:

```
let y = 1 + x
in ( let x = 3
     in (x + y) * (x + 2)
   )
```

but unfortunately the scoping is wrong and the initial x does not have a binding. We could change the order of the definitions and rewrite to:

```
let x = 3
in ( let y = 1 + x
     in (x + y) * (x + 2)
   )
```

In this particular example the above trick will work but it will only be possible to rearrange equations in this way if there *is* an order where each object being defined only depends on previous ones. When mutually recursive objects are defined this will not be the case. We shall look at recursion shortly; but the reordering solution is in any case unsatisfactory because it introduces an unpleasant asymmetry. We should try to treat these as the *simultaneous* declarations that they are.

We therefore try a different tack. In the above example, rewrite the equations as

```
let (x,y) = (3,1 + x)
in (x + y) * (x + 2)
```

It can now be seen that we are making a (recursive) definition of a tuple whose elements we call x and y. Let us therefore look at a simpler non-recursive example for the moment — say for instance

```
let (x,y) = (3,5)
in (x + y) * (x + 2)
```

We would like to translate this into:

$$(\lambda\ (x,y).\ (x\ +\ y)\ *\ (x\ +\ 2))\,(3,5)$$

and it would not be difficult to extend the λ-calculus to include such structured patterns. But instead we can give a new name, l say, to the pair (x,y) and then refer, by using selector functions, to *first* l or *second* l whenever we mean x or y respectively. Thus:

$$(\lambda\ l.(primMulInt\ (primPlusInt\ (first\ l))\ (second\ l))\ (primPlusInt\ (first\ l)\ 2))\,(3,5)$$

and in general, for any non-recursive set of definitions:

$$
\left.
\begin{array}{l}
\text{E where } V_1 = F_1 \\
\qquad\quad\ \ V_2 = F_2 \\
\qquad\qquad\quad \cdot \\
\qquad\qquad\quad \cdot \\
\qquad\quad\ \ V_n = F_n
\end{array}
\right\}
\Rightarrow (\lambda\ L\ .\ E')(F_1',F_2',\ldots,F_n')
$$

where L is chosen not to interfere with the other variables present and E' is obtained by the usual translation process but with V_1 replaced by *(first l)*, V_2 by *(second l)*, ... (for suitable selectors *first, second,...*) wherever the V_i appear in E.

We have been much more informal in this explanation of how to translate clauses with multiple local definitions than in the earlier parts of the chapter. The reason is that there we were laying theoretical foundations whereas here we are showing how that theory can be used in practice.

5.10.4 Recursion

So far we have dodged the issue of recursion. Before we see how to cope with it let us have a look at just what we mean when we write a recursive equation. Here are some equations which a mathematician might write:

$$x \quad = \quad 2x^2\text{-}1 \qquad (1)$$
$$f\,x \quad = \quad f\,x + 1 \qquad (2)$$
$$g\,x \quad = \quad g\,x \qquad (3)$$

$$h\,x \quad = \begin{cases} 1 & \textit{if } x=0 \\ h\,3 & \textit{if } x=1 \\ h\,(x\text{-}2) & \textit{if } x>1 \end{cases} \qquad (4)$$

$$fact\,x \quad = \begin{cases} 1 & \textit{if } x=0 \\ x\,fact(x\text{-}1) & \textit{otherwise} \end{cases} \qquad (5)$$

What are the solutions, if any, of these equations? The first is to be solved for x, presumably a floating point number and has the solutions $x=1.0$ and $x=-0.5$. The solutions of equations (2) to (5) are meant to be *functions* however. We will treat them, moreover, as functions from the domain of integers to the range of integers in cases (2), (3) and (4) but allow the range to be floating point for (5).

The equation (2) doesn't have a solution for f. Equation (3) goes to the opposite extreme — any function is its solution. Equation (4) has as a solution:

$$h\,x \ = \begin{cases} 1 & \textit{if } x{\geq}0 \textit{ and } x \textit{ is even} \\ \textit{undefined} & \textit{otherwise} \end{cases}$$

But that is not the *only* solution. Another is:

$$h\,x = 1 \textit{ for all } x$$

and yet a third is:

$$h\,x \ = \begin{cases} 1 & \textit{if } x{\geq}0 \textit{ and } x \textit{ is even} \\ a & \textit{if } x{>}0 \textit{ and } x \textit{ is odd} \\ b & \textit{otherwise} \end{cases}$$

for arbitrary a and b. Likewise with the *fact* equation (5), there are a number of solutions. The obvious one is:

$$fact\,x \ = \begin{cases} x(x\text{-}1)(x\text{-}2)\ldots1 & \textit{if } x{\geq}0 \\ \textit{undefined} & \textit{otherwise} \end{cases}$$

but we can make the value when $x=-1$ any arbitrary integer, say a, and then arrange for the values when $x=-2,-3,-4,\ldots$ to be $-a, a/2, -a/6,\ldots$ and the resulting function will be a solution of (5).

Why then do we pick certain solutions as the correct ones? Partly because we want to know which solution a computer would find. In Haskell the above equations might be written:

```
x          = 2*x*x - 1
f x        = f x + 1
g x        = g x
h 0        = 1
h 1        = 3
h x | x>1  = h (x-2)
fact 0     = 1.0
fact x     = x * fact (x-1)
```

If we try to run this by printing x or evaluating one of the functions for selected values of its argument we will get the following:

```
x?
```

will send the computer into a loop. Why? Because we proceed by replacing the left hand side by the right aiming at a normal form:

$$x \xrightarrow{\beta} 2*x*x - 1 \xrightarrow{\beta} 2*(2*x*x - 1)*(2*x*x - 1) - 1 \ldots$$

In this case no normal form is arrived at. But wait! We stated earlier that a program that went into a loop had as its value the undefined object. It would seem that neither the solution x=1.0 nor x=-0.5 is being chosen by the computer but a *third* solution, x=*undefined*, one that we as mathematicians missed — for indeed it *is* a solution. If we plug this into the right hand side we square the undefined object getting the undefined object and if we double that and subtract 1 we still get the undefined object, which is what is on the left hand side.

The Haskell version of equation can be activated by typing, for instance:

```
f 1?
```

and once again the computation does not terminate:

$$f\,1 \xrightarrow{\beta} f\,1 + 1 \xrightarrow{\beta} f\,1 + 1 + 1 \ldots$$

Again we see that there *is* a solution to the equation which we thought was insoluble. The solution is f=*undefined*.

The undefined object plays such a key rôle in this kind of analysis that we use a special symbol for it:

$$\perp$$

pronounced 'bottom'. It now becomes clear that (3), which has any object as its solution has ⊥ as a particular solution. It will be solved by choosing ⊥ as the preferred answer (see below for the reason for this.) What about (4)? Is ⊥ a solution here? At last the answer is no, for if we were to apply the ⊥ function to 0 we would get ⊥ as the answer — not 1.

Nevertheless we saw that (4) had more than one solution and we again ask which one will be selected by the Haskell version. It is obvious (and can be proved rigorously by induction) that h x will give 1 for all non-negative even x; and it will give ⊥ for all other values of x. In the case of (5), the factorial function, the Haskell solution is undefined on negative arguments. In fact in all cases it is evident that the computer inserts *no arbitrary information* into its solution. Although it will not choose ⊥ as a solution (it is not) it will choose that solution that is *least well defined*.

In fact this is a manifestation of the second law of thermodynamics — that no computer can manufacture information, only process it and possibly destroy it. Note that all this assumes that there exists a partial ordering on solutions which determines when one solution is less well defined than another. This *algebra of domains* has been studied intensively in the last few years chiefly in connection with the denotational semantics of computer languages. We shall talk about the *less well defined* relation in chapter 9. For a more detailed treatment readers should consult Stoy [stoy77] or Schmidt [schm86].

Let us now come back and see how all this is relevant to recursive equations. The equations permitted in Haskell are restricted to a form designed to allow replacement of objects on the left of the equations by the corresponding expressions on the right. In fact all the equations expressible in Haskell are of the form:

```
f = ... f ...
```

or can easily be manipulated into this form. We shall see the details below. If we take that for granted for the moment, we can see that the solution we want is in each case going to be a *fixed point* of the function $\lambda f.(...f...)$.

DEFN 5.12:   A fixed point of a function F is a value x such that $F\ x = x$

In fact the desired solution of our equation will be the *least fixed point*, the one without any arbitrary information. For example let us look at the function h which was defined by equation (4) above. The three Haskell equations which were used to define h can be rewritten using λ-calculus conditionals as:

$$h = \lambda x. \ \ \textit{if } x{=}0 \textit{ then 1 else}$$
$$\textit{if } x{=}1 \textit{ then h 3 else}$$
$$h \ (x{-}2)$$

and we can rewrite this by abstracting the h, as:

$$h = \lambda h. \ (\lambda x. \ \ \textit{if } x{=}0 \textit{ then 1 else}$$
$$\textit{if } x{=}1 \textit{ then h 3 else}$$
$$h(x{-}2)$$
$$) \ h$$

and this is now in the form we want where f is defined as a (non-recursive) function H applied to h where H is the function:

$$\lambda h. \ (\lambda x. \ \ \textit{if } x{=}0 \textit{ then 1 else}$$
$$\textit{if } x{=}1 \textit{ then h 3 else}$$
$$h \ (x{-}2)$$
$$)$$

It is this function that we wish to find the fixed point of.

Luckily there is a λ-expression which is custom built to find minimum fixed points (the ones with no arbitrary information). We want to find a λ-expression Y which is such that for all H

$$Y H = H (Y H)$$

Y is said to be a *fixed point finder* since the equation means that $Y H$ is a fixed point of H. This of course is itself a recursive definition and we wish to find a non-recursive one. One such λ-expression is defined by

$$Y = \lambda H.(\lambda x.(H (x x))) (\lambda x.(H (x x)))$$

We can see that this works because, for any H:

$$
\begin{aligned}
Y H \quad &\overset{\beta}{\Rightarrow} (\lambda x.(H (x x))) (\lambda x.(H (x x))) \\
&= Z \ \text{(say)} \\
&\overset{\beta}{\Rightarrow} (H ((\lambda x.(H (x x))) (\lambda x.(H (x x))))) \\
&= H \ Z \\
&= H \ (Y \ H)
\end{aligned}
$$

Note in passing that Y is not a normal form and indeed has no normal form. This means that any reduction scheme which uses Y must do at least some normal order reduction when Y is applied, as applicative order reduction will diverge at this point.

Thus the solution to a recursive definitional equation of the form

$$f=\ldots f \ldots$$

is

$$f=Y(\lambda f.\ldots f \ldots)$$

Mutual recursion is no great difficulty. We couple the method used in the previous section to deal with simultaneous definitions with the fixed point trick. An example is easily generalised:

```
f = ... f ... g ...
g = ... f ... g ...
```

is converted first to:

```
(f,g)  =  (... f ... g ... ,  ... f ... g ...)
```

and then to

```
fg = (... (first fg) ... (second fg) ...,
     ... (first fg) ... (second fg) ...)
```

which is now a recursive definition of a single entity `fg` with solution:

$$fg = Y(\ \lambda fg\ .\ (\ ...\ (first\ fg)\ ...\ (second\ fg)\ ...,$$
$$...\ (first\ fg)\ ...\ (second\ fg)\ ...))$$

5.10.5 Constructed Values

We have already assumed that the λ-calculus is augmented with constants. To deal with data structures, we shall also assume the addition of some tuple making and tuple accessing functions. As with constants these are not *strictly* needed. Church shows how to simulate tuples with pure λ-expressions, but this is an academic exercise and here we mean to be pragmatic.

Algebraic data types can be translated into these augmented λ-expressions by making the constructor functions for a given type build tuples with an extra field called a *tag*. The tag holds some coded representation, say an integer, which represents which constructor constructed the value. Thus, for lists say, we could use a tag of 0 for `[]` and a tag of 1 for `a:b`. Thus, for instance, the list `['a','b']` would be represented by the tuple structure `(1,'a',(1,'b',(0)))`[1].

5.10.6 Patterns

λ-expressions do not allow patterns after the λ so we have to describe how to translate patterns into pure λ-expressions. We will not go into great detail but point out that sets of equations with patterns on the left can be rewritten as single equations with `case` expressions on the right. For instance

```
length []    = 0
length (h:t) = 1 + length t
```

can be rewritten as:

```
length x = case x of
           [] -> 0
           (h:t) -> 1 + length t
```

The Haskell report contains details of how every expression may be rewritten into a *kernel language* which consists of very simple expressions (near to the λ-calculus + `case` matching). This kind of simple expression can in turn be written in terms of predicate functions which test which kind of list is present (`isnil` and `iscons`) and selector functions (`hd` and `tl`) which retrieve components from structures:

```
length x = if isnil  x then 0                    else
           if iscons x then 1 + length (tl x) else
           matcherror
```

---

[1]We have to cheat slightly here. The (0) represents a tuple with one element. Haskell only allows tuples with 2 or more elements, but that doesn't mean that augmented λ-calculus cannot have monopoles.

where we have introduced the selectors and predicates explicitly. These in turn can be translated into expressions using the tuples we introduced in the last section and the tuple selectors `first`, which retrieves the tag, `second`, `third`,... which retrieve the fields of the tuple, so that we get:

```
length x = if first(x)=0 then 0                              else
           if first(x)=1 then 1 + length (third x) else
           matcherror
```

Such predicates and selectors will be manufactured by the compiler for every algebraic data type or predeclared tuple type in the program. For details the reader should consult chapter 5 in [peyt87].

5.10.7 Overloading

Before leaving this chapter and its description of how to translate Haskell programs into lambda expressions we shall have a short look at overloading. Again we will only give an outline of a method for dealing with overloaded operators.

We have seen in section 5.10 above that operators like + have to get translated into calls of primitive functions like `primPlusInt`. With overloaded operators, we have to decide at some point which of these will be called. When a class `instance` is defined, the compilation system will find out which actual functions are going to be used to implement the operators. It makes a tuple out of these which is called a *dictionary* [wadl88]. Any overloaded function will be called by passing it an extra parameter, hidden from the user, which is the dictionary defining all the operations for this particular call of the function. When a `class` declaration is made, the system finds out which operations will be defined with each instance of the class and the compiler can then translate each operator into an access function which will select the appropriate function from the dictionary.

Consider as an example a heavily simplified[1] definition of the `Integral` class :

```
class Integral a where
(+),(*) :: a -> a -> a
negate  :: a -> a
```

When this declaration is made, the compiler will recognise that any overloaded function such as:

```
f x = x+x*x
```

which uses operators from this class will actually be compiled as:

```
f dict x = x+x*x where
                  ((+),(*),negate) = dict
```

---

[1]In fact these operators belong to the Num class which is a super-class of Integral. See Appendix D

When an instance of the class is declared, for example:

```
instance Integral Int where
  (+)    = primPlusInt
  (*)    = primMulIint
  negate = primNegInt
```

the dictionary for this instance is manufactured:

```
dictInt = (primPlusInt,primMulIint,primNegInt)
```

and whenever the function is called in an `Int` context, this dictionary will be passed in. If it is known that i is an `Int`, then the expression:

```
f i
```

for example, would be compiled into

```
f dictInt i
```

Clearly a number of optimizations can be made. For instance, if it is known at compile time which instances are needed in certain places, then no dictionaries will be needed. If, for example, the call above had been

```
f(i+j)
```

where j is also known to be `Int`, the compiler could produce

```
f dictInt (i `primPlusInt` j)
```

rather than

```
f dictInt (i + j) where ((+),(*),negate) = dictInt
```

In this instance the compiler can do some early evaluation to access elements of a known dictionary. We give no further details here, merely pointing out that this mechanism is powerful enough to cope with the translation of *ad hoc* polymorphism as defined in Haskell into λ-expressions.

5.11 SUMMARY

In this chapter we have seen how the λ-calculus lies behind much of the applicative programming style that we have been exploring. We have seen that the action of functional application, the cornerstone of applicative computing, can be modelled using the λ-calculus. In particular the model rests upon the ideas of substitution, conversion and reduction. We have seen that there are different orders of reduction which naturally correspond to certain well known orders of parameter evaluation in mainstream computing. And we have seen how to take Haskell programs and desugar them into λ-calculus expressions. In fact Haskell is a syntactic variant of the λ-calculus designed to be more readable without losing the expressive power of pure λ-calculus.

5.12 EXERCISES

1.   What are the bound and free variables in the following expressions and their sub-expressions? Show the scope of each bound variable.

a) $(\lambda x. x)(y\ z)$

b) $(\lambda x. x\ y)(\lambda z.z\ x)$

c) $\lambda x\ y\ z.\ x\ z\ (y\ z)$

d) $\lambda x\ y.\ x\ (\lambda x.\ x)\ (\lambda y.\ x\ y)$

2.   What is the effect of the following substitutions?

a) $x[x := y]$

b) $(\lambda x.\ x\ y)[x := y]$

c) $(\lambda x.\ x\ y)[y := x]$

d) $((\lambda x.\ x\ y)(\lambda z.z\ x))[x := y]$

e) $((\lambda x.\ x\ y)(\lambda z.z\ x))[x := z\ y]$

f) $((\lambda p.\ p\ (p\ q))\ (\lambda r.p\ r))[q := p\ r]$

3.   If

$$
\begin{array}{rcl}
I & = & \lambda\ x\ .\ x \\
K & = & \lambda\ x\ y\ .\ x \\
S & = & \lambda\ x\ y\ z\ .\ x\ z\ (y\ z) \\
B & = & \lambda\ x\ y\ z\ .\ x\ (y\ z) \\
C & = & \lambda\ x\ y\ z\ .\ (x\ z)\ y
\end{array}
$$

reduce the following λ-expressions to normal form:

a) $I\ I$

b) $I\ I\ I$

c) $K\ K$

d) $K\ K\ K$

e) $S\ (S\ S)$

f) $S\ (S\ S)\ (S\ S)\ (S\ S)\ S\ S$

g) $S\ times\ (B\ f\ (C\ minus\ one))$

4.   Show, with the above definitions of S, K, I, B and C that:

a) $S\ K\ K \simeq I$

b) $S\ (K\ S)\ K \simeq B$

c) $B (B I) (B K I) \simeq \lambda x y.y x \simeq C I$

5. We shall see later (chapter 7) that any closed λ-expression (one without free variables — also known as a *combinator*) can be converted to a λ-expression containing only combinations of the combinators S, K and I. a) above shows that we can do without I. In fact a single combinator is enough. Let $X = \lambda x$. $x K S K$. Show that

a) $X X X \simeq K$

b) $X (X X) \simeq S$

Combinators like X are called *bases*. By applying them to themselves a few times, show that $\lambda x. x (x S (K K)) K$ and $\lambda x. x (x S (K (K (K I)))) K$ are both bases.

6. Let S be as above and

$$
\begin{array}{rcl}
S^1 & = & S \\
S^i & = & S^{i-1}S \qquad i > 1 \\
S_1 & = & S \\
S_2 & = & S S \\
S_i & = & SS(S_{i-2}) \quad i > 2
\end{array}
$$

Show that $S^i \simeq S_i$. (This example requires the use of induction. See Chapter 9).

7. Convert the following Haskell programs into pure λ-calculus. Assume type Int in all cases

a) ```
let x = 2 in x+1
```

b) ```
let f x = x+y where y=5 in f 2 * f 3
```

c) ```
let f x = x+y
      y   = 5
in f 2 * f 3
```

d) ```
let f x = g where g y = x-y in f 2 3 * f 3 2
```

d) ```
let f x y = x-y in f 2 3 * f 3 2
```

8. Give solutions for the following equations. Which ones contain minimal information?

a) $x=1$

b) $x=x+1$

c) $x=x$

d) $f(x)=1$

e) $f(x)= if (x=1 \text{ or } x=2) \text{ then } 1 \text{ else } f(x-1)+f(x-2)$
```

9.   Show that

a)   If $W = \lambda x. x\, x$ then $W \lambda a\, b.b\, (a\, a\, b)$ is a fixed point finder.

b)   If Y_0 is any fixed point finder then the sequence $Y_{i+1} = G(Y_i)$ generates other fixed point finders where $G = \lambda Y\, H.H\, (Y\, H)$.

10. Write a Haskell program which will reduce a λ-expression to normal form (if it has one) and shows each individual reduction step in the reduction.

11. Carry out exercise 7. again but assuming that overloading is present.

Chapter 6

Applicative Implementation

6.1 INTRODUCTION

One of the central reasons which we considered in chapter 1 for the importance of applicative programming was that research was being done on unconventional hardware, much of it to exploit parallelism, in order to overcome the problems of the von Neumann bottleneck. At present however such hardware is not available, even as a research tool, to many of us and we have to make do with traditional machinery. This means that if we want to experiment with applicative programming techniques and methods and to develop environments in which applicative work can be carried out, we will have to implement such tools on Von Neumann hardware using imperative techniques. This chapter looks at techniques of this kind in detail. Our first attempts to look at how a program runs will concentrate on applicative order evaluations. In chapter 8 we will extend our view to consider implementation of normal order evaluation.

6.2 THE SECD MACHINE

Our aim will be to investigate various internal syntactic methods of storing applicative programs, the conversion of source programs into such internal forms and their *evaluation* to yield printable values (normal forms). We see therefore that there will be a *compilation* stage (conversion of source programs to internal form); and an *execution* stage (evaluation of the internal forms).

It is not our intention to say much in this book about compilation. Many books are already available on this subject, for example [davi81]. We are, however, more concerned here with semantics than syntax and we shall therefore concentrate on the execution or evaluation phase. However we should note that it will be of concern to us to choose a set of internal forms which are appropriate to the semantics of applicative programming; so that even if we do not have machines that are directly capable of executing applicative programs, we will be able to *simulate* at least some of their aspects easily and efficiently. This will have the added benefit that we can design such machines to our own tastes since they are only present in software anyway. We will therefore be considering a number of different possible internal architectures. Variations will be reflected in the data structures used in our simulations of such *soft* or *abstract* machines.

In chapter 5 we saw that it was possible to consider Haskell programs as sugared λ-expressions. It would therefore seem to make sense to propose some efficient internal representation of λ-expressions as a possible internal form of Haskell programs. The execution of such internal programs would then correspond directly to the conversion (principally β-reduction) of λ-expressions to normal form.

Perhaps the most obvious internal representation of λ-expressions is as a string of characters. The algorithms for doing substitution which were developed in chapter 5 would then be of use in successively replacing sub-strings representing redexes by their reduced form. To ensure applicative order evaluation innermost redexes would be reduced first. When a state was reached when there were no redexes, the resulting normal form would be printed as the result. Note that special action would have to be taken to reduce expressions representing combinations with a rator which was a standard abstraction like $+$[1].

The above method of reduction based on copying strings is, for obvious reasons, known as *string reduction*(see chapter 8 for further discussion). It has, however, a number of drawbacks. It uses a representation which is not structured in any way which is natural to the tasks of finding and replacing redexes. Another serious inefficiency is that, if an argument appears more than once in the body of an abstraction, then, when substitution for it takes place during application to an operand, it will be copied *each time* it appears. This is very wasteful of space and a method which *shares* storage for such objects is vastly preferable. Such a method is now presented. It is based on a machine developed by Landin [land65] which was specifically designed to model the λ-calculus.

Landin proposed a machine to interpret internally represented λ-expressions called the *SECD* machine. There are four chief components to it:

- A Stack   *S*

- An Environment   *E*

- A Code vector   *C*

- A Dump   *D*

The names *S*, *E*, *C* and *D* are traditional, following Landin's paper in which some of the original ideas of applicative programming were first proposed. The four components collectively keep a track of the *state* of the SECD machine. Let us take the components one by one, but not in the order above.

---

[1]The techniques described in this chapter are not specific to implementations of Haskell. They are applicable to a wide range of functional programming languages. Each will have its own set of primitive operations implemented in machine code. Substitute `primAddInt` ... or the functions appropriate to the language of your choice.

Firstly, the *C* component — the *code*. Conventional computers have a program which is internally represented by a code vector which is composed of a list of transformations to be carried out on the state of the machine. Each transformation is specified by a single machine code instruction and the machine normally has a hardware register which keeps a track of what instruction to carry out next. Now, as has been repeatedly stated in the first few chapters, applicative programs don't *do* anything. They merely describe some canonical value. How shall we interpret this in an imperative framework? If we have to evaluate some such expression as x+y which is composed of subexpressions x and y then, in the absence of the ability to evaluate these in parallel, we must evaluate them in series. Consequently what we *do* is evaluate objects (x and y) or apply machine code functions (+) to them. The code therefore consists at any moment of a list of instructions either to *load* and evaluate an object or to carry out a primitive operation such as addition on some already evaluated object(s). The things to be evaluated will be (pointers to) internal forms of λ-expressions and these will be held in some structured form to be discussed below. The primitive operations such as *load* and *add* will have individual op-codes.

We talked above of a *load* operation. Where do objects get loaded to? The answer to this question allows us to introduce the second component of the SECD machine: the *stack S*. As the operation of loading x+y will break down into loading first x, then y and finally doing an addition, we must keep the values of x and y somewhere until it is time to do the addition. One choice is to use a stack. Then, when primitive operations come to be carried out, they can find their operands on the top of the stack, already evaluated, and the operations can then be carried out and will place their results back on the stack. Thus we see that the whole idea of the SECD machine is that it *transfers unevaluated objects on C to the stack S, evaluating them (to normal form) as it goes.* The compiler, when presented with a Haskell expression to evaluate, will generate a single *load* instruction which refers to the data structure which is the internal representation of the expression. When the SECD machine starts, *C* only contains this one instruction — to load the evaluated expression onto the stack. The stack will be empty when the machine starts and, when it stops, it will have a single value on *S* which is the normal form of the original expression. The final action of the SECD machine before a return is made to the compiler to fetch another expression for evaluation is to print the single item left on *S*.

We now come to a third component of an SECD machine's state — the *environment, E*. We have seen that when expressions are loaded they are broken up into their sub-parts each of which will in turn be loaded. But this process can only go so far. Ultimately expressions are made up of objects of two kinds which are not decomposable further. If such an object is a constant it presents no problem because it is already in normal form and the action of loading merely consists of moving it from *C* to *S*. But in the case of variables, how are we to evaluate these before they get their normal value placed on the stack? The fact of the matter is that variables have different values in different parts of a Haskell expression depending on the values of the variables defined by an equation in scope at these places. The way we keep a track of these values is to keep them in a model of an environment. This is an associative store which provides a mapping from identifiers to their current value. The environment is maintained by adding an association whenever a binding takes place — that is, when a function is applied to an argument and a β-reduction is about to take place. Then the formal parameter name is bound to the actual argument.

The final component of the SECD machine's state is the *dump*, D. This component is the one which controls function calling in applicative languages. The basic idea is that, when a function is called, a completely new piece of program corresponding to the body of that function, (i.e. a new C) is executed using a purely local stack and in a completely different environment in which variables are bound to the values which were in force at the point the function was defined rather than those at the time of calling. We therefore need to save the old values of S, E and C so that they can be resumed when the function call has finished. We use D to save these old values. In fact D will keep an old value of D itself as well as the other three components so that the dump consists of a complete SECD machine state which tells the machine how to return from a subroutine. It plays the same part as a *return* address does in a conventional implementation of subroutine calling.

We shall use the technique of *operational semantics* [reyn72] for describing how the machine works. This method consists of showing how the *state* of the machine (the SECD quadruple in our case) is transformed to a new state in each possible different case of the *code* part of the state. We shall show this by giving a *state transition function* called do. This function will be described below in Haskell and operates on SECD quadruples to produce new ones. The operation of the SECD machine can then be viewed as a sequence of applications of this do function until some termination condition is obtained. Termination presumably occurs when all the code (initially the single expression in C) has been executed and a single resulting value remains on the the stack S. The initial state of the SECD machine is

```
( [] , es , [c] , EmptyDump )
```

where es represents an environment in which various *standard* objects are represented. These will include such constant machine coded standard functions as those for doing arithmetic. The other three components show an empty stack, [], since no values have been transferred there yet from C; an empty dump, EmptyDump, because one of these is only present when we have entered a subroutine (function); and a code component C which consists of a list with one member, c, — the internal representation (placed there by the compiler) of the single expression to be evaluated.

The final state, reached before the answer is printed, will be in the form

```
( [s] , es , [] , EmptyDump )
```

where S is a list containing the single value, s, of the original expression that was in C; es is as before; C contains nothing further to evaluate and is therefore the empty list; and D is empty as before.

6.3 REPRESENTATION

We have actually jumped ahead in deciding how to represent things internally. We have evidently already decided to represent the SECD state as a *tuple* of four elements. Other ways could have been chosen. For instance we might have imagined that the state should be held as a pair of pairs:

```
( ( S , E ) , ( C , D ) )
```

or some other way. We also seem quite naturally to have assumed that at least S and C will themselves be lists — S being the empty list to start with and having one element at the end; C being a singleton list to start with and empty at the end. We could certainly have used an abstract data type for each of these — we saw one such for stacks in section 4.5.

In a certain sense these representations *do not matter* — we may only be interested in the abstract transformations. In an actual software implementation or perhaps even in a piece of custom built hardware, the values of S, E, C and D will probably be in *registers*. In real implementations the state of the machine is *distributed*; it is not one list but is found in a real hardware store at various locations in that store.

It is a matter of convenience that we use Haskell itself to explain how a machine for evaluating Haskell works. That said, it should be pointed out that there is a fine dividing line to be drawn between *abstract* definitions of languages and machines and *concrete* representations of how to implement them. Abstract definitions have the advantage that they should not be dependent on extra knowledge of how a particular piece of hardware or software works and that they should therefore be understandable by everyone; but concrete representations allow more details to be given of how real implementations can be engineered to be more useful and efficient.

We have tried in this first attempt at describing an implementation to stay very near to an abstract definition — using Haskell to describe the workings of Haskell — but nevertheless we make no apology for making some concrete decisions. We will assume that:

An SECD quadruple is represented by a 4-tuple.

S and C are themselves lists of values and instructions respectively.

D is either EmptyDump when the machine is not executing a subroutine or is another SECD quadruple when it is:

For the moment we will represent the environment E by a list of Name-Value pairs.

```
type Stack = [ Value ]
type Env   = [ (Name,Value) ]
type Code  = [ Instr ]
data Dump  = EmptyDump | Quadruple (Stack,Env,Code,Dump)

type Name = [ Char ]
```

All we need from an environment is to look it up to find the Value of an object in the environment. We also need to be able to create new environments out of old ones by binding objects to values. These two can be represented by functions lookup and declare which will be described below.

The data type `Value` contains the objects that can be the results of evaluation. As these are the normal forms of expressions to be evaluated, we could have used the same data type for `Value` as for code items, `Instr`. But we will keep them separate so that it is always obvious which items are evaluated and which still to be evaluated:

```
data Value = IntValue   Int   |
             FloatValue Float |
             CharValue  Char  |
             BoolValue  Bool
```

We shall extend this definition later. The type `Instr` of instructions is now discussed.

6.4 OPERATIONAL SEMANTICS OF THE SECD MACHINE

We now embark on giving the individual cases of SECD transitions for the various possible instructions on the *C* code list.

Let us see just what kind of objects would be generated by a compiler. At a basic level we have seen in chapter 5 that the only λ-expressions we *need* to be able to represent are identifiers, abstractions and combinations. However in a more realistic situation we will, for efficiency's sake, make a compiler produce other objects which represent special cases of common λ-expressions represented in a way which allows quicker access to, and more compact representation of, the information. We have already mentioned for instance that *constants* of various types will be added to our pool of λ-expressions though it is theoretically possible to use certain λ-expressions as constants and others as operators which act on them in a way consistent with the rules of algebra. As another example consider expressions like x+y. A formally correct way of treating this expression would be to consider it as an abstraction `adder` applied to x and y: `adder x y` and use the mechanism for application to get the value of the function. We shall use a more direct method. By allowing our SECD machine to have other operations besides application at the lowest level we can treat `adder` as a binary operator which expects to find its two arguments on the stack and returns the result of adding them to the stack.

Our basic set of instructions will then be:

```
data Instr = LoadInt Int        |
             LoadFloat Float     |
             LoadChar Char       |
             LoadBool Bool       |  -- to load constants
             LoadVar Name        |  -- to load a variable
             Add Instr Instr     |  -- binary operations
             .
             .
             Negate Instr        |  -- unary operations
             .
             .
             LoadAbs Name Instr  |  -- to load an abstraction
             LoadAppl Instr Instr   -- to load an application
```

For example the Haskell program `let x=1 in x+2` would be converted to the instruction:

```
(LoadAppl (LoadAbstr "x" (Add (LoadVar "x")(LoadInt 2)))
          (LoadInt 1)
)
```

corresponding to the λ-expression:

$$(\lambda x . (x+2)) 1$$

Let us now consider each possible class of λ-expression in turn.

1. Constants

In fact everything in Haskell is a constant! What is meant here is a primitive sub-expression in Haskell which is self descriptive like `1`, `True` or `'*'`. In other languages these are sometimes called *literals*. When such a constant appears in the code to be evaluated, we need do nothing except transfer it to the stack. We will presume that the compiler has marked each constant with its type by using one of the constructors `LoadInt`, `LoadFloat`,.... This will accompany the constant wherever it goes. This aspect allows our SECD machine to cope with dynamically typed applicative languages. In an SECD implementation of a functional language such as Haskell which is type-checked at compile time it would not be necessary to tag constants in this way.

We represent the action of the machine on encountering a particular kind of λ-expression on *C* by one or more Haskell equations giving a clause in the definition of a function `do`. For constants the state transitions given in Figure 6.1 are appropriate.

```
do ( S , E , (LoadInt   const):C , D ) =
                     (IntValue   const:S , E , C , D)
do ( S , E , (LoadFloat const):C , D ) =
                     (FloatValue const:S , E , C , D)
do ( S , E , (LoadChar  const):C , D ) =
                     (CharValue  const:S , E , C , D)
do ( S , E , (LoadBool  const):C , D ) =
                     (BoolValue  const:S , E , C , D)
```

Figure 6.1 Loading constants (literals) to the stack

In each case we are taking the constant off the *C* list and putting it on the stack *S*.

2. Variables

The second simplest case that has to be dealt with is that of the variables (or more properly speaking *identifiers*) which name the objects they are bound to. To find out what they are bound to, the current environment must be

inspected. The resulting value will then be put on the stack. The compiler will
tag identifiers with the constructor `Loadvar`.

```
do ( S , E , (Loadvar x):C , D ) =
               ( lookup x E : S  , E , C , D )
```

Figure 6.2 Loading variables (identifiers) to the stack

As we stated earlier, our first attempt at an implementation of an environment
will be just a list of identifier-value pairs. Hence the `lookup` function can be
coded by:

```
lookup name [] = error "Unbound variable"
lookup name ( (n,val):env ) | name==n   = val
                            | otherwise = lookup name env
```

Note the call of `error`. This represents $\bot$ in one of its manifestations and a
message will be issued telling the user that the identifier in question is not in
scope. In order to extract the maximum information out of a situation like this,
an *error value* could be allowed to propagate through the system. Thus we
could put it on the stack and make it interact with other objects in the system
under the proviso that when it does (for instance when it might be added to
something else) the answer obtained will itself be the error value. Thus a
trace-back of a chain of subexpressions containing the error would be
obtained. To implement this properly, we should introduce the extra error
object to the type `Value`:

```
data Value = IntValue   Int   |
             FloatValue Float |
             CharValue  Char  |
             BoolValue  Bool  |
             ErrorValue
```

This would entail adding clauses to the `do` function to deal with interaction
with `Errorvalue` and other values but we will not give further details here.
An interesting exposition of this kind of modification to interpreters can be
found in [wadl90].

The presence of unbound variables could, in fact, only happen with a
dynamically checked language. Haskell is statically checked and any unbound
variables would be found by the compiler, so the first clause of the `lookup`
function would be unnecessary.

3. Simple Expressions

From variables and constants we can, with the addition of the standard
operators, make more complicated expressions. As stated before it would be
possible to treat these operators as functions in the same way as other user
defined objects (see Case 2), but we prefer the more efficient method of
treating these operators as built in. What we must do is to delay the action of
the operator until after its operands have been evaluated. This means
arranging for such operands to be found by the operator on the stack after
they have been evaluated. For example: Suppose that the expression `x+y`

needed evaluation. The compiler must be made to represent this expression as
`Add (Loadvar "x")(Loadvar "y")` and when the machine finds such a
representation at the start of *C*, it must take it off and put back the operator
and the two operands. The operator is changed to `DoAdd` which actually
carries out the addition when the two operands have been evaluated and are
found on top of the stack. Thus we get:

```
do ( S , E , (Add e1 e2):C , D ) =
              (S , E , e2:e1:DoAdd:C , D)
do ( (IntValue v1) : (IntValue v2) : S , E , DoAdd:C , D ) =
              (IntValue (v1+v2) : S , E , C , D)
do ( (FloatValue v1):(FloatValue v2):S , E , DoAdd:C , D ) =
              (FloatValue (v1+v2):S , E , C , D)
```

Figure 6.3 Addition

We can treat all binary operators in the same way and all unary operators in a
similar uniform way. We have to extend our definition of the kinds of
instructions to:

```
data Instr = LoadInt Int          |
             LoadFloat Float      |
             LoadChar Char        |
             LoadBool Bool        | -- to load constants
             LoadVar Name         | -- to load a variable
             Add Instr Instr      | -- binary operations
             .
             .
             Negate Instr         | -- unary operations
             .
             .
             DoAdd                | -- to add stack elements
             .
             .
             DoNegate             | -- to negate an element
             .
             .
             LoadAbs Name Instr   | -- to load an abstraction
             LoadAppl Instr Instr   -- to load an application
```

We have defined the effect of the operator + in Haskell (or whatever
functional language is being implemented) by doing the operation (`v1+v2`
above) using the built-in (overloaded) addition facilities of Haskell itself. The
trouble about that is that we are using Haskell itself to describe how a
particular implementation of Haskell works. It is being used both as language
and as meta-language. It can be a confusing practice to use the abstruse
semantic features of a language to describe the language itself. We stand in
danger of not explaining anything at all. Reynolds [reyn72] describes the
dangers of this kind of method very well as well as giving a first class account
in great detail of how interpreters (for hypothetical machines like the SECD
machine) work.

We shall continue to use Haskell as a meta-language but we should be clear that this is just a descriptive trick and we should really enter some machine code routine here to do the addition at the very lowest level. A similar routine must be available for each possible basic Haskell operator.

4. Non-strict Operations

The above method has to be altered slightly in the case of built-in non-strict operators such as the ternary *conditional* operator. For strict operators we wish to evaluate the operands before applying the operator but with non-strict operators we may not want to evaluate all the operands. For instance the expression if test then left else right in Haskell can be thought of as the application of a ternary operator cond to the three arguments test, left and right: but we certainly don't want to evaluate both left and right and we can only find out which to evaluate *after* the test has been calculated. When we come to look at the implementation of lazy evaluation in chapter 8 we will see that a coherent mechanism can be given for evaluating all kinds of operators, both strict and non-strict. In the meantime, however, we must treat each non-strict operator in its own piecemeal fashion. As pointed out in chapter 5 the fixed point finder Y described there has no normal form and must therefore be treated non-strictly. We will deal with recursion in a special way in Case 9.

If the compiler produces Cond test left right as the instruction representing the above expression, then we can implement conditionals by:

```
do ( S , E , (Cond test left right ):C , D ) =
        (S , E , test:(Switch left right):C , D)
do ( (BoolValue True ):S , E , (Switch left right):C , D ) =
        (S , E , left :C , D)
do ( (BoolValue False):S , E , (Switch left right):C , D ) =
        (S , E , right:C , D)
```

Figure 6.4 Conditionals

Notice how the evaluation of one of left or right is delayed until the instruction Switch is encountered and then one of the operands is abandoned. We have to augment the type Instr once again:

```
Instr = ...                   |
        Cond Instr Instr Instr |   -- for conditional
        Switch Instr Instr     |   -- to make a choice
```

A similar kind of thing can be done for the logical operators && and ||. These do not *need* to be non-strict but efficiency is gained if they are. In the expression x&&y we do not need to evaluate y if we have already found that x is False. Similarly the second arm of a disjunction need not be evaluated if the first has value True. Thus it is better to treat each of these operators in its own way. Suppose that the compiler produces `Or e1 e2` and `And e1 e2`. The appropriate transformations can then be written:

```
do ( S , E , And e1 e2:C , D) = (S , E , e1:(And2 e2):C , D)
do ( S , E , Or  e1 e2:C , D) = (S , E , e1:(Or2  e2):C , D)
do (BoolVal False:S , E , (And2 e2):C , D) =
                                (BoolVal False:S , E , C , D)
do (BoolVal True:S , E , (And2 e2):C , D) =
                                (S , E , e2:C , D)
do (BoolVal True:S , E , (Or2  e2):C , D) =
                                (BoolVal True :S , E , C , D)
do (BoolVal False:S , E , (Or2  e2):C , D) =
                                (S , E , e2:C , D)
```

Figure 6.5 Non-strict logical operations

with the addition of the following instructions:

```
Instr = ...                  |
        And  Instr Instr | -- for logical connectives
        Or   Instr Instr |
        And2 Instr       | -- for second argument id needed
        Or2  Instr
```

5. Combinations

A combination represents the application of a function to an argument. We can treat this as a simple expression in the same way as in case 3 since the compiler must remember that there is an invisible application operator between the rator and the rand. Thus:

```
do ( S , E , LoadAppl rator,rand:C , D ) =
                (S , E , rand:rator:Apply:C , D)
```

Figure 6.6 Combinations

and the actual application is delayed until the rator and the rand have both been evaluated and put on the stack. Case 7 below deals with this.

6. Abstractions

What is the value of a λ-abstraction? It is not a printable object. We cannot do anything with a function except apply it and it is at the point of application and only then that we will need to get inside its body to be able to execute it. At application time, however, we will need something more. Function application involves changing the environment to the one in force at the textual position of the abstraction. To be able to access that environment at application time, the value placed on the stack when an abstraction is evaluated must consist of a package consisting of three items:

- The body of the abstraction — the code to be evaluated at call.
- The environment in which to evaluate the body.
- The variable of abstraction — so that it can be bound to the actual parameter when calling.

Such a package is called a *closure* and is (in an operational sense) the value of a λ-abstraction. It contains all the algorithmic information needed to make a function work. Thus the appropriate transformation is:

```
do ( S , E , (LoadAbs var body):C , D ) =
            ( Clos body E var:S , E , C , D )
```

Figure 6.7 Abstractions

where `Clos` is a new closure constructor added to the Value type:

```
data Value = IntValue    Int   |
             FloatValue Float |
             CharValue  Char  |
             BoolValue  Bool  |
             Clos Instr Env Name
```

7. The Point of Application

Now we can see what happens when an application actually takes place. We will have a closure on the stack and, below that, the actual argument to which the function is to be applied (see Case 5). The application is signalled by having the `Apply` object on the code list, C. What we have to do is to simulate entering a subroutine. We are going to abandon temporarily the current SECD state and change to one in which a different environment entirely is operating and different code is being executed. There will be a new empty stack upon which to evaluate the sub-expression represented by the body of the function being applied. However we will eventually need to return to (just after) the point of application so that the result of the application can be used. To be able to effect this return, we push down the current state into the dump, D and prepare for execution of the body by binding the formal and actual parameters together. This is done using the `declare` function which returns the new environment. Hence:

```
do ( Clos body newE formal:actual:S ,
        E ,
            Apply:C ,
              D )
    =
    ( [] ,
            declare formal actual newE ,
              [body] ,
                 Quadruple (S,E,C,D) )
```

Figure 6.8 Applying a closure

This transformation is the crux of how we implement function calls and will repay careful examination. Here is a definition of `declare` which is correct in the context of the simple minded approach we are taking to the representation of environments. It merely extends the list of bound pairs:

```
declare formal actual E = (formal,actual):E
```

8. Returning

The penultimate case we have to deal with involves returning from a subroutine. When does this happen? There is no explicit `Return` instruction in the code repertoire of the SECD machine: but the end of a subroutine is reached when there is nothing left on *C* to be evaluated, i.e. when it is `[]`. At that point one of two things can happen depending upon the state of *D*. If *D* is `EmptyDump`, the machine is executing at the top level and it stops. The controlling process must arrange for the single object left on the stack to be printed and we regard this as happening externally to the working of the SECD machine.

If, however, *D* contains a pushed down SECD state, a `Quadruple`, that must be restored and the result of the subroutine expression evaluation made available to the calling routine:

```
do ( [value] , oldE , [] , Quadruple (S,E,C,D) ) =
                (value:S , E , C , D)
```
Figure 6.9 Returning from a function call

9. Recursion

When a recursive definition is encountered, an object must be put on the stack which involves a closure in which the embedded environment contains a binding of the name to the recursive object itself. This presents some special problems which we now discuss.

We will assume that when the compiler encounters a definition of the form:

f = E *involving* f

it will generate a structure of the form `Fix f E'` where, as usual E' is what the compiler generates for E. The SECD machine will have to deal with such an object as follows:

```
do ( S , E , (Fix var body):C , D ) =
             (S , newE , body:(Fixup var):C , D)
             where newE = declare var Guess E
```
Figure 6.10 Encountering recursion

What is happening here is that the machine is going to evaluate the body of the recursive definition in an environment where the name (var) is bound to a estimated value which will later be fixed up as follows:

```
do ( v:S , E , Fixup var:C , D ) =
                    (v:S , fixenv E var v , C , D)
```

Figure 6.11 Carrying out the recursion

The function `fixenv` cannot be implemented in Haskell as it involves finding the binding of the `var` on the environment E and *overwriting* the Guess found there with the v on the stack.

It is not good enough merely to make a *new copy* of the environment E but with the guess replaced by the value because this would not change any references to the guess inside v (which as stated above is going to be a closure for a recursive function). The implementation must involve *overwriting* so that all internal structures that point to (share) the guess will end up sharing the recursive value.

This may appear like cheating but we must realise that our implementation language will not actually be Haskell itself. We have used Haskell as a matter of convenience only and it is not convenient in this case! What may indeed be a justified criticism is that applicative languages are not as powerful as we thought. We shall see however that when we replace applicative order evaluation by normal order this problem need not arise.

6.5 AN IMPROVED SECD MACHINE

In this section we will show how to improve the SECD machine in a number of ways. One of the classical methods of improving the performance of any computer language is to transfer as much work as possible from execution time to compile time. In this way actions performed many times in a loop at run time can sometimes be reduced to a single action at compile time.

In the machine described above there is one outstanding place where such *factorisation* can be done; and that is in the traversal of the data structure built by the compiler for an expression involving prefixed and infixed operators. Consider for example the transformation:

```
do ( S , E , (Add e1 e2):C , D ) =
                    (S , E , e2:e1:DoAdd:C , D)
```

This really does no useful work at all but merely flattens a tree-like structure:

and turns it into a linear list:

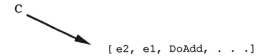

C

[e2, e1, DoAdd, . . .]

so that the machine can encounter the primitive actions to be carried out one at a time.

This flattening can be done for *all* strict operators and is a well known technique called translation to *Reverse Polish* (see for instance [rand64]) which can be carried out at compile time so w ask the compiler to produce:

(S , E , e1:e2:DoAdd:C , D)

in the first place (and indeed e1 and e2 may themselves be expressions which can be flattened.)

The linearising effect of writing in Reverse Polish notation is so effective that the code produced can be written in a much more conventional way as *assembly code* for our hypothetical machine. Let us call it the SECD2 machine [turn75] to distinguish it from the first one, whose operational semantics have already been given earlier in this chapter. A summary of implementation in terms of SECD2 now follows.

6.6 SECD2 MACHINE CODE

As explained above, there is an instruction for each strict operation in the Haskell language. These are parameterless and operate on operands found at the top of the stack. For example there is PLUS which adds the top two elements and leaves the result on the stack in their place[1]. (It also checks, for a dynamically typed language, that the elements being added are indeed numbers by looking at their constructor tags and that, if an 'overflow' occurs, an error is signalled. In either case an 'error value' is left on the stack). There is a whole host of such instructions : PLUS, MINUS, TIMES, EQUAL, LESS, GREATER, CONS1, CONS2,..., FIRST, SECOND, ... where the CONSs are for building tuples of various sizes and the FIRST, SECOND... are for accessing fields of tuples.

Operands are dealt with by an LDC instruction which loads a constant (with its type tag) onto the stack and by LOOKUP which is used to place on the stack the value associated with a name in the current environment.

---

[1]Again we are neglecting overloading. We presume that the compiler has identified all the built in functions for the language being implemented.

Thus for instance the code generated by the compiler for the Haskell expression:

```
3 + x
```

would be:

```
LDC        3
LOOKUP     x
PLUS
```

The environment can be controlled and manipulated with three instructions: DECL, DECLGUESS and TIEKNOT which we now explain The first of these represents a further flattening of the code so that an explicit binding such as occurs in definitions:

```
name = expression
```

is dealt with in two parts in the code. First comes the code for the expression which leaves the value on the stack. Then there is an instruction

```
DECL name
```

which takes an item off the stack and augments the environment by binding name to that item. So for example the declaration:

```
x = y + 2 * z
```

compiles to:

```
LOOKUP     y
LDC        2
LOOKUP     z
TIMES
PLUS
DECL       x
```

For recursive declarations of the form name = expression the instruction:

```
DECLGUESS name
```

is used instead of DECL.

DECLGUESS makes a dummy entry in the environment, binding the name to a dummy Guess entry. This binding happens *before* the expression is evaluated and afterwards it is fixed up by a

```
TIEKNOT    name
```

which overwrites the Guess value with the value of the expression which is now to be found on top of the stack.This value is, of course, usually a closure referring to the environment itself so that a knot gets tied by making the environment have a reference to itself embedded within it.

Conditionals are dealt with by a branching instruction:

```
FORK       label
```

This takes the top element off the stack and inspects whether it is True or False. If neither an error is signalled. If False, a jump is made to the machine code instruction at the given label. If True the next instruction in sequence is obeyed. It will be the first of the sequence representing the value of the left arm of the conditional. At the end of this sequence of instructions will be an unconditional jump

```
GOTO      label
```

to the common continuation of the two arms[1]. For instance

```
(if x>y then 1 else 2) + z
```

would give the code

```
        LOOKUP      x
        LOOKUP      y
        GREATER
        FORK        L1
        LDC         1
        GOTO        L2
   L1   LDC         2
   L2   LOOKUP      z
        PLUS
```

A slightly simplified *closure* mechanism is possible with the aid of the DECL instruction described above. Before, a closure consisted of three things:

- The environment in which the closure was formed.

- The body to be executed in that environment when the function is called.

- The name of the formal parameter — to be bound to the actual argument at call time.

With this scheme, however, we can conflate the last two by making the first instruction of the body a DECL instruction which does the binding.

Before giving an example of this we must, however, complete the discussion of the function calling mechanism. We need to consider two further aspects, closure formation and application of a closure to an argument. Closures may be formed by using a

```
LOADFN      body
```

instruction which places a closure consisting of the environment and the address of the body on the stack. This happens when a functional object appears in the program either by declaration or anonymously.

Functions are *applied* by the execution of an APPLY instruction which effectively makes entry to a subroutine. APPLY is a zero-address instruction which expects to find two items on the stack — a closure and an actual parameter to apply it to.

---

[1]This represents a slight variation of Turner's original SECD machine implementation [turn75].

These are removed and the current SECD quadruple pushed down onto D to provide state information which will be used on returning from the subroutine. The actual parameter is replaced on the stack so that the DECL instruction in the body can find it there and after the environment has been updated to the value found inside the closure, a jump is made to the body pointed at by the closure.

When a function has performed its work and has left the value of its result on the stack, it must return to the point of calling. There is a RETURN instruction which is placed at the end of the code of a subroutine implementing such a function[1].

Let us now look at an example of the definition and application of a function using the instructions described above. Consider the simple definition:

```
f x = x + 1
```

This would be implemented as:

```
        LOADFN      L1    This creates a closure
                          for \ x -> x+1
        DECL        f     This binds f to it
          .
          .
L1      DECL        x     This is the body. It binds
                          x to the actual parameter
        LOOKUP      x
        LDC         1
        PLUS
        RETURN
```

A call of `f` such as

```
f ( a + b )
```

then gets compiled to:

```
        LOOKUP      f
        LOOKUP      a
        LOOKUP      b
        PLUS
        APPLY
```

Had the function `f` been a recursive one, the LOADFN L1 and DECL f instructions would have been replaced by:

```
        DECLGUESS       f
        LOADFN          L1
        TIEKNOT         f
```

All the discussion about function entry suggests that this particular method looks more and more like the implementation of a conventional stack orientated machine. This can be further emphasised when it is realised that the dump D can be

---

[1]The original machine [turn75] joined all the instructions for a function into a linked list and the RETURN instruction was *implicit* in that a return to the calling routine was made automatically when the end of the linked list of instructions was reached.

implemented by placing the values E, C and D on the main stack instead of on a special push down list D. These values stored on the stack constitute the base of a *stack frame* [rand64] or a *mark stack control word* where C is a *return address*, D is a *dynamic link* pointing back down the stack to the previous stack frame and, although it may not be immediately obvious, E does the same work as a *static link*. In a stack based implementation of a block structured language, the static link points to another further down the stack and they form a *static chain* of stack frames; it is arranged that all accessible variables are stored on the stack in these linked stack frames. Thus the chain gives access to the values of variables in the current environment.

For further efficiency we now introduce a second mechanism for subroutine entry (besides the APPLY instruction). This is to deal with local definitions of the form:

```
let name = E2 in E1
```

As we have seen when studying the translation of Haskell to λ-expressions, this could be handled as if it were *(λ name.E1)E2* and by then compiling code to apply this function to its argument. However to treat it in this way is wasteful. We set up a subroutine and then call it (once only) immediately. We therefore prefer to take a more direct approach and consider this construct to be more analogous to entering a block than to entering a subroutine.

In order to make sure that name has a limited scope, we enter a block using the instruction:

```
BLOCK      blockaddress
```

and it is only when executing this block that name will be in the environment. It is quite natural to treat these *explicit* bindings (of name to E2) in a separate way from bindings that occur dynamically if and when a function is applied to an argument appearing in a different part of the program from the function body's definition. As an example consider:

```
(let x = 2 in x + 1) - 3
```

The code generated for this will be:

```
        BLOCK     L1     to evaluate the bit
                         in brackets
        LDC       3
        MINUS
          .
          .
          .
L1      LDC       2
        DECL      x      x=2
        LOOKUP    x
        LDC       1
        PLUS             x+1
        RETURN
```

6.7 DROPPING STITCHES

A number of other variations can be made to the SECD2 machine to make it more efficient. One is the technique known as *tail recursion*. It has also been referred to as *dropping stitches*. In chapter 3 we gave an example of a program to calculate quotients by repeated subtraction and showed that it could be written in a form where tail recursion was evident — that is, a form where the last thing that a function was doing was calling another (often itself). If that is implemented exactly as specified in the last section, then a wasteful extra stack frame is set up. In such a tail recursive situation we can replace an APPLY followed immediately by a RETURN by a jump (a GOTO) directly to the code indicated by the closure in question. Before the jump is made, however, the actual parameter of the function being called will *overwrite* that of the function doing the call and the environment register will be updated by that found in the closure. When the subroutine called by the APPLY finishes execution, its RETURN will now act as a return for the calling function as well. This then not only has both the advantage of saving stack frames but of returning directly through two or more levels of subroutine calls at once.

6.8 FURTHER IMPROVEMENTS

Without going into great detail we mention that considerable gains can be made by optimising the way that the environment is organised. We have assumed up till now that it is a list of pairs each associating a name with a value. The time to look up such an environment will be proportional to the length of the environment and, on average, the list will be scanned half way down before the identifier being sought is discovered. This may be improved in a number of ways. A fairly simple improvement would be, for instance, to replace the linear list by a binary tree sorted by the name of the identifiers. Using this method look-up of the tree takes a time proportional, on average, to the logarithm of the size of the environment.

Well known techniques are available for getting rid of the names of identifiers completely after compile time and replacing them by numbers (offsets from the base of a stack frame which is now being used to store the environment as well as the intermediate results of calculations). This means that look-up will take a *constant* time. The interested reader should consult [rand64, morr77 and davi79] for details.

6.9 SUMMARY

In this chapter we have seen how a custom designed SECD machine can execute applicative programs and we have studied its operational semantics extensively. We have seen several improvements that can be made to it such as factoring out its tree flattening aspect and carrying that out at compile time, replacing tree-like code with linear code of a more conventional nature.

One thing that is evident about the variations on the SECD machine that we have studied, however, is that it operates in applicative order — it evaluates arguments to functions before the functions are executed. In the next chapter we shall see some of the advantages of normal order evaluation and we shall then examine how such an order of evaluation can be implemented.

6.10 EXERCISES

1. What code is generated for the SECD machine for the following Haskell programs?

   a) `(1+2)*(3-4)`

   b) `let x = 2 in x + 1`

   c)
   ```
   let f y = y-3
       x   = 2
   in f x + 1
   ```

   d)
   ```
   let succ = add 1 where add x y = x+y
   in succ 3
   ```

   e)
   ```
   let fib 0 = 1
       fib 1 = 1
       fib n = fib(n-1) + fib(n-2)
   in fib 3
   ```

2. With the same examples show the successive states of the SECD machine as the code is executed.

3. With the same examples show what code would be generated for the SECD2 machine.

4. With the same examples show the execution as the SECD2 machine runs the programs.

Chapter 7

Lazy Evaluation

7.1 INTRODUCTION

We have so far made no use of the fact explained in chapter 5 that some reductions terminate when evaluated in normal order even though they do not in applicative order. In this chapter we show how this can be of use and indeed how it leads us to some new powerful programming techniques.

Recall that

$$W \equiv ((\lambda x.\ x\ x)\ (\lambda x.\ x\ x))$$

has no normal form (and so no order of reduction will terminate) and yet

$$X \equiv (\lambda\ y.z)((\lambda\ x.\ x\ x)\ (\lambda\ x.\ x\ x))$$

does have a normal form:

$$z$$

because it can 'throw away' its argument y. However that normal form will not be found if, as happens when X is reduced in applicative order, the process attempts to reduce W *before* carrying out the binding of x to W.

In its simplest form this corresponds to seemingly useless Haskell programs like:

```
let f x = 3
        y = y
in f y
```

where the definition of y would make the evaluation process loop if it were carried out in applicative order. As it happens however Haskell (and several other functional programming languages) performs evaluation in normal order and so, because y is never needed during the evaluation of f y it is never evaluated and the

131

correct answer, 3, is printed. This mode of operation, when implemented efficiently, is sometimes called *lazy evaluation* because nothing (e.g. y) is evaluated until it is needed[1]. We shall see later that it can also be arranged that nothing gets evaluated more than once. At any stage of evaluation, only the parts of an object which are needed are evaluated and then only as much as needed. This is called evaluation to *Weak Head Normal Form (WHNF).* forms} Now the above may seem like a rather pathological example as nothing very useful is being described. Surely no-one would write a non-terminating definition like y = y, at least not intentionally. That may be so, but consider a slight variation:

```
let f x = 3
        y = some expression
    in f y
```

where some expression might take a *very long time* to evaluate. We still want to avoid carrying out this expensive evaluation if possible, even though we might be able to prove that it will eventually terminate, because we can see that it is useless. We shall see below, however, that there are definitions which do not terminate at all which can be very useful indeed.

A further objection to the rather simplistic example above might be that one would not often write functions like f x = 3 which do not make use of their argument. But in fact many functions, though they may not be quite as simple as this one, make use of their argument or arguments only on some occasions. Take for instance

```
f x y = if x>0 then y else 0
```

which only makes use of y if x happens to be positive. Why should extra work be done, then, in computing y at all, when it might turn out not to be needed? The conditional function

```
cond test x y = if test then x else y
```

which is, in a sense, an abstraction of all the testing which ever happens in a computer, only needs to calculate one of x and y. So why calculate both?

We shall see (section 8.5.1) that constant functions like f x = 3 are not so useless after all and that *all* functions may be transformed into a combination of constant functions (the function k introduced in section 3.10.3) and others which merely distribute their argument.

7.2 INFINITE OBJECTS

The above discussion is a rather negative one. What are the positive benefits of delayed (lazy) evaluation? We often talk about objects which are infinite in size, for instance sets like the *positive integers* or the *prime numbers* and a chemist might talk about *the paraffins*. Note that nobody wants to write down or even calculate all the prime numbers but they may want to make a selection from among them — and no chemist wants to write down the formulae of all the paraffins far less synthesise

---

[1]But the term *lazy evaluation* really refers to an implementation technique which we will see more of in chapter 8 while the term *normal order* refers to an order of evaluation, however implemented.

them all but may want to make a choice of one or two of them or describe some common property of all or some of them. It is therefore useful to be able to *describe* infinite sets and other infinite (or very large) objects even though we will never want to *calculate* the whole of them. Lazy evaluation allows this kind of description to be made in Haskell. For instance the definition:

```
inf = 1 : inf
```

describes a very simple infinite object. It is plainly a list; and its first element is 1 and its tail is the same as the whole list itself. Thus inf must be the infinite list all of whose elements are 1. Of course we never calculate the whole of the list; but we can quite easily ask for any given element of it, for example:

```
inf !! 5
```

will find the sixth of the infinite list of 1s (remember that list subscripts start at 0). As a matter of fact we can even request the whole list and Haskell will attempt to print it. It will, in the process, go into a loop, printing a single 1 on each cycle. Luckily implementations of Haskell usually have a method of interrupting such loops. Let us stress that this kind of loop is not the reason for being able to describe infinite objects. Rather it is annoying and unnatural to have to have to impose a limit on the size of objects in advance of knowing how much of them will be wanted. Such a limit is nearly always arbitrary and, in any case, the responsible programmer is obliged to associate all sorts of error detecting code to make sure that the limit is not overstepped.

One might object that inf should not be calculable *at all* on a computer. After all if one made the definition:

```
x = 1+x
```

one would not expect it to terminate. But : is not the same kind of operator as +. Adding is a *strict* operation[1] (see section 5.9 for a discussion of this term). We can only carry it out if we know the values of both the numbers being added. On the other hand : is *non-strict*, like the cond function above. We only cons two elements together to make a structure which we can access later — and then we might not want to access all of it. We might only want to take its head or its tail but we do not know in advance which, if any, of these will be needed.

A more interesting example of an infinite object is furnished by using a function. Consider:

```
from n = n : from(n+1)
nats   = from 0
```

---

[1]The kinds of basic addition built in to Haskell are strict. It would be possible for a user to define an overloaded + on some type which was non-strict.

Then we can see that:

```
nats = from 0
     = 0 : from 1
     = 0 : 1 : from 2
     = 0 : 1 : 2 : from 3
     = 0 : 1 : 2 : 3 : from 4
     = ...
       .
       .
       .
```

Lists and streams of consecutive numbers are common enough for Haskell to have a special notation for them. The list of integers from n to m can be written [n..m] and the stream of integers starting at n can be written [n..] so that this is another way of writing from n. We can even write arithmetic sequences with an increment different from 1 by placing the optional increment after the starting value and a comma. For example [1,3..15] represents the list [1,3,5,7,9,11,13,15] and [2,5..] represents the stream [2,5,8,11,14, ...].

We have described the list of non-negative integers (the *natural numbers*) in order. Actually it is very easy to define a list of any kind where each element is related to the previous one. Suppose that each member, x, of a series is followed by $f\,x$ and that the first element of the series is a. We are therefore trying to describe the series:

$$a\,,f\,a\,,f^2\,a\,,f^3\,a\,,...$$

We can implement this general series in Haskell by a function

```
    series f a = a : series f (f a)
```

For instance the natural numbers could equally easily be described by

```
    nats = series (+ 1) 0
```

and the infinite list of ones by

```
    inf = series (\ i -> i) 1
```

where (\ i -> i) is the identity function (see section 5.2 for the Haskell version of λ notation). The powers of n might be

```
    powers n = series (* n) 1
```

The series function for producing infinite series can be used as a model for *generating functions* to produce infinite objects of shapes other than the linear lists shown above. As another example suppose that we wish to describe labelled trees:

```
    data Tree t = Label t [Tree t]
```

That is, such a tree is has a label of type t and a list of subtrees. Then the function:

```
    gentree f a = Label a (map (gentree f) (f a))
```

will generate the (possibly infinite) tree rooted at label a and using f to generate, for each label, a list of the labels of its successor subtrees. This kind of generating function was first used by Burge [burg75b] and we shall discuss some more of his ideas in the next section.

Those who are a little perplexed by infinite objects may be reassured if they realise that Haskell contains infinite objects anyway — the functions.

A function over an infinite set like the natural numbers contains an infinite amount of information in it, the mapping giving the element of the domain corresponding to each member of the range (subject of course to resource limitations on the equipment being used to work out the algorithm given for the function which is *always* finite). Such a function is never applied to all its arguments and so its information is never provided all at once. But of course we never want it all at once. In a similar fashion we never want all the information locked up in an infinite data object. As a matter of fact mathematicians sometimes consider functions as infinite sets, each element of the set being a pair associating an element of the range with an element of the domain. And, *vice versa*, lists can be thought of as functions mapping subscripts (taken from the positive integers) onto elements of the list.

7.3 STREAMS

The above examples are a good introduction to an idea described and developed in detail by Burge in [burg75a] and [burg75b]. This is to write functions which act not on single objects but on whole *streams* of objects. These streams might or might not be infinite. As a matter of fact we have already met some stream functions in chapter 3 — map, filter and fold. The function map f maps a stream into another all of whose elements are applications of f to elements of the original stream. The function filter p takes a stream and produces another which contains only the elements of the original which satisfy property p. And foldr f and foldl f take a stream and 'fold it up' by inserting the function f between pairs of elements. The fold operations do not, like map and filter, produce new streams (unless one is dealing with streams of streams); instead they 'reduce the dimensionality' of a stream. The folds are usually only applied to finite streams as their result (unless the inserted function is non-strict) depends on the values of all the elements of the stream. However there are other functions which can operate on infinite streams to produce finite values. The most obvious of these is the function hd which takes a stream's first element! There are other useful ones which generalise this kind of operation. We can of course access *any* element of a stream (see the end of the last section); and it might be advantageous to have a function take to take the first n elements of a stream:

```
take 0 _     = []
take _ []    = []
take n (h:t) = h:take (n-1) t
```

More generally the answer may depend on many elements of the stream. Consider, for instance, a function to find the *limit* of a stream: the point, if any, to which the elements of the stream tend, as the stream is generated. There is a more complicated formal definition of this concept, but we will not use it here as it is hardly constructive. Instead we will be content with a technique which looks at sufficient elements until some criterion has been met like 'two consecutive elements are equal' or 'two consecutive elements are within ε of each other'. Whatever the criterion, we can parameterise it, passing it on to the `limit` function:

```
limit crit (h:t) | crit (h:t) = h
                 | otherwise   = limit crit t
```

This example again points out a desire for a facility to be able to name both a whole pattern and its parts. In the above, if `list` were an alternate name for the pattern `(h:t)`, we could have written the guard on the first equation as `crit list`. Using as-patterns (see section 5.6) the example could be written:

```
limit crit list@(h:t) | crit list  = h
                      | otherwise   = limit crit t
```

A stream which has become well known as a seminal example is the infinite stream of prime numbers. Turner introduced this as a calculable concept in his first manual of the SASL language [turn76]. Its calculation is based on the Sieve of Eratosthenes which takes the primes discovered so far and filters out their multiples from the infinite list of integers:

```
primes        = sieve [2..]
sieve (p:nos) = p:sieve (remove (multsof p) nos)
                where multsof p n = n `rem` p == 0
```

The function `remove` can be found in section 3.10.2. It is the dual of `filter` but filters elements out rather than in.

7.3.1 Stream diagrams

Turner [turn85] also gives as an example a solution to a problem which is useful to illustrate a way that some stream problems can be visualised as a set of interconnected processes.

The problem (attributed to Hamming) is to generate in increasing order the sequence of all positive integers divisible by only the primes 2, 3 and 5. Dijkstra [dijk76] neatly axiomatises this as follows:

- The value *1* is in the sequence.

- If *x* is in the sequence, so are *2x*, *3x* and *5x* .

- No other items are in the sequence.

but this is hardly an algorithmic solution. If we try to form a queue by starting with element *1* and successively generating the new elements which arise by applying axiom 2 to elements at the start of the queue and adding them to the end, one does indeed get all the elements but not in the desired order. Moreover some of the elements appear twice:

$$1, 2, 3, 5, 4, 6, 10, 6, 9, 15, 10, 15, 25, 8, ...$$

Taking a different tack, let us consider that H is the desired sequence which we will model as an infinite stream; and that t2, t3 and t5 are stream functions which each take the stream H and produce streams h2, h3 and h5 which are the same as H but with the elements multiplied by 2, 3 or 5 respectively. We can represent this diagrammatically as shown in Figure 7.1:

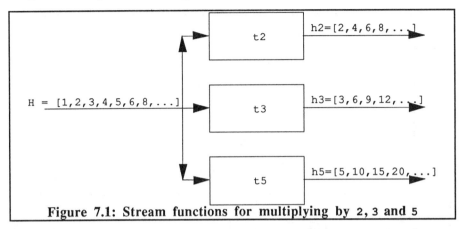

Figure 7.1: Stream functions for multiplying by 2, 3 and 5

Here streams are represented by lines and boxes stand for stream functions. One can imagine that each box represents a process which takes data as it arrives and produces a stream of values in its output. Those familiar with dataflow diagrams [ping86] will note a similarity.

The functions can be programmed by:

```
t2 (h:t) = 2*h : t2 t
t3 (h:t) = 3*h : t3 t
t5 (h:t) = 5*h : t5 t
```

or, by abstraction:

```
times n (h:t) = n*h : times n t
```

and the connections are made by:

```
h2 = times 2 H
h3 = times 3 H
h5 = times 5 H
```

We can now process these derived streams further by feeding them into boxes which will produce streams with the elements merged to preserve ascending order and remove duplicates as shown in Figure 7.2:

The merge stream function is easily programmed by:

```
merge l1@(h1:t1) l2@(h2:t2) | h1<h2     = h1:merge t1 l2
                            | h1==h2    =    merge t1 l2
                            | otherwise = h2:merge l1 t2

h23  = merge h2  h3
h235 = merge h23 h5
```

and what we have managed to get out at the end is a stream identical to the original H except that it needs a 1 at the front — see Figure 7.3:

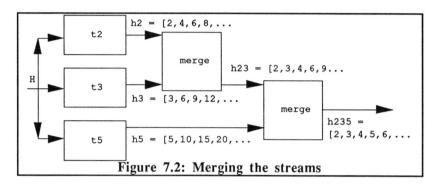

Figure 7.2: Merging the streams

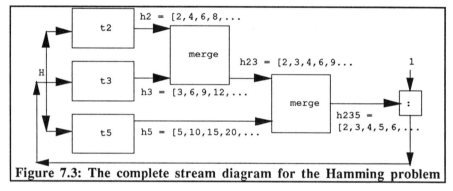

Figure 7.3: The complete stream diagram for the Hamming problem

so the recursion is completed with the definitions:

```
H = 1 : h235
```

and the whole problem is solved with a set of mutually recursive stream equations:

```
H    = 1 : h235
h2   = times 2 H
h3   = times 3 H
h5   = times 5 H
h23  = merge h2 h3
h235 = merge h23 h5
```

The analogy which forces itself upon one here is that of a number of independent pieces of electronic black boxes connected along communication channels by physical pieces of wire. Jones has made the analogy into a reality by constructing a model operating system(see [jone84] and [jone89]) which depends on hardware implemented, separate, independent stream processors connected by physical wires.

7.4 LIST COMPREHENSIONS

We saw in section 3.11 how to use list comprehensions to describe certain objects. This notation's use is not restricted to finite sets. Here for instance is the primes example (see section 7.3) which we gave before but couched as a set expression:

```
primes = sieve [2..]
sieve (prime:rest) =
     prime : sieve [ r | r <- rest , r `rem` prime /= 0]
```

When we were describing Zermello-Fränkel notation in section 3.11 one of the names for the notation was 'set abstraction'. The differences between list comprehensions and true sets come into sharp focus when we try to extend this kind of expression to cope with infinite lazy data structures.

One difference is that sets do not have duplicate elements, but these lists might. It is, of course, possible to write a function which will remove the duplicates from a list (provided the members of the list are comparable — this is not possible for lists of functions, for example). The following one works for finite lists:

```
nub []                     = []
nub (h:t) | member h t = nub t
          | otherwise  = h:nub t
```

but a slightly more awkward one must be used if infinite streams could be involved, because set membership testing is only possible on finite sets (one would have to test for membership arbitrarily far into an infinite set):

```
nub = rm []
where rm sofar []                      = []
      rm sofar (h:t) | member h sofar = rm sofar t
                     | otherwise      = h:rm (h:sofar) t
```

Here `sofar` holds onto a list of elements found so far. This list will remain finite but will get longer and longer as time goes on and the `rm` function eats further and further into the list. This is an example of what has become known as a *space leak*[1][wadl87] and it is representative of a much larger problem which has not been fully explored, that of the *complexity* of lazy evaluation style programming (that is, how long a problem takes to run and how much computer space it uses in relation to the size of the supplied data). Because of this particular space leak, many functional programming languages which use a version of ZF-notation do not eliminate duplicates from lists produced as the result of executing a set expression.

7.4.1 Diagonalisation

Another problem which occurs with laziness, where more than one list is concerned, is connected with *fairness*. Lazy lists, either using the notation of

---

[1]An alternative definition of `nub` which works on infinite lists (and which also has a space leak) is given in the Haskell report:

```
nub []    = []
nub (x:xs) = x : nub (filter (/= x) xs)
```

comprehensions or otherwise, can only be infinite in a *countable* sense. For instance, we have no way of writing an expression for 'The set of all functions f such that f 3 = 4'. This is not merely because we have not based the set on another one as with ZF notation, but also because there are an uncountably infinite number of functions which satisfy the equation.

So if we are restricted to describing countably infinite sets, we would certainly like to make sure that every member of the set in question is generated in a finite time (even if that time is very long). This is referred to as *fairness*. Consider the following expression

```
cart s t = [ (x,y) | x <- s , y <- t ]
```

which at first sight appears to represent a function to calculate the Cartesian product of the sets s and t. Indeed this function works fine when the sets involved are finite, but it does not work if t is an infinite set, because items are generated in an order which selects every possible pairing of the elements of t with the first element of s before moving on to the next one. If s and t are both the infinite list of natural numbers in ascending order, for instance, the values generated by the above expression would be [(0,0),(1,0),(2,0),…] and it would be an infinite amount of time before we reached (0,1) and so on. KRC and an early version of Turner's later language Miranda [turn85b] both solved this problem by using a built-in *diagonalisation* of sets so that elements were not chosen in the obvious 'inside out looping' way, when more than one generator was involved. For answers to be predictable, however, users should know what diagonalisation algorithm is being used and for this reason later versions of Miranda and other languages which have adopted this notation (e.g. Haskell [huda91]) have abandoned automatic diagonalisation in favour of users supplying their own. Here, for instance, is just one way of producing a diagonalisation of the Cartesian product of the set of natural numbers (from 0 — see above) with itself so that every pair appears in a finite amount of time

```
intpairs = [(x,n-x) | n <- [0..] , x <- [0..n] ]
```

and this can be used to select subscripts to index into any two sets to produce *their* Cartesian product (see Ex. 7).

7.5 INPUT/OUTPUT IN FUNCTIONAL PROGRAMMING

Some first time functional programmers, especially those who come to the style from the imperative style rather than learning it from scratch, are confused by interactive input/output. At first there does not seem to be any. We define black box functions and then apply them to some input, which is presented, *as a whole*, as an actual parameter to the function. In fact the input is presented *as part of the program* and there is no distinction between data and program. Even the separate presentation of the functional definitions is additional sugar as they could all be defined in a let clause as part of the expression to be evaluated.

Similarly, the output is, at least conceptually, presented all at once as the single result emanating from the black box.

This is all very fine theoretically, but in reality programmers want to be able to *interact* with a running program and enter data depending on results reported so far;

and this means that we would like a functional program to accept its input piecemeal and produce output as it becomes available. In fact this facility is exactly what normal order evaluation in association with a read-evaluate-print cycle provides. Only that part of an object which is required for output is evaluated, and this in turn will mean that only the input necessary to calculate that part of the output will be read in.

Ideally we would want this laziness to be extended to the expressions read in by the compiler so that even the compiler itself would be lazy. But in practice most functional programming systems available today treat the compilation phase as separate from the execution phase.

Lazy input/output is achieved in Haskell in the following manner: Imagine that the functional program and the operating system are two processes communicating via streams:

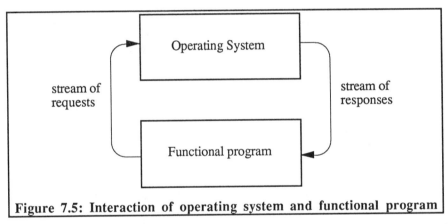

Figure 7.5: Interaction of operating system and functional program

With this model we see that a functional program as a whole can still be thought of as a single function mapping one input to one output, but the input and output are slightly more complicated. Each is a stream and the type of the program may be thought of as:

```
[Response] -> [Request]
```

At first this seems slightly counter-intuitive until it is realised that the requests can be thought of as commands to the operating system whose type is:

```
[Request] -> [Response]
```

though it is slightly misleading to think of the system as having a type at all as it is not guaranteed (and indeed is extremely unlikely) to be purely functional — for instance, the system may be responding to requests from more than one program running concurrently. On the other hand the *program is* purely functional and as such is referentially transparent. The ith response is the reply to the ith request[1].

The kinds of request available to Haskell include the following:

```
data Request = ReadFile    String         |    -- filename
               WriteFile   String String   |
                   -- filename and string to be written
               ReadChan    String         |    -- channel name
               AppendChan String String   |
                   -- channel name and string to be appended
                 .
                 .
                 .
```

and the possible responses include:

```
data Response = Success          |  -- a successful write
                Str String       |  -- a successful read and
                                    -- its result
                Failure IOError     -- a fail and the reason
                   .
                   .
                   .
data IOError = WriteError  String |  -- further details of
               ReadError   String |  -- different kinds of
               SearchError String |  -- failure are found
               OtherError  String |  -- in the String
                 .
                 .
                 .
```

Mostly, these are self describing, but we must say what the difference between a file and a channel is.

The *channels* include *standard input* (stdin) and *standard output* (stdout) and are one-way communications media which are normally set up beforehand. They read from or write to *agents* such as line printers, networks and human beings. They cannot be deleted or created and they represent lazy streams of characters which are conceptually infinitely long. AppendChan cname str evaluates str hyper-strictly (that is, it evaluates it fully so that it can be printed and not just to weak head normal form) and appends it to the end of channel cname. ReadChan cname opens cname for input. Input channels can only be read once in a program and are designed so that the characters on the streams that they return in the response, once consumed, are not available again. If standard channel input and output occur to the same agent, for instance to a user sitting at a workstation, it will be interleaved properly in the sense that no responses will appear on the screen before the user's requests.

---

[1]In fact the ith response *depends on* the whole history of the interaction, that is, ulimately, the initial state of the system when the program started and all of the requests up to and including the ith. It is a mistake to think of the ith response as the *value* of the ith request, only the reply to it.

Files are mappings between file names and strings which are their contents. ReadFile fname will produce a response Str s where s is the contents of the file, (unless it is unreadable when a Failure response will occur). WriteFile fname s will overwrite the file fname with the string s, creating the file if necessary (and if possible — for the usual system reasons files may not be creatable or writable and a Failure will then occur). Unlike channels, files can be read more than once. If a write intervenes between two reads, the results will give different results, but the first read is not changed and is purely static. This means that one has to imagine that the whole file is read at once and (a copy of) its value as a string frozen to preserve referential transparency.

Hudak [huda89] gives the following example (slightly modified here) of an interaction which asks the user for a filename and then prints the file back:

```
main resps =
  [ AppendChan stdout "please type a filename",
    case resps!!0 of Success -> ReadChannel stdin,
    AppendChan stdout fileName,
    case resps!!2 of Success -> ReadFile fileName,
    AppendChan stdout
              (case resps!!3 of
               Failure ioerror -> "Can't open "++ fileName
               Str fileContents -> fileContents
              )
  ] where (fileName:_) = case (resps!!1) of
                         Str userInput -> lines userInput
```

Here lines is a prelude function which breaks a stream of characters up into a stream of lines. Notice that all input/outut described here is of strings of characters. (Binary I/O is also available in Haskell but we will not discuss it here). Haskell provides a number of prelude functions to aid turning strings into other values and *vice-versa* including lines and show which was mentioned in section 2.11. Others are read which converts a string into an object of another appropriate type and is therefore the input analogue of show.

At first sight, the following program, which expresses members of the response stream directly, looks like a better version of the above:

```
main ( Success : Str userInput : Success : fCont : _ ) =
  [ AppendChan stdout "please type a filename",
    ReadChannel stdin,
    AppendChan stdout fileName,
    ReadFile fileName,
    AppendChan stdout
              (case fCont of
               Failure ioerror -> "Can't open "++ fileName
               Str fileContents -> fileContents
              )
  ] where (fileName:_) = lines userInput
```

but there is a *synchronisation* problem with this version. The trouble arises because this main program first tries to make sure that the response stream conforms in shape to the pattern (Success : Str userInput : Success : fCont : _) before it does anything else. This means that the program must make sure that there are at least four responses *before issuing any requests*! This will clearly lead to some sort of deadlock. In the first, more cumbersome, version, this is prevented by the laziness and the fact that elements of the response list are examined in order interleaved with making the requests.

7.6 IRREFUTABLE PATTERNS

For the above reason and others, Haskell allows a kind of pattern called an *irrefutable* pattern which is even lazier than normal and matches and binds its variables in a different order. No pattern matching is done unless and until it needs to be, by accessing one of the variables in it. All variable names and the wild card pattern, _, are automatically irrefutable — they *always* match anyway. Other patterns can be marked irrefutable by placing the special reserved operator ~ before the pattern. Consider the following example:

```
f   (h:t) = 3
f   []    = 4

g ~(h:t)  = 3
g   []    = 4
```

The function f pattern matches before doing anything else, so f [] = 4, but g does not bother to pattern match before using its first clause to give g [] = 3. At first this does not seem terribly useful, but this is a pathological example. Consider the further rewriting of the file copying example as follows:

```
main ~(Success: ~(Str userInput: ~(Success: ~(fCont: _ )))) =
     [ AppendChan stdout "please type a filename",
       ReadChannel stdin,
       AppendChan stdout fileName,
       ReadFile fileName,
       AppendChan stdout
              (case fCont of
               Failure ioerror -> "Can't open "++ fileName
               Str fileContents -> fileContents
               )
     ] where (fileName:_) = lines userInput
```

Here all the substreams of the responses have been made irrefutable so no pattern matching occurs until userInput is required because fileName in the third request is defined in terms of it. Similarly, use of fCont in the last request triggers the pattern matching down to the last response which, by this time, will be available anyway.

Haskell supports a second style of input/output programming, the continuation style. We refer readers to the Haskell report for details.

7.7 MODULARITY

One of the best reasons for normal order evaluation schemes is described in a paper by Hughes [hugh89] where he emphasises the idea of modularity as one central to the design of well-structured software in the large. He describes two kinds of modularity for composing programs together. One is the use of higher order functions and their composition and the other is the use of lazy evaluation. It may sometimes be possible to modularise a program into small parts, only if they interact with one and other in a lazy way. For instance, consider the limit function which we defined above in section 7.3. It was rather a naive one and could easily be replaced with a more realistic one from a numerical analyst's point of view. This can be done without considering the generating function which will be used to produce the stream whose limit is desired (if indeed a generating function is used at all). Later the modularly designed functions can be composed by, for instance:

```
limit . (series f)
```

The fact that the generation of the series can be separated from the taking of the limit is a great advantage which would be largely negated if one were not allowed to use lazy evaluation to describe the whole (infinite) series.

Hughes gives a more comprehensive example of a chain of functions composed with one another in which the first function needs to interact lazily with the last and points out that the whole chain would have to be programmed as one giant function if it were not possible to modularise using lazy stream functions. The example is from artificial intelligence and shows how to evaluate positions in a game such as chess based on looking ahead to find what possible later positions are available. The modularised function will be applied to a position to evaluate how good it is. The decomposition is a chain of 4 functions:

```
val = maximise.(maptree staticval).(prune 5).(gentree moves)
```

We do not give details of these functions here but in summary:

- `moves` is a function that maps a position onto its list of successor positions

- `gentree`, as defined in section 7.2, is used to make the infinite tree (or certainly, in a non-trivial game, the very large tree) of positions

- `prune` throws away all sub-trees below the depth given as its first argument. This will make the tree finite but it might still be much too big to have in main store all at once. So it will still be advantageous to examine those bits of it which are needed all at once.

- `maptree` is a function on trees analogous to `map` on lists. It applies its functional argument to every node in the tree. In this case that argument is `staticval`

- `staticval` is a static evaluation function. The `val` function is a dynamic evaluation function which finds the value of a position dependent on the values of its successor positions. Sooner or later we must ask for a static value calculated *on its own merits*, without examining any further down the tree of positions.

- `maximise` takes the tree of static values and uses one of the well known techniques (see e.g. [nils71] or [rich83]) for extracting a minimax value from the tree, bearing in mind that one of the opponents playing the game will choose moves to attempt to maximise the value of the position arrived at while the other will try to minimise the value.

If this function were not decomposed, it would have to be written monolithically and would have been very much harder to debug and maintain. It is only laziness which allows the functions to be separated out without putting an arbitrary limit on

the size of trees to be searched and having to place intermediate results in a file store
with all that that implies in the way of 'flattening' the tree on output and rebuilding
its structure again on input.

7.8 MEMO FUNCTIONS

An idea due to Michie [mich68] is interesting in the context of lazy evaluation. This
is a mechanism which replaces, wherever possible, computation of a function using
its user supplied algorithm with looking up the function in a table. Suppose that we
have a function `f` which, for simplicity, we will assume maps the natural numbers
into other values. Let us augment its definition with a definition of `flist`:

```
flist = [ f x | x <- [0..] ]
```

so that `flist` is the infinite list of all the values calculated by applying `f`. This list
is, of course, evaluated lazily and only the elements which we need are ever
calculated. To make use of this memoised table of values, we need now to replace
every call of `f` by an index into `flist`. If the value does not already exist in the
table, laziness ensures that it will be calculated and placed there; subsequent calls on
the function with the same argument will not be calculated again except insofar as
we have to perform the table lookup. To look up `flist !! n` takes a time
proportional to `n` and this will obviously be of advantage if the complexity of the
calculation of `f` is higher than this. Indeed if we could implement memo functions
using a language with lazy arrays[1] rather than lazy lists, we might be able to achieve
constant lookup time.

As an example, here is a way of calculating Fibonacci numbers

```
flist = [ fib x | x <- [0..] ]
fib 0 = 1
fib 1 = 1
fib n = flist !! (n-1) + flist !! (n-2)
```

The more direct way of calculating these numbers

```
fib 0 = 1
fib 1 = 1
fib n = fib (n-1) + fib(n-2)
```

is exponentially complex in time and in cases like this, it is well worth the trouble of
memoizing.

Memoizing is, of course, a simple program transformation technique. We shall be
talking more about such techniques in chapter 10.

---

[1]Haskell's arrays are lazy in the sense that no element of an array is evaluated until another value
needs to look at it, but they are not open ended in the same way as streams. When an array is first
created, its size is strictly evaluated and used to get the right amount of contiguous storage for the
array elements. Thus arrays cannot be used for memo functions without extra effort.

7.9 SUMMARY

In this chapter we have looked at a powerful facility which allows the representation in functional languages of infinite lists and other infinite data structures. These, we found, could sometimes be programmed using stream functions and these, in turn, can be visualised using stream diagrams. We saw that the ZF notation could be used for infinite lists but that this raised two problems, that of eliminating duplicates and that of diagonalising so that every element of a set was generated in a finite time. Input/Output was examined because laziness, in cooperation with the careful use of irrefutable patterns, provides the synchronisation necessary to allow interaction. A program transformation technique, memoisation, was examined which allows functions of the natural numbers to be calculated in linear time. We saw that laziness contributes significantly to the modularity of programs making them easier to prototype and develop.

7.10 EXERCISES

Readers should at this stage review the exercises given in chapters 3 and 4 in the light of the concept of laziness. Many useful functions extend automatically to lazy cases and insight into their working and usefulness may be gained in this way.

We now present some exercises which are specifically geared to lazy evaluation.

1.   Write programs to generate the following infinite objects:

 a)   The negative integers.

 b)   The infinite list of positive powers of two.

 c)   The terms of the series which sums to e^x, viz:

$$1 + \frac{x}{1!} + \frac{x^2}{2!} + \dots$$

 d)   The terms of the partial sums of the previous series so that the nth term in this new list is the sum of the first n terms of the first list.

 e)   An infinite list of rational numbers, in which every rational is guaranteed to be calculated in finite time reduced to its lowest terms and appears only once in the list.

2.   If you have not done so already, use a list comprehension to make the same lists as in the previous question.

3.   Generalise the idea of partial sums suggested in exercise 1d above.

4.   Produce a stream diagram for generating Fibonnacci numbers with two copies of the stream, one delayed by one element and so solve the problem by adding the elements pairwise.

5.   Investigate why it is difficult to make a stream diagram out of the 'primes' example?

6.   Turner [turn82a] gives an interesting example of a lazy list, being the digits of
      e. He points out that *e* = *2.1111...* if each of the digits after the point is
      written in a different base, the first in base *2=2!*, the next in base *6=3!*, the
      next in base *24=4!* and so on. The normal way of changing the base of a
      number is to keep multiplying it by the base and finding what its integral part
      is. Adapt this to converting from a changing base to base *10* (or to any
      constant base) and hence write a program which will produce the digits of *e*
      one at a time.

7.   An example in section 7.4.1 showed how to calculate indices into the
      Cartesian product of two sets. Complete the example to calculate the product
      itself. Can you extend it to produce the Cartesian product of any number of
      sets?

8.   Write a function which takes a set (implemented as a list) and produces its
      power set — the set of all its subsets. It should operate fairly on infinite lists,
      producing every finite subset in a finite amount of time.

Chapter 8

Implementation of Lazy
Evaluation

8.1 INTRODUCTION

Before we get into the details of particular methods of implementation of lazy evaluation, let us pause a moment to see if we really need to provide *any* new mechanism at all. Let us examine what occurs if we try to execute, say:

```
let  loop  = loop
     f x y = y
in f loop 3
```

using a SECD-machine operating in applicative order. Before f is entered, the machine will attempt to place the value of loop on the stack, and this will involve an infinite computation. What we would like to do is arrange that this attempt to evaluate the parameter of a function should be *delayed* until *after* the function is entered. It is inside the function that information resides that allows the machine to decide when and if a parameter is needed at all. Well, have we a mechanism which allows us to delay evaluation? The answer to this rhetorical question is 'yes'. There are expressions in Haskell that do not get evaluated until we explicitly force their evaluation, and those are the bodies of functions. They are only executed when we call the functions. This suggests that if we replace (or rather, get the compiler to replace) each actual parameter by a function to calculate the actual parameter and each occurrence of every formal parameter by a call to evaluate the corresponding function, we should be able to delay evaluation until a parameter is really needed (if it is at all).

149

So, for instance, in the above case, the program is transformed by the compiler into:

```
let loop = loop
    fnloop() = loop
    fn3() = 3
    f x y = y()
in f fnloop fn3
```

Note the use of a dummy () parameter (called a *trivial expression* in Haskell — it has type Unit and is the only value with this type) with the invented functions. The only reason for making them functions at all is to delay evaluation of the body. They do not need parameters for any other reason. In general, each definition

```
f x = expr
```

would be replaced by the compiler by a definition

```
f x = expr'
```

where expr' is expr[x := x()]. All calls to

```
f expr
```

would be replaced by

```
let fnexpr() = expr in f fnexpr
```

To do this transformation properly, however, we need to make a similar transformation not only at binding time when functions are called but also where definitions bind a name to an expression (see section 2.4), so that definitions of the form name = value need to be replaced by name() = value thus delaying the evaluation of value; Occurrences of name then have to be replaced by name() in order to force the evaluation.

Some readers may recognise this mechanism as the one known as *call by name* which was the default parameter passing method of Algol 60 [naur63] and it is interesting to note in passing that a strict implementation of that language allowed some bizarre effects because of the interaction of the parameter evaluation with side effects (for instance the so called 'Jensen's Device' [sebe89]).

8.2 LAZY EVALUATION

The interaction of parameter evaluation with side-effects is of no interest to us here, as there are no side-effects in functional programming. But call by name also gave rise to heavy criticism of Algol even when viewed separately from interactions with side-effects, partly because the above features were rather obscure in their operation and tended to be used by aficionados of technique much more than by straightforward programmers. Another (perhaps more important) reason for rejecting call by name, certainly for us as applicative programmers, is that it is *highly inefficient*, so much so that its use can change the time complexity of a program drastically, sometimes making otherwise linear time programs into ones that execute in exponential time. This is because, with call by name, *every* time a formal parameter is met in the body of a function, one has in effect to call a function (called a *thunk* [inge61] or a *suspension*) to go back to evaluate the actual parameter. If the actual parameter itself contains formal parameters at its own scoping level, *it* will now call a thunk to evaluate it and progress may be suspended for some time while control is passed back and forward between different levels of scope. This gives rise to a style of programming in which the various functions of a program communicate with each other as co-routines, each one suspending its operation while another works out the value of a parameter before passing control back after other possible suspensions of control.

Luckily, we can rectify this unfortunate situation but only in an applicative context. The key lies with the referential transparency of applicative programs which allows the replacement of any expression with another having the same value. This means that suspensions to calculate values of formal parameters can be *overwritten* by those values as soon as they become known. Subsequent requests for the value of the parameter can find that value already present in the location which used to hold the suspension[1]. So we now find that we have the best of both worlds: not only do parameters which are not needed not get evaluated, but ones which are only get evaluated once. This is known as *call by need*, a term invented by Wadsworth who first discovered the technique [wads71]. It later became known as *lazy* evaluation when, nearly contemporaneously, it was first used for serious applicative programming by Henderson and Morris [hend76], Turner [turn76] and Friedman and Wise [frie76]. As a point of nomenclature note that just as call by need is also called lazy evaluation, call by value is equivalent to so called *eager evaluation*.

If readers refer back to case 4 in section 6.4 they will see that, while looking at the operational semantics of the SECD machine, we had to treat non-strict operations like the conditional and the Boolean operators && and || in a special way. We can now see that in a lazy implementation based on suspensions, we can treat every function in the same way. Indeed *all* functions are treated as potentially non-strict and their argument is automatically suspended. Later, if and when it is needed, it will be *unsuspended* (strictly evaluated).

It is perhaps important to note that the technique of overwriting suspensions by equivalent values is not in itself the same as lazy evaluation which stipulates, in addition, that the evaluation must be carried out in normal order (enter all functions before their parameter has been evaluated). Other evaluation orders can also make use of overwriting. For instance, if several processors are available, we might decide to evaluate several redexes in parallel (see chapter 11). It will still be of advantage to replace suspensions by their values so that all processes can benefit.

8.3 ADAPTING THE SECD MACHINE

In this section we shall see what changes need to be made to the SECD machine to allow lazy evaluation to be integrated into it. An applicative order SECD machine operates essentially in reverse Polish. Applications f x are evaluated by the sequence: evaluate f, evaluate x and then apply. To make this run in normal order, we only need to change this to: evaluate f, suspend x and then apply. But inside each function f we need to plant code to unsuspend the suspensions (by calling a

---

[1]Compare this to memoising which we saw as a programming technique in section 7.8.

thunk) and then we need to arrange for the resulting value to overwrite the suspension.

This can best be organised by extending the universe of represented values to include suspensions. We have seen above that suspensions are like functions with a dummy variable and this suggests that we should implement them in nearly the same way as closures (see case 6 in section 6.4). To recap, closures consist of three parts:

- The body of the abstraction — the code to be evaluated at call.

- The environment in which to evaluate the body.

- The variable of abstraction — so that it can be bound to the actual parameter when calling.

Suspensions can be somewhat simpler because the dummy () argument we introduced above was artificial in that it was used purely to allow us to make a source transformation and keep within the Haskell context. In the SECD-machine we do not need the argument at all, so that a suspension will consist of only two parts:

- The actual parameter body — the code to be evaluated at call.

- The environment in which to evaluate the actual parameter.

When the time comes to evaluate a formal parameter, the suspension is called in a very similar manner to applying a closure except that no variable is bound. There is slightly more to it, however. When we need the value of a parameter, it may either be the first time we have seen it, in which case it will still be a suspension; or it will already have been evaluated, in which case it will be a more ordinary type of object, a floating point number or character or other type of object. This suggests that we may have to have some way of *tagging* objects with a bit to detect whether they are suspensions or not. We can introduce two new operations into the improved SECD-machine that we described in 6.5 to deal with suspension evaluation. First an instruction STRICT which looks at the item on top of the stack, S, decides if it is a suspension or not, and, if so, calls it to evaluate it; but, if not, merely ignores it. The second instruction, OVERWRITE, usually follows immediately after a STRICT instruction. It will find a suspension and a value on the stack and will overwrite the first with the second, updating the tag which distinguishes between the two kinds of object.

We will not go into further detail with this method here, but refer the readers to [davi89] for a more exact description (and where a more efficient method of representing environments is also presented). Henderson [hend80] also describes a lazy SECD machine in detail.

8.4 GRAPH REDUCTION

Adapting the SECD-machine is not the only way of implementing lazy evaluation. The idea of *overwriting* an object with another of the same value which we saw in section 8.2 can be carried further.

The two SECD machines described in chapter 6 both work by *interpretation*. That is, the SECD-machine program, which is a tree in the first version and a (nearly) linear set of instructions in the second, and which lives in the C component of the state of the machine, is fixed and immutable. Its sole job is to load an object, the single result, onto the S component of the state. This it does by executing the individual instructions on the tree program or linear program each of which in turn has the job of manipulating the stack. So the program and the data are kept rigourously apart in C and S. The other two components are for book-keeping.

However, another way of operating is to make little distinction between program and data. Here, the object to be evaluated can be directly manipulated (selectively overwritten) so that redexes within it are continually being reduced *in place* by literal substitution of arguments for all occurrences of a bound variable in the body of an abstraction [wegn68].

Let us go back to first principles and consider the evaluation of pure λ-expressions. In particular let us look at how applications of abstractions to their arguments are reduced. When this happens, the body of the abstraction is copied out with the variable of abstraction replaced at each of its occurrences with the argument of the application. If we do this symbolically on paper, the copying of the argument happens literally and if the argument appears several times in the body of the abstraction, the body's length may, at least early in the chain of reductions, grow alarmingly. This kind of implementation of reduction is called *string reduction* and it is akin to macro expansion (see [cole76] for instance). It is clearly impractical except in the smallest of examples.

If, however, we examine this idea we see that, provided we store expressions to be reduced in a structured form, we can replace sub-expressions by pointers to them and so several instances of a variable of abstraction can be replaced during reduction by a pointer to a single instance of the actual argument. In this way an expression stored first as an expression tree gets transformed by successive reductions through a sequence of graphs in which common sub-expressions can be shared by several nodes. This method of implementing reduction is called *graph reduction* and it represents a considerable efficiency advance over string reduction both in space (since nodes are shared) and time (because a single node which is a candidate for reduction will only be reduced once).

In the remainder of this chapter we will illustrate this method by showing how it works in two famous implementations of functional languages, the first using combinators to implement SASL and the second using supercombinators to implement a language called lazy ML. The techniques in both these implementations could easily be extended to the evaluation of Haskell expressions.

8.5 TURNER'S COMBINATOR MACHINE

In this section we are going to describe an implementation technique for evaluating SASL expressions which Turner [turn79b] used. It is based on *SKI-combinators* as the underlying representation of expressions instead of λ-expressions.

8.5.1 Combinators

Most implementations of conventional programming languages use the concept of an environment which allows us to associate names with values (the *E* component of an SECD machine). This implementation, however, uses a result due to Schönfinkel [schö24] which allows us to transform a program so that it contains *no* bound variable names. Consequently we do not need an environment in which to look them up. As we shall see, we can process a λ-expression so that it is replaced by a *combinator expression* which does not contain bound variable names. This transformation can be thought of as a kind of compilation; Turner directly compiled SASL [turn79a] into combinator expressions without going through the intermediate stage of producing λ-expressions. As Turner's paper [turn79b] is very famous and a model of clarity, we shall not hesitate in what follows to use some of the examples that he gives there.

Removal of the environment has some major advantages. It is not just that a whole component conveniently vanishes from the state of the computation. Graph reduction based on full λ-expressions (as opposed to combinators which we will discuss in the rest of this chapter) requires a large amount of copying, even when sharing is fully exploited. Consider the curried application add 3 4 when the definition add x y = x+y is in force. When add is applied to its first argument, the body of the λ-expression λ x.λ y. (x+y) has to be *copied* once while substituting 3 for x and the result has to be copied again when y is bound to 4. Function bodies have to be copied in case they are used again with different bindings. All this copying is unavoidable when doing graph reduction on λ-expressions with free variables present. So we now proceed to show how to get rid of variables. We shall see in section 8.6 how to reduce expressions to forms in which all variables are bound at the point of application, so that only a single copy has to be made.

8.5.2 Translation of Haskell to Combinators

Consider the following functions:

$$S\,x\,y\,z\ =\ (x\,z)\,(y\,z)$$
$$K\,x\,y\ =\ x$$
$$I\,x\ =\ x$$

Functions such as this which have no free variables are called *combinators*. The first, *S*, is used to distribute its third argument to its first two. The second, *K*, throws away its second argument, and the third, *I*, is the identity function. Turner shows that it is possible to rewrite user definitions in terms of these combinators in such a way as to get rid of parameters. They can then be executed using the defining equations for *S*, *K* and *I* as basic instructions for a combinator machine which rewrites combinator expressions.

We now show that we can use these combinators to transform applicative expressions in the following way. Suppose we have a function defined by

$$f\,x = E$$

We show how this may be transformed by *abstracting x* from the defining expression as follows. We write $F \equiv [x]E$ to mean '*x* abstracted from *e*' so that the resulting expression contains no free occurrences of *x* but still has the same effect, if applied, as the function f. If we can manage to do this, we can say that F and f are extensionally equal (see section 5.7). Thus we require:

$$([x] E) x = E \qquad \text{(extensionality)}$$

Note that $[x] E$ behaves in a similar way to $\lambda x . E$; but $[x]$ is a compile time textual operation which removes x from E in the way to be described in the next paragraph, rather than binding it at run time.

The abstraction transformation is carried out using the following rules operated repeatedly until x no longer occurs free in the expression.

$$[x] (e_1 e_2) \quad \Rightarrow \quad S ([x] e_1) ([x] e_2) \qquad (8.1)$$
$$[x] x \quad \Rightarrow \quad I \qquad (8.2)$$
$$[x] y \quad \Rightarrow \quad K \, y \qquad (8.3)$$

where y is either a variable different from x or is a constant. For these to work properly we have to prove in each case that the functions on the left have the same effect as those on the right. We take each equation in turn and apply left and right hand sides to arbitrary x:

8.1 L.H.S. $=$ $([x] (e_1 e_2)) x$

$=$ $e_1 e_2$ (extensionality)

R.H.S. $=$ $S ([x] e_1) ([x] e_2)$

$=$ $(([x] e_1)x)(([x] e_1)x)$ (defn. of S)

$=$ $e_1 e_2$ (extensionality, twice)

8.2 L.H.S. $=$ $([x] x) x$

$=$ x (extensionality)

R.H.S. $=$ $I x$

$=$ x (defn of I)

8.3 L.H.S. $=$ $([x] y) x$

$=$ y (extensionality)

R.H.S. $=$ $K \, y \, x$

$=$ y (defn of K)

Let us try to apply this to a concrete example. Consider the SASL[1] definition

```
succ x = 1+x
```

First rewrite the definition in a curried form using a prefixed operator `plus` instead of infixed +.

---

[1]SASL is similar in its syntax to Haskell. Where it differs we shall indicate.

```
succ x = plus 1 x
```

We now have to abstract x from the right hand side using the above rules. We get

$$[x](plus\ 1\ x) \quad\Rightarrow\quad S([x](plus\ 1))([x]x)$$
$$\Rightarrow\quad S(S(K\ plus)(K\ 1))I$$

so the definition of succ can be replaced[1] by

```
succ = S(S(K plus)(K 1))I
```

and we leave it as an exercise to show that this exhibits the same behaviour as the original definition. Also as an exercise, the reader should verify that the classical definition of factorial

```
fac x = if x==0 then 1 else x * fac(x-1)
```

leads to the definition in terms of combinators:

```
fac = S(S(S(K cond) (S(S(K eq) (K 0)) I))
        (K 1)) (S(S(K times)I) (S(K fac)
        (S(S(K minus)I) (K 1))))
```

as given in Turner's paper.

As we can see, quite small definitions may lead to large combinator expressions. We should not worry too much about this as the combinator form is really a kind of machine code for a special graph reduction machine. But we note that in fact the successor function can be defined with

```
succ = plus 1
```

so it is fair to assume that optimisations are possible. Turner discusses some of these, using some other combinators:

$$B\ x\ y\ z = x\ (y\ z)$$

$$C\ x\ y\ z\ =\ x\ z\ y$$

and the additional transformation rules:

$$S\ (K\ e_1)(K\ e_2) \quad\Rightarrow\quad K\ (e_1\ e_2) \qquad (8.4)$$
$$S\ (K\ e)\ I \quad\Rightarrow\quad e \qquad (8.5)$$
$$S\ (K\ e_1)\ e_2 \quad\Rightarrow\quad B\ e_1\ e_2 \qquad (8.6)$$
$$S\ e_1\ (K\ e_2) \quad\Rightarrow\quad C\ e_1\ e_2 \qquad (8.7)$$

where the last two rules only apply if no earlier one does.

---

[1]These replacements are supposed to be done by the compiler after any type checking has been done. In fact the replacements may introduce combinator expressions which are not themselves typeable, but that is immaterial to the user who does not see the transformations taking place.

With this in mind, the reader should verify that the code for `fac` now reduces to:

```
fac = S(C(B cond(eq 0)) 1)
          (S times(B fac(C minus 1)))
```

Functions of several variables are no problem as we would first abstract with respect to the later variables and so on backwards, so that, for instance:

```
avge x y = (x+y)/2
```

reduces, by first abstracting `y` (treating `x` as a constant) to get

```
avge x = C (B divide (plus x)) 2
```

and then abstracting the resulting expression with `x` to

```
avge = C(B C(B(B divide) plus)) 2
```

It can be shown that the size of combinator expression grows as the square of the number of arguments being used to abstract. Turner invented further optimisations to cope with this problem which he reported in [turn79c].

Non-recursive local definitions of the kind `let x = e1 in e2` are easily dealt with by abstracting `x` from `e2` and applying the resulting function to `e1`, i.e. by treating it as `([x] e2)e1`. This is a little more complicated in the case of recursive definitions which we deal with below.

Turner covers a number of other forms in his paper including a combinator, *P* (pair), for the primitive constructor[1] `:`. He also discusses pattern matching, but we will not consider that here. We will, however, talk about recursion. Readers will have noted that when the recursive function `fac` was defined above, the name `fac` was not abstracted out and Turner treated definitions at the top level differently from others. We stated earlier that the concept of an environment could be got rid of by using this abstraction technique and that is so, but Turner retains the top level environment as this is one which, being globally available, need not be an explicit part of the state of the machine. While a particular expression is evaluated, it does not change as functions at various scoping levels are entered and left. In fact the whole concept of scoping level has vanished, and it is convenient to retain the outer layer of names. The compiler will, of course, change these to some form of index into an array of top level names. These names, however, could also in principle have been abstracted away using the technique we now describe for local recursion.

Recursive local definitions of the kind `let f = e1 in e2`, (or using `where`) where `e1` involves `f`, are dealt with in a similar way to that used for recursion when translating to λ-expressions (see section 5.10.4). We saw there that the solution to a definitional equation of the form

$$f = e_1$$

---

[1]The only constructor operator in SASL is `:`. Extra constructors in other languages such as Haskell can be treated in an exactly similar fashion.

is

$$f = Y(\lambda f . e_1)$$

where Y is a fixed point finder. We replace that with

$$f=Y([f] e_1)$$

So, for instance if the definition of an infinite list of 1's:

```
x = 1:x
```

is made locally, it is treated as Y([x] (P 1 x)) which is just Y(P 1).

There are a number of ways in which we can implement Y. We saw in 5.10.4 that there are non-recursive λ-expressions which act as fixed point finders. We could abstract the bound variables out of one of these expressions and hence obtain an implementation using the combinators S, K and I. We could also implement recursion by using a pointer within the recursive expression to the expression itself. All fixed point finders have to satisfy the equation

$$Y H = H (Y H)$$

so we could implement Y by using this as the defining equation and reducing it in the same way as we reduce other combinators (see below). We shall see the solution used by Turner when we discuss the actual representation and interpretation of combinator expressions in the next section.

8.5.3 Interpreting Combinator Expressions

To evaluate combinator expressions, we have to implement the reductions described in the defining equations for S, K and I by turning them into rewrite rules. Moreover we have to make sure that, for lazy evaluation, reductions are carried out in normal order. In addition, we have to implement combinators for the built-in functions such as addition, subtraction, and other arithmetic and logical operations; also conditionals, and the optimising combinators B and C.

Some of the reduction rules not detailed previously are given below:

```
plus x y          ⇒     x + y
cond True x y     ⇒     x
cond False x y    ⇒     y
and True y        ⇒     y
and False y       ⇒     False
or True y         ⇒     True
or False y        ⇒     y
hd(P x y)         ⇒     x
tl(P x y)         ⇒     y
```

The basic data structure in Turner's SK Reduction Machine is a node with two fields which represents the first field (or what it points at) being applied to the second field (or what it points at). Thus, for instance, $S\ x\ y\ z$ is represented by the data structure:

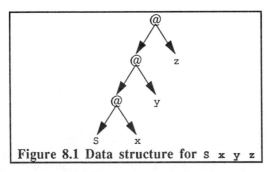

Figure 8.1 Data structure for s x y z

We have pointed out earlier that combinator reduction can proceed lazily by overwriting redex nodes with the equivalent reduced expression. Thus each of the reduction rules represents an overwriting of a node in the graph which matches the left hand side, by the equivalent right hand side. For instance $S\ x\ y\ z$ reduces as follows

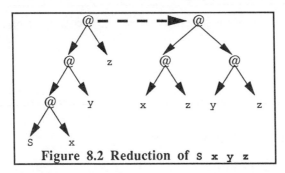

Figure 8.2 Reduction of s x y z

where the broad dotted arrow means that the node at the right is the same physical node as that on the left, but with the indicated overwritten contents. The other two nodes, x z and y z are new space dynamically allocated when the reduction takes place.

We need to organise things so that evaluation proceeds in normal order. This can be done by descending the left pointers in the graph, until a combinator is discovered. At this point, if that combinator can take part in a reduction, it does so, the resulting overwrite takes place and evaluation proceeds from that point in a similar fashion. This continues until nothing further can be done and the result, the single object left on the stack, is printed[1].

---

[1]If the result is a structure (h : t in SASL, but this could be generalised for languages like Haskell with other shaped structures), the printing routine will have to call on the evaluator to unsuspend the fields (head and tail in SASL) before printing them, and this in turn may involve further evaluation. The lazy evaluation is said to be *print driven*. Only those parts of the result needed by the user are evaluated.

Turner gives the example:

```
succ 2 where succ x = 1+x
```

which compiles to:

```
C I 2 (plus 1)
```

and this transforms at run time as follows:

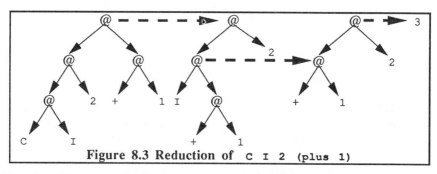

Figure 8.3 Reduction of `C I 2 (plus 1)`

The Y combinator can be implemented, as we said above, by using the reduction sequence

$$Y f = f\,(Y f)$$

i.e. as follows:

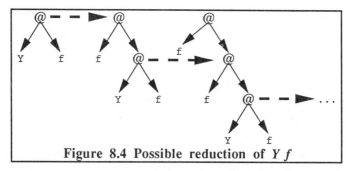

Figure 8.4 Possible reduction of $Y f$

where there may be intermediate reductions of the expression f before each unwinding of the recursion happens. But, as a copy of the original graph appears as a sub-graph of subsequent graphs in the (infinite) reduction sequence, we can tie the knot by making the sub-graph coincide with the graph itself as follows:

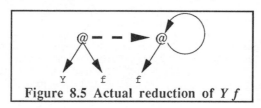

Figure 8.5 Actual reduction of $Y f$

8.5.4 Book-keeping

Arranging the normal order reductions described above is not difficult with the aid of a *left ancestors stack*. The stack starts by containing a single entry, a pointer to the expression being evaluated. So long as the expression at the front of the stack is an application node (an @), a new node is pushed onto the stack, a pointer to the left descendant of the original. In this way a whole chain of pointers to the left *spine* of the node to be evaluated is created, so that when we eventually arrive at a node which is a combinator name rather than an application node, we can apply the combinator, knowing that its arguments can be reached through the pointers immediately behind the front of the stack. As an example, it is instructive to see what happens to the stack as the expression c I 2 (plus 1) starts evaluation. For convenience, we draw the stack growing downwards. The stack starts off pointing at the expression itself as shown in (a) and eventually, as the spine is traversed, turns into (b).

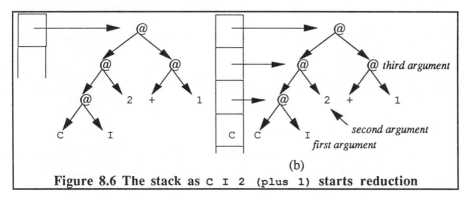

(b)

Figure 8.6 The stack as c I 2 (plus 1) **starts reduction**

At this stage, the hardware of the combinator machine takes over and a machine code routine is invoked to deal with the *C* combinator. This creates a new application node for I (plus 1) and overwrites the node pointed at by the fourth top element in the stack, the top of the spine, with the application of the new node to 2. At the same time, the piece of graph thus constructed is descended along its spine, so that the machine is ready to proceed further by further stacking of left descendants until another combinator is reached. The positions before and after are as follows:

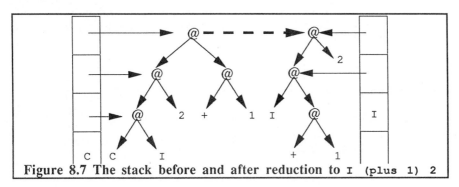

Figure 8.7 The stack before and after reduction to I (plus 1) 2

8.6 THE G-MACHINE

Turner's paper on combinator reduction made a major impact on applicative programming for two important reasons. One was due to the efficiency gained by not doing expensive environment look-ups and this we have stressed above. In addition, the graph rewriting that takes place means that sometimes expressions which are shared by several different parts of the program are only evaluated once. But we have seen that graph rewriting is not unique to the SKI combinator machine — the SECD machine can be modified to take advantage of this optimisation — and its technique for getting rid of variables is not the only one that is available. We describe now the work done by Johnsson and his colleagues [john87] on the applicative language Lazy ML (LML). It has been pointed out that the granularity of the Turner combinator implementation is rather fine in that the method breaks down expressions into very small parts each of which, when executed by the machine, constitute an atomic action. Johnsson in a series of important papers [john84, john85 and john86] and culminating in his thesis [john87] describes a method which uses *supercombinators* which are combinators abstracted from the users' programs and specialised to their particular needs[1]. In this way the granularity of actions is better suited to the users' needs.

Johnsson assumes that by the time a program is executed it will have the form of a series of (possibly mutually recursive) definitions of combinators (functions without free variables) whose bodies contain no λ-expressions. In addition any expression to be evaluated is assumed not to contain λ-expressions. Since users commonly want to write expressions containing local definitions and since these contain λ-expressions implicitly, a transformation (see below) is applied by the compiler to *λ-lift* local definitions out to the top level. This transformation, moreover, removes any references to non-local variables thus forcing all defined functions to be combinators.

The advantage of using combinators is the same as with Turner's implementation. The environment component of the underlying machine is not needed and this in turn means that closures are unnecessary. By allowing user defined combinators, names *are* re-introduced, but they are all local arguments to the functions defined and can be looked up on a stack (as indeed the variables in Turner's implementation of S, K, I and his other basic combinators are all found by looking at the pointers to the spine on the stack).

The combinators in Turner's machine were built-in to it, but with users inventing their own, they now have to be compiled down to some lower level code. A definition of a combinator

```
f x1 x2 … xi = e
```

gets compiled into code that will perform the rewriting of the call

```
f e1 e2 … ei
```

---

[1]The term *supercombinator* was coined by John Hughes [hugh82, hugh83].

into:

```
e [x1 := e1] [x2 := e2] … [xi := ei]
```

so that an application of f to all its parameters is rewritten to the right hand side of the definition with all the actual parameters being substituted for the formals (with sharing so that all occurrences of a formal parameter point at a single actual parameter). The abstract machine invented by Johnsson for this purpose is called the *G-machine* and it has some similarities to the SECD machine. Johnsson compiles G-machine code further to machine code for a number of real machines, but that will not concern us here.

8.7 TRANSFORMATION TO SUPER-COMBINATORS

Let us first examine the transformations made to a program to ensure that all functions are moulded into combinators. Johnsson presents a number of different strategies and we will only look at the simplest here. It is in principle the same as the one described by Hughes in his work on supercombinators [hugh83] and it involves introducing extra parameters to functions so that any variables free in the original are bound by applying the new function (a combinator) to the value of the free variable. The transformation is as follows. Suppose that $\lambda x.e$ is an abstraction with e containing references to a free variable y. In this case we replace $\lambda x.e$ with the semantically equivalent expression $(\lambda y.\lambda x.e)y$ and then, provided that e now contains only bound variables, the λ-expression is given a new machine generated name, F say, and this is λ-*lifted* out to the top level as a definition of a new combinator, $F\ y\ x = e$. The original expression is transformed to $F\ y$. If e still has free variables after y has been abstracted, the process is repeated as many times as needed before the lifting of the new combinator. Let us see an example of this. Consider the following definition in Haskell:

```
f x = (a-x) / (a+x)
    where a = exp x
```

There is an implied λ-expression here as this is regarded to be

```
f x = (\ a -> (a-x) / (a+x)) (exp x)
```

which has x as a free variable in the λ-expression which must therefore be rewritten as

```
(\ x -> \ a -> (a-x) / (a+x)) x
```

Now the λ-expression is a combinator to which we can give an internal name so that the whole transformation turns into a definition of the pair of super-combinators:

```
f x = F x (exp x)
F x a = (a-x) / (a+x)
```

In the G-machine implemented by Johnsson, things are a little more complicated than this, especially where recursive functions are concerned. But these are matters of detail which will not be considered here. In principle we have enough to make a complete transformation to combinators using the fixed point combinator, Y, to effect recursion. This is the method that Hughes uses [hugh83], but Johnsson prefers to leave recursive functions as they are as far as possible since the

G-machine handles them well. The reader is referred to [john85] or [john87] for further details of the optimisations that can be made to recursive functions.

8.8 PROGRAMS FOR THE G-MACHINE

We now consider how an equation defining a combinator can be turned into a sequence of G-machine instructions for rewriting a graph node denoting an application of that combinator into its new form. Essentially what such a sequence of instructions has to do is regard the left hand side of a defining equation as a template which is to match a node of the graph under consideration and the right hand side as a template for replacing it with the formal parameters being replaced by the actual ones.

As in Turner's machine, a stack is used to point at the spine of a graph being evaluated and so, when an application is about to take place, the actual parameters are all made available by unwinding the graph to expose its spine.

A slight reorganisation of the stack then takes place so that the parameters are available *directly* rather than indirectly through the application nodes on the spine. This is shown as follows:

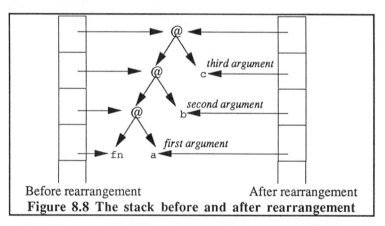

Before rearrangement   After rearrangement

Figure 8.8 The stack before and after rearrangement

The function being applied is not, of course, restricted to a predefined subset of machine combinators. Instead each named user super-combinator corresponds to an address of some code which builds a graph to overwrite the appropriate application node on the graph. This rebuilding will be done by picking up the actual parameters and essentially using them to make a copy of the right hand side of the definition with the substitutions made. As an example, consider the generation function for making streams which we looked at in section 7.2.

```
series f a = a : series f (f a)
```

The code that is generated for the G-machine is very similar to that generated for an SECD machine at first sight. It is a reverse Polish representation of the right hand side of the definition.

In this case the code will be:

```
series : PUSH 1            !stack a
         PUSHFUN series    !stack series
         PUSH 2            !stack f
         MKAP              !construct (series f)
         PUSH 2            !stack f
         PUSH 4            !stack a
         MKAP              !construct (f a)
         MKAP              !construct (series f(f a))
         CONS              !construct a:(series f(f a))
         UPDATE 3          !over-write the original node
         RET 2             !return the answer to caller
```

Objects are addressed relative to the top of the stack (shown at the bottom) which has address 0 so that a *seems* to have a different address in lines 1 and 6. We can summarise the actions of the various instructions shown in this example as follows:

PUSH n   is used for loading (pointers to) arguments onto the stack so that new graphs can be built with them. It takes the argument found n cells from the top of the stack and pushes a copy of it onto the stack.

PUSHFUN f   is similar and is used for loading a pointer to the code for the top level combinator f onto the stack.

MKAP   is a zero address instruction which builds a new application node in the graph with pointers to the rator and rand found on the stack. These are popped and (a pointer to) the resulting node pushed onto the stack.

CONS   is similar but builds a list node instead with head and tail found on the stack. Similar instructions could be used for more general constructors.

UPDATE n   is used to overwrite the node n elements down the stack with the one on top of the stack, which is then popped.

RET n   is used to return the value found n nodes down the stack as the result of this evaluation. As we shall see, the rewriting of a node is initiated with a call of EVAL and this in effect calls a subroutine, RET returns from the subroutine and has to transmit a value back to the calling routine. Each subroutine has its own stack frame and this instruction transfers the value back to the top of the stack in the caller's stack frame.

Note that it is the main business of a subroutine to *build* a subgraph, and the act of overwriting the initial graph with the result is the only piece of *evaluation* normally done. This is the way that computation makes progress. However there are places where one wants to *force* evaluation. For instance, what caused the function we have been talking about to be called in the first place? What asked for a piece of graph to be reduced?

At the most basic level, when a user wants to print the value of an expression, we arrange that the evaluation is started by making the print routine start evaluating the graph handed to it by the compiler. This is done by loading a pointer to the graph onto the stack and then performing an EVAL instruction. This instruction is used whenever a piece of graph has to be forced to be evaluated. It operates as follows:

EVAL   causes a new stack frame to be started and a function to be entered. The graph to be evaluated is copied in to be the single object on the new frame, and then the old machine state is saved on a dump as with the SECD machine. EVAL then causes the spine of the tree to be traversed to build the structure which was shown in Fig. 8.8 and the function found at the leftmost node to be entered. When a rewrite has been completed by executing the subroutine, a further unwinding and rearranging of the graph may be needed if it is still not in normal form.

Using this scheme, lazy evaluation is catered for by suspending rewriting of parts of the graph until they are really needed. For instance, when a list node is constructed (corresponding to the operator :) its head and tail are not evaluated further. It is only when we attempt to access the head or tail of such a node that an explicit EVAL instruction will be compiled into the code that needs to access the list node. In fact, without any of the optimisation that we describe below, whenever *any* basic operation is carried out — one that is built-in, not described by a user's program — then a call of EVAL is needed to calculate its argument(s). This is exactly the same as with Turner's machine.

Many optimisations can be made to the above scheme, but we will look at one in detail. On many occasions, the rewriting scheme constructs a new graph merely to re-traverse it and take it apart again to EVAL it. Johnsson uses the following example. Consider the definition

```
succ n = n+1
```

As we have shown above, code for this would be compiled which, when executed with the function being applied to an expression e, would build the following graph:

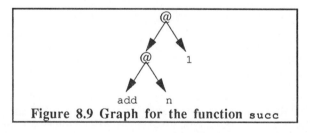

Figure 8.9 Graph for the function succ

This requires the primitive built-in function add to evaluate e (and the constant 1) before proceeding further. So the graph is scanned for evaluation immediately after it is built.

Instead of making code for building the tree and then scanning it, the LML compiler plants code to evaluate the expression n+1 in the first place. The code is as follows:

```
succ:   PUSH 0          !stack graph for n
        EVAL            !evaluate it
        GET             !get the value to the V-stack
        PUSHBASIC 1     !stack 1 on the V-stack
        ADD             !n+1 on the V-stack
        MKINT           !make it into a graph on the graph stack
        UPDATE 2        !over-write the original node
        RET 1           !return the answer to caller
```

Note that arithmetic (all strict evaluation in fact) is carried out on a separate stack called the *V-stack* and instructions are available for manipulating that in reverse Polish. GET loads a value from a graph onto the V-stack. ADD is a zero address instruction operating on the top two elements of the V-stack in the way such instructions do. MKINT pops an integer from the V-stack, makes a single-cell graph from it and stacks (a pointer to) it on the main stack.

Below is listed a more complete set of instructions for the G-machine divided into the two different kinds we have talked about, those for constructing graphs and those for evaluating on the V-stack.

• **Graph Construction and Manipulation**

PUSHINT i   Constructs a graph node with the integer i in it. Pushes a pointer to it onto the (main) stack. Similar instructions are available for all the basic types. This code is generated when the compiler discovers a literal in a context where it need not be strictly evaluated.

PUSHFUN f   Constructs a graph node containing the entry point of a top level user function or λ-lifted function, f. Pushes a pointer to it onto the stack.

PUSH i   Pushes a copy of the object i elements down the stack onto the top of it. The compiler generates this when a formal parameter is used in a graph building context.

CONS   Constructs a graph representing a list using the top two elements of the stack as head and tail. The elements are not strictly evaluated by this instruction. The pointer to the result replaces the head and tail.

MKAP   Construct an application node from a rator and rand on the stack and replaces them with the result.

MKINT   This instruction is used to pop a value from the V-stack and construct a graph node containing an integer. A similar instruction is used to construct basic graphs of other types.

HD   Checks that the top item of the stack is a list node — issuing an error message if it is not — and extracts the left element from it. This result replaces the original on the stack.

TL   As above, but selects the right hand element.

• **Evaluation**

EVAL   This is generated by the compiler whenever it needs to specify strict evaluation, for instance after the two above instructions. It will also be used to force evaluation of graphs before a basic strict operation such as addition. When executed it does one of two things, depending on the type of node found on the top of the stack. If it is anything but an application node, the graph has already been evaluated — some other part of the main graph must have been sharing it — and the item is placed on the stack without further evaluation.

If, however, it is a graph containing an application node, it 'calls a subroutine' by using the dump as in an SECD-machine to push down the old stack and return address, effectively starting a new stack frame. It then *unwinds* the graph as described above, traversing down the left spine of the graph stacking items until a node is found which is an entry point to a top level function. At this point the pointers to its arguments are rearranged as described in Figure 8.8 so that they are directly accessible from the stack and a jump is made to the code for the function.

PUSHBASIC i   Pushes the literal integer i onto the V-stack. Similar instructions are available for all the basic types. This code is generated when the compiler discovers a literal in a context where it needs to be strictly evaluated.

ADD   A zero address instruction which adds the top elements of the V-stack and replaces them with the result. Similar instructions for other operations on values of all basic types are available.

JFALSE l   Used for implementing conditionals, this is placed after the evaluation of the test. It pops a Boolean value from the V-stack and, if discovered to be False, jumps to the code labelled l.

JUMP l   This is planted after the first arm of a conditional to implement a jump round the second arm to label l.

GET   This is used to transfer an item from the stack of graph pointers to the V-stack

For a complete list and further explanation, readers should consult the theses of Augustsson [augu87] and Johnsson [john87] and their eminently readable joint description in [augu89].

8.9 STRICTNESS ANALYSIS

It will probably be evident, especially when one considers the EVAL instruction, that lazy evaluation, though a powerful technique semantically, is difficult and potentially inefficient to implement. The inefficiency lies mainly in the fact that since items of graph get evaluated at most once, we have to keep a track of this and dynamically test such items to see whether or not they have been evaluated. It would therefore be of great advantage to know statically, at compile time, whether items needed to be strictly evaluated.

Consider the expression:

```
if n > 0 then n+x else n-x
```

It is clear that, whether n is greater than 0 or not, it will have been strictly evaluated by the time that one of the branches, whichever it is, is evaluated. On the other hand, nothing can be gleaned from the information in this example about whether x has been evaluated. We can still, however, deduce that x will *need* to be evaluated. Supposing, for example, that the expression is part of the definition:

```
f x n = if n > 0 then n+x else n-x
```

we can see at compile time that f is a strict function and we might as well pass its parameters by value rather than by need, saving all the testing that would otherwise be necessary inside the body of the function to see if n or x was already evaluated.

Things are not always so easy, however. Consider instead:

```
f x y n = if n > 0 then n+x else n-y
```

Here we know that n needs strictly evaluated, but we do not know which of x and y will be needed. We therefore have to compile checks into the code to find out at run time what their evaluation status is. Some of these kinds of problems can be solved by doing *strictness analysis*. which attempts to discover at compile time whether certain expressions are bound to be strictly evaluated at run time.

Bloss and Hudak [blos86] have identified four questions to ask whose answers provide useful information when an expression exp is evaluated:

- What definitely *will* be evaluated after exp is evaluated?

- What definitely *will not* be evaluated after exp is evaluated?

- What definitely *was* evaluated before exp was evaluated?

- What definitely *was not* evaluated before exp was evaluated?

These questions are considered by the related technique called *path analysis* which can be used to discover other kinds of information. For instance it can tell in some cases whether it is safe to update a data structure *in place* rather than making a copy of it [blos89]. Conceptually functional programming involves no updating, but if an update would make the implementation more efficient while preserving the safe referential transparency of the original, there is no reason why this should not be done. It is clear that this would allow space to be saved in certain circumstances. It would also save time as space needs to be allocated dynamically and periodic expensive garbage collections will be necessary.

Both strictness analysis and path analysis are still under active investigation — see for instance [clac85] and [blos88]. These are complex problems, especially in the presence of higher order functions which are particularly difficult to reason about and we shall not enter into the details here. A good introduction is to be found in [peyt87] and some recent research work on it can be found in [clac85] and [hugh87] as well as in the work previously cited by Bloss and Hudak [blos86, blos89].

8.10 FURTHER DEVELOPMENTS

Lazy evaluation and its implementation is a huge and growing subject and we cannot give every detail of it here, but it is worth pointing the reader to at least some of the recent developments which have been made. A number of these are gathered together in an edition of the Computer Journal which was devoted to the subject in April 1989 [comp89]. In addition [peyt87] is an encyclopaedic reference to lazy evaluation and its implementation by graph reduction.

8.11 SUMMARY

In this chapter we have seen several methods for implementing lazy evaluation. First we saw that the SECD machine could be easily modified to cope with delayed and forced evaluation by using suspensions. These act as shareable graph nodes which can be overwritten with values when needed.

We examined Turner's combinator machine which relies on the abstraction of variables from expressions at compile time rather than using λ as a run time abstraction operator. We examined optimisations to the basic machine and a mechanism for interpreting combinator expressions.

We looked at the G-machine which allows a larger granularity by turning user definitions into combinators using λ-lifting and then compiling graph rewriting code from the resulting top-level definitions. An optimisation for using a second stack to evaluate arithmetic and other strict expressions was discussed.

A brief look at strictness and path analysis concluded the chapter.

8.12 EXERCISES

1. Reduce the expression $(\lambda x. x(a\ x))((\lambda z.\ z\ b)c)$ to normal form using

    a) string reduction

    b) graph reduction

    and trying both types of reduction in both applicative and normal order. Try to estimate the saving, if any, in space and number of reduction steps.

2. Show that the definition

    ```
    succ = S(S(K plus)(K 1))I
    ```

    performs in the same way as the original definition of `succ` given in section 8.5.

3. Verify that the classical definition

    ```
    fac x = if x==0 then 1 else x * fac(x-1)
    ```

leads to the definition in terms of combinators:

```
fac = S(S(S(K cond) (S(S(K eq) I) (K 0)))
          (K 1)) (S(S(K times)I) (S(K fac)
          (S(S(K minus)I) (K 1)))))
```

and show that this works when applied to 1.

4. Show that using the optimisations given in equations (8.4), (8.5), (8.6) and
    (8.7) leads to reduced combinator expressions for succ and fac as presented
    in unoptimised form in exercises 2 and 3. Comment on what happens if you
    define succ with

    ```
    succ x = x+1
    ```

    What can you say about simplification of combinator expressions containing
    commutative operators like +?

5. Show, by successive abstractions that

    ```
    avge x y = (x+y)/2
    ```

    reduces to

    ```
    avge = C(B C(B(B divide) plus)) 2
    ```

    You are advised to perform optimisations as you go along the transformation
    sequence, otherwise the intermediate steps can become very large.

6. Write Haskell programs which will perform the operations of abstraction and
    optimisation described in this chapter on a simple representation for
    unsugared λ-expressions. Count the number of application nodes generated in
    each case. Try to make some empirical estimate of the complexity of the
    unoptimised and optimised methods.

7. Investigate the evaluation of avge 2 4 where avge is as defined in Ex. 5.
    Keep a careful note of which cells get overwritten, which are new cells, and
    which can be freed (assuming that nothing else is pointing to them) for re-use
    by a garbage collector.

8. This example is due to Hughes [hugh83]. Consider the recursive definition of
    a function that selects the nth element of a sequence:

    ```
    el n s = if n==1 then hd s else el (n-1) (tl s)
    ```

    Convert this to λ-expression form as shown in section 5.10.1 and remove the
    recursion using the Y fixed point finder. Use the techniques described in this
    chapter for converting λ-expressions with free variables into combinators to
    transform the definition to pure combinator form. Does it make any difference
    in which order the free variables are abstracted?

Chapter 9

Correctness

9.1 INTRODUCTION

One of the advantages which was claimed for functional programming in the introductory chapter was that proving the correctness of programs is greatly facilitated. In this chapter this is expanded upon and details are given of how proofs that functional programs have certain properties may be carried out.

The software industry suffers from an enormous problem to do with *formality*. Many programmers are not mathematicians or logicians and they do not feel at home with a formal approach to the subject. This is especially true with respect to using any new notation. It is therefore extremely difficult to persuade practitioners to use, for instance, the Hoare axiomatic scheme [hoar69] for proving properties about imperative programs, because it involves learning a new notation, or even two new notations, not to mention the new methodology of manipulating such notation. Consider for example the following assertion taken at random from a proof of correctness of a Pascal program:

$$\{t=x_0 \ \& \ x=y_0\} \quad \text{y} \ := \ \text{t} \quad \{y=x_0 \ \& \ x=y_0\}$$

This asserts that if $t=x_0 \ \& \ x=y_0$ was the case before the assignment was executed, then $y=x_0 \ \& \ x=y_0$ will be the case after. The y := t is written in the programmer's own Pascal notation and the $t=x_0 \ \& \ x=y_0$ and $y=x_0 \ \& \ x=y_0$ (called the *pre-* and *post-conditions*) are both statements of the classical logical language known as *predicate calculus*, a language which the programmer has to learn in addition to mastering the programming language. The whole assertion consisting of both pre- and post-conditions and the Pascal statement forms a term of a third *language of assertions*, and proofs in this system consist of terms from this language, each one being an *axiom* of the system or following by strict deduction from a previous term or terms in the proof using *rules of inference*.

173

The methodology associated with generating proofs will also be new to programmers. A great deal of this involves, in the Hoare scheme, the attaching of *invariants* to execution loops in the program (facts which are both pre- and post-conditions of the loop). Quite often the finding of such invariants requires a spark of intuition, especially if the proof is not generated by the programmer. Further details may be obtained from a number of text books, e.g. [grie81]

In proofs of functional programs, things are somewhat simpler. We will still have to have sparks of intuition from time to time. Programmers still have to know how the program works to be able to prove a point about any reasonably complicated function. But because functional programs are written as equations which have been designed to obey the rules of logic, programmers do not have to learn a new proof language. Proofs can be carried out using the functional language itself. This distinct advantage is gained because of the properties of equality and substitution which are applicable to referentially transparent expressions are well known to most programmers even from school days, even though they probably did not know them by these names.

9.2 MATHEMATICAL INDUCTION

However, as we said above, some methods and principles still have to be learned. One that is very prevalent in correctness proofs, both imperative and functional, is the use of various principles of *induction*. One of these principles is called the *Principle of Mathematical Induction*, a method of proof which is unfortunately often misunderstood. This book is not meant to be a course in mathematics, but we shall give a small example here to show how easy it is to use the principle. The principle works approximately as follows. If you want to prove something about every natural number (non-negative integer) then you prove the fact about some small number, typically *1* or *0* and then prove that, *if* it is true for an arbitrary number *k* *then* it will be true for *k+1*. These two necessary steps are called the *base* and the *induction step*. They are sufficient to show that the fact is true for every natural number greater than or equal to the base number. An informal proof proceeds as follows. We know that it is true for (say) *0* (by the base). Therefore, it is true for *1* (by the induction). Therefore it is true for *2* (by the induction) *etc....*

For instance, suppose we wanted to prove that:

$$1+2+3...+n = \frac{n(n+1)}{2}$$

We shall use a base *n=1*. Clearly the proposition is true for *n=1* because

$$1 = \frac{1(1+1)}{2}$$

and *if* it is true for *n=k*:

$$1+2+3...+k = \frac{k(k+1)}{2} \qquad \text{(hypothesis)}$$

then, adding *k+1* to each side:

$$1+2+3\ldots+k+(k+1) \;=\; \frac{k(k+1)}{2}+(k+1)$$
$$=\;(k+1)(\tfrac{k}{2}+1)$$
$$=\;\frac{(k+1)(k+2)}{2}$$
$$=\;\frac{(k+1)((k+1)+1)}{2}$$

so that, under the assumption or *hypothesis* that it was true for *n=k*, we see that it will then be true for *n=k+1*.

Some people have a deep seated mistrust of this method of argument which assumes what we want to know for a particular value and then proves that it will be true for the next value. There seems to be a deep-seated psychological 'block' against using what looks like the theorem we are trying to prove as a hypothesis[1]. It is, however, quite in order to do this *so long as the base case is proved separately*. The psychology is probably similar to that shown by beginners when first asked to use a recursive method to code a function, who also find it bizarre to be able to call the function which is being defined. This similarity is no accident. In chapter 3 we emphasised the base-and-induction method of *designing* recursive functions and we shall now see that the equation(s) written in Haskell as base cases will be used to *prove* the base case of an inductive proof and the inductive case(s) to prove the inductive step.

Consider for example the factorial function:

```
fac 0 = 1              -- base
fac n = n * fac(n - 1) -- induction
                       -- (n /= 0 implicitly)
```

Suppose we wish to prove that this algorithm is correct — i.e. that

$$\text{fac } n = n! = n*(n-1)*(n-2)\ldots*1 \text{ for } n \geq 0$$

Firstly, by the base equation, it is true for n=0 if we assume that the product of no numbers at all is 1, the unit of multiplication. Now make the hypothesis, or assumption, that it is true for n=k so

$$\text{fac } k = k*(k-1)*(k-2)\ldots*1$$

and so, making use of the inductive equation and substituting n=k+1 in it:

$$
\begin{aligned}
\text{fac } (k+1) \quad &= \quad (k+1) \;*\; \text{fac}(k) \\
&= \quad (k+1)*k*(k-1)*(k-2)\ldots 1 \\
&= \quad (k+1)\,!
\end{aligned}
$$

---

[1]The block is not quite so solid as that experienced by some people when using the *reductio ad absurdum* method of argument, where we assume the *opposite* of what we want to prove and show that this leads to an absurdity. A whole branch of logic called intuitionist or constructive logic, has been based on the rejection of this kind of argument.

which completes the proof. The proof of correctness of this function and many others like it is, indeed, so intimately linked with its recursively inductive definition that it may appear as if we have not really done anything at all, that the proof is vacuous. This is a consequence of the fact that many specifications of functions are the same as their implementations, and so proofs are trivial.

Not all proofs are so straightforward, however. Some do require the spark of intuition we talked about in the introduction. Turner [turn82] gives an example which connects two definitions of the Fibonacci function:

```
fib 0 = 0
fib 1 = 1
fib n = fib(n-1) + fib(n-2)     -- n not 0 or 1
```

This definition could be regarded as a specification, but unless memoised (see section 7.8), it is extremely inefficient because of the large number of calls needed (exponential in n). More efficient is the following algorithm which keeps a note of enough information in its extra parameters to be able to calculate a value with a much smaller number of calls proportional to n:

```
fib' a b 0 = a
fib' a b n = fib' b (a+b) (n-1)     -- n not 0
```

and we then claim that:

THEOREM 9.1:   `fib' 0 1 n = fib n`   for all $n \geq 0$

The proof of this example requires a flash of inspiration to notice that it is a special case of a more general theorem:

THEOREM 9.2:   `fib' (fib i) (fib (i+1)) n = fib (i+n)` for all $n \geq 0, i \geq 0$

Actually the inventor of the algorithm should have no difficulty in framing this more general theorem as it says how the algorithm works! It will clearly be much easier for programmers to prove the correctness of their own algorithms as they presumably know how they work. Some would go further than that and say it is the *duty* of programmers to prove the correctness of the work they produce. Certain government bodies are beginning to *insist* on correctness proofs for all safety critical software.

In the following proof of the revised Fibonacci algorithm we have annotated the lines to show how they are derived. This is a common aid used to allow easy following of proofs by anyone who wants to verify them[1]. When we refer to defining equations, we mention the case being used. When we use the hypothesis

---

[1]Verification might be made automatically.

during an induction step, we use, by convention, the (Latin) abbreviation *Ex. Hyp.* which merely stands for *By hypothesis.*

Proof of: `fib' (fib i) (fib (i+1)) n = fib (i+n)` for all $n \geq 0$, $i \geq 0$

Base: $n=0$

```
fib' (fib i) (fib (i+1)) 0 =   fib i for all i ≥ 0 (By fib' a b 0)
                           =   fib (i+n) for all i ≥ 0
```

Induction: Assume that the statement is true for $n=k$

If `fib' (fib i) (fib (i+1)) k = fib (i+k)` for all $i \geq 0$ and some $k \geq 0$
then   `fib' (fib i) (fib (i+1)) (k+1)`
```
    =   fib' (fib (i+1)) (fib i + fib (i+1)) k      for all i ≥ 0
                                          (By fib' a b n)
    =   fib' (fib (i+1)) (fib (i+2)) k
                                          (By fib n)
    =   fib (i+1+k)                       (Ex hyp.)
```

and now using the theorem with $i=0$, we can demonstrate our original claim that

$$\texttt{fib' 0 1 n = fib n} \text{ for all } n \geq 0$$

9.3 INDUCTION ON LISTS

The examples in the last section all prove propositions about numbers but it is perfectly possible to extend it to other data structures and we shall see that in full generality in the next section. But let us see first how the extension works for lists. One way is to say that a theorem to be proved about a list, should work for zero length lists and if true for length *n*, prove also to be true for length *n+1*. Thus it should often be possible to do list induction by doing mathematical induction on their length. To formalise this we need to recall the definition of the length of a list which we saw in section 5.10.6:

```
length []    = 0
length (h:t) = 1 + length t
```

Now, as an example, suppose that we define an infix append function in the obvious way:

```
[]    ++ x = x
(h:t) ++ x = h : t ++ x
```

and wish to prove some properties of this function. For instance, we should be able to say that:

THEOREM 9.3:   `length (a ++ b) = length a + length b`

The proof by induction on the length of *a* is quite easy:

Base: `length a = 0, a=[]:`

`length([] ++ b)`	`=`	`length b`	**(By** `[] ++ x`**)**
	`=`	`0 + length b`	**(By** arithmetic**)**
	`=`	`length [] + length b`	**(By** `length []`**)**

Induction: Assume true for lists, a of length *k*

If	`length(a ++ b)`	`= length a + length b`	
then	`length((h:a) ++ b)`	`= length (h:a ++ b)`	**(By** `(h:t) ++ x`**)**
		`= 1 + length(a ++ b)`	**(By** `length(h:t)` **)**

and so it is true for lists of length *k+1*.

9.4 STRUCTURAL INDUCTION

In the above example, we showed that it is possible to consider induction on lists as if it was mathematical induction. We now show how to generalise mathematical induction so that both it and list induction are special cases of a technique called *structural induction*, a method which is applicable to any algebraic data type.

Just as with mathematical induction, it is necessary with structural induction to prove the theorem in question in base cases and inductive cases. In an algebraic data type definition (see section 4.4), a type *T* is a union of of several possible structures, some of which involve *T* itself and some of which are defined in terms of other types. The former we shall call *recursive* cases and the latter *atomic*. Base cases in a proof have to be demonstrated for all values of the atomic structures. Inductive cases demonstrate that, if the relevant property holds for sub-structures, it will hold for values made from them using the constructor functions of the data type.

To make this clear let us take as an example the definition of labelled binary trees given in section 4.4:

```
data Tree t = Tip | Node t (Tree t) (Tree t)
```

Any theorem we want to prove about such trees will have a base case which must be proved about the tip nodes and an inductive case which, under the assumption that it holds for two trees, a and b, proves that it holds for `Node val a b`. Here, for instance, is a function which makes the mirror image of a tree:

```
reflect Tip = Tip
reflect (Node lab left right) =
  Node lab (reflect right) (reflect left)
```

Let us prove that:

THEOREM 9.4:   For all trees t, `reflect (reflect t) = t`.

Base: `reflect (reflect Tip)` `=` `reflect Tip`
                                            `=` `Tip` **(By** `reflect Tip` twice**)**

Induction: `reflect (reflect (Node v l r))`
`= reflect (Node v (reflect r) (reflect l))`
(By `reflect (Node ...)`**)**
`= Node v (reflect (reflect l)) (reflect (reflect r))`
(By `reflect (Node ...)`**)**
`= Node v l r` (**Ex hyp.**)

When we remember (see section 4.4) that the natural numbers can be defined by the algebraic data type:

```
Nat = Zero | Succ Nat
```

we can see how list induction (Base case `[]` and Inductive case `h:t`) and mathematical induction (Base case `zero` and Inductive case `Succ k`) are both specific instances of Structural Induction.

Clearly, there is a huge variety of theorems we can prove about the functions which we define and some will be more useful than others. Those that relate a functional definition to a specification will be especially valuable, but we shall see that there are a variety of theorems which can be used for improving functional definitions by allowing semantics preserving transformations of them to make them run faster. We shall see more of this in chapter 10 but will give a short example here. With the usual definition of map

```
map f []      = []
map f (hd:tl) = f hd:map f tl
```

we can prove the following:

THEOREM 9.5:   `(map f).(map g) = map (f.g)`

This is a useful theorem to prove because applying the left hand side means two traversals of a list, but if we replace it by the right hand side only one will be required. Darlington [darl82b] calls this optimisation *loop fusion*. The proof is as follows:

Base: `((map f).(map g)) []` `= map f (map g [])`
(By the properties of composition**)**
`= map f []`   **(By** `map f []`**)**
`= []`   **(By** `map f []`**)**
`= map(f.g) []`   **(By** `map f []`**)**

Induction:
If `((map f).(map g)) t` `= map (f.g) t`
then `((map f).(map g)) (h:t)` `= map f (map g (h:t))`
(By the properties of composition**)**
`= map f (g h : map g t)`
(By `map f (h:t)`**)**
`= f (g h) : (map f (map g t))`
(By map f (h:t)**)**
`= (f.g) h : (((map f) . (map g)) t)`
(By the properties of composition twice**)**
`= (f.g) h : map(f.g) t`
(**Ex hyp.**)
`= map(f.g) (h:t)`
(By `map f (h:t)`**)**

We could give endless examples of such proofs. A number are to be found in [bird86].

9.5 INDUCTION ON FUNCTIONS

In the sections above, we have seen that proofs about structures of various kinds are made by showing how proofs of smaller structures lead to proofs of larger ones. Sometimes we would like to be able to prove properties of *functions* in a similar way, but at first sight this seems a little difficult as functions seem 'atomic' and do not seem to have any internal structure. There are no sub-functions that we can break a function into. Remember not to confuse a function with an algorithm which implements it. The algorithm does have (syntactic) structure, but it is not this that we want to analyse. The methods of *fixed point induction* essentially replace this missing internal structure by a sequence of *approximations* to the function, which, in the limit, converge onto the function itself. These are approximations in an information theoretic sense. Each one in the sequence contains more information than the last, until ultimately all the information in the desired function is reached. We try to arrange that a property we want to prove about the function in question can be proved about each of the estimates in this *chain* of better and better approximations. A base case is provided by ⊥ which we saw in section 5.10.4 represents a complete absence of information. How shall we find a sequence of approximations to a function which we want to prove something about?

9.6 APPROXIMATION AND DOMAINS

First let us digress on just what we mean by approximation, and by one object containing less information than another — particularly some function being an estimate of another. The following gives a non-rigorous introduction to *domain* theory. Those who wish to see a more mathematically formal treatment should consult [stoy77].

For simple types of objects, integers say, it does not usually make sense to say that one contains less information than the other. The number *1* may be less than *2* but it is not any less well defined. In fact they are both fully defined. However there is an integer which is less well defined than either of them or than any of the 'ordinary' integers. Consider the Haskell definitions:

```
x = 1
y = y + 1
```

The recursive definition of y is a device to make y an undefined object, ⊥. This object does contain less information than other integers. When a value, y, contains less information than another, x, we write

$$y \sqsubseteq x$$

and the symbols ⊑, ⊒ and ⊐ have obvious meanings — but note that $x \not\sqsubseteq y$ does not necessarily imply $x \sqsupseteq y$ — try x=2 and y=3. We can illustrate the relationship between such objects by drawing a graph in which objects lower down contain less information than those higher up if they are joined to them by an edge of the graph. The following figure shows such a *partial ordered set* for the integers:

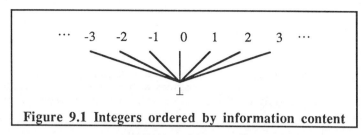

Figure 9.1 Integers ordered by information content

A set of objects which is augmented and structured by adding objects containing partial information (or a total lack of information) is called a *domain* [scot76] and one in which none of the original elements of the corresponding set is comparable with any other is called a *flat domain*. When more complicated types of object are considered, domains with more than two layers of definedness become evident. Consider, for instance, the set of pairs of Booleans. Representing truth and falsity by t and f, the elements are (t,t), (t,f), (f,t) and (f,f) but when either or both of the elements of the pair is allowed to be ⊥, the set extends to a domain with the extra elements (t,⊥), (⊥,t), (f,⊥), (⊥,f) and (⊥,⊥) provided that we can then sensibly define a relation ⊑ on pairs. This we can do by defining

$$(x,y) \sqsubseteq (X,Y) \Leftrightarrow x \sqsubseteq X \text{ and } y \sqsubseteq Y$$

and then

$$(x,y) \sqsubset (X,Y) \Leftrightarrow (x,y) \sqsubseteq (X,Y) \text{ and } (x,y) \neq (X,Y)$$

The relation between the information content of the possible pairs can be viewed as in Figure 9.2

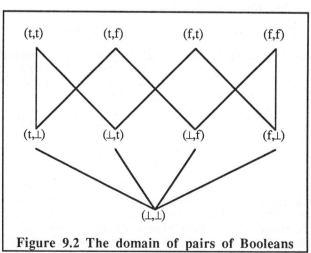

Figure 9.2 The domain of pairs of Booleans

We can further extend this concept of comparability of objects by their information content to *functions* by defining an appropriate ⊑ relation. Functions can be partially defined in the sense that they only apply to certain values. The `factorial` function, for instance, is not usually defined on the negative integers. If we make the Haskell definition

```
f 1 = 1
f 2 = 2
f 3 = 6
```

`f` is only defined on the three values 1, 2 and 3 and we can say, for other values x, that $f\ x = \bot$. However we can see that `f` agrees with `factorial` wherever they are defined and we can sensibly say that $f \sqsubseteq$ `factorial`. The appropriate definition for the general case is

$$f \sqsubseteq g \iff f\,x \sqsubseteq g\,x\,for\,all\,x$$

With this general description of a partial ordering by information content on functions, we can proceed to demonstrate a sequence of better and better approximations to any computable function in the following way.

9.7 CHAINS OF APPROXIMATIONS

Recall from 5.10.4 that any function (whether recursive or not)

$$f = \lambda x \,.\, e$$

can be written as the solution of fixed point equation:

$$f = fix\ (\lambda f \,.\, \lambda x \,.\, e)$$

where

$$fix\ h = h\ (fix\ h)$$

Expanding this last equation we find that

$$fix\ h = h\ (fix\ h) = h\ (\ h\ (fix\ h)) = h\ (\ h\ (\ h\ (fix\ h)))\ \ldots$$

A popular way to try to solve similar equations (involving real numbers rather that functions) is to insert a guess at the answer into one side of the equation and extract a new guess (a better one, it is hoped) from the other side. We also hope that this process will converge to a solution if each successive guess is used to calculate a better one. In the present case, an appropriate first guess at a function which is a solution of the fixed point equation is $\bot$. This gives rise to the sequence of approximants:

$$\bot\,,h\,(\bot)\,,h\,(\,h\,(\bot))\,,h\,(\,h\,(\,h\,(\bot)))\ \ldots$$

We now have to ask whether each term of this sequence does indeed represent a better guess at the solution and whether the sequence does converge. Luckily, where 'better' is interpreted in terms of $\sqsubseteq$ the answer is *yes* as far as the class of computable functions we are interested in is concerned. Scott's domain theory is a rigorous mathematical one and we shall not go into great detail about it. We merely give some intuitive indication about why the above results may hold.

Firstly, it is at least reasonable to expect that any function we are interested in will be be *monotonic* in the following sense. Imagine that a function is a black box processing information. One manifestation of the second law of thermodynamics says that the less information we put in, the less we get out. That is to say that there are no two arguments x and y such that both $x \sqsubseteq y$ and $f x \sqsupseteq f y$. The law of monotonicity is a little more powerful than this and is written as:

$$x \sqsubseteq y \Rightarrow f x \sqsubseteq f y$$

It can be shown to hold for all computable functions. This law allows us to apply h to both sides of the relation

$$\bot \sqsubseteq h(\bot)$$

to yield

$$h(\bot) \sqsubseteq h(h(\bot))$$

and then

$$h(h(\bot)) \sqsubseteq h(h(h(\bot)))$$

and so on so that we do find that

$$\bot \sqsubseteq h(\bot) \sqsubseteq h(h(\bot)) \sqsubseteq h(h(h(\bot))) \ldots$$

Our sequence of guesses does monotonically increase; or at least never decreases.

The second requirement of our sequence of guesses is also true. Scott's theory allows us to prove, for *continuous* functions (which include the computable ones) that the sequence of guesses above not only converges to a limit, but that that limit is a fixed point, f, of the function h which we want to find.

As an example, let us try to convince ourselves that this process works by applying it to the fact function:

$$fact\ x = if\ x{=}0\ then\ 1\ else\ x * fact(x{-}1)$$

The usual pair of equations has been rewritten as a conditional here so that we can easily solve it by applying a fixed point operator:

$$fact = fix\ h = h(fix\ h)$$

where

$$h = \lambda fact\ .\ \lambda x\ .\ (if\ x{=}0\ then\ 1\ else\ x * fact\ (x{-}1))$$

We now form, in succession:

$$fact_0 = \perp$$

which is the totally undefined function, and:

$$
\begin{aligned}
fact_1 \quad &= \quad h\,fact_0 \\
&= \quad \lambda x \,.\, (if\ x{=}0\ then1\ else\ x * fact_0\ (x{-}1)) \\
&= \quad \lambda x \,.\, (if\ x{=}0\ then1\ else\ x * \perp (x{-}1)) \\
&= \quad \lambda x \,.\, (if\ x{=}0\ then1\ else\ x * \perp) \\
&= \quad \lambda x \,.\, (if\ x{=}0\ then1\ else\ \perp)
\end{aligned}
$$

which is the function undefined everywhere except at $x{=}0$ where it agrees with factorial.

$$
\begin{aligned}
fact_2 \quad &= \quad h\,fact_1 \\
&= \quad \lambda x \,.\, (if\ x{=}0\ then\ 1\ else\ x * fact_1\ (x{-}1)) \\
&= \quad \lambda x \,.\, (if\ x{=}0\ then\ 1\ else\ x * \\
&\qquad\quad (\lambda x \,.\, if\ x{=}0\ then\ 1\ else\ \perp)\ (x{-}1)) \\
&= \quad \lambda x \,.\, (if\ x{=}0\ then\ 1\ else\ x * \\
&\qquad\quad (if\ (x{-}1){=}0\ then\ 1\ else\ \perp)) \\
&= \quad \lambda x \,.\, (if\ x{=}0\ then\ 1\ else\ if\ x{=}1\ then\ 1\ else\ \perp)
\end{aligned}
$$

$fact_2$ is the function undefined everywhere except at $x{=}0$ and $x{=}1$ where it agrees with factorial. We find that a whole succession of approximations:

$$fact_3 = h\,fact_2$$

$$fact_4 = h\,fact_3$$

$$fact_5 = h\,fact_4$$

$$\vdots$$

are generated, each defined at one more integer than the last and each agreeing with factorial wherever they are both defined. It is not difficult to see that factorial can be considered to be the limit of this succession of partial functions.

9.8 FIXED POINT INDUCTION

Let us recapitulate at this point. We wanted to try to invest functions with some structure so that we would be able to make inductive arguments on a chain of approximations converging to the function. We have shown that we can find such a natural sequence of approximants. It only remains for us to frame a suitable induction law. Without further justification, the following theorem turns out to be useful[1].

THEOREM 9.6:   The Principle of Fixed Point Induction

If property P is chain complete, then, to prove that $P(fix\ h)$ it suffices to show that $P(\perp)$ and that if $P(X)$ then $P(h(X))$

Here, we require to prove something, P, about an object f (usually a function) which is given as the fixed point of a function h. This induction principle says that, provided that P is suitable in a manner described below, all we need to do is show that P holds for all approximations to f:

$$\perp,\ h\perp,\ h(h\perp),\ \dots$$

The idea of *chain completeness* (sometimes called *directed completeness*) of a property is an unfortunate intrusion into what is otherwise a simple and powerful principle. Technically speaking, a property is chain complete if, when it applies to a chain of objects, each of which is ⊑ the next, we can deduce that it applies to the limit of that chain.

Not every property is chain complete but luckily a great many important properties are. Equalities and inequalities (in the information theoretic sense, ⊑) that relate continuous functions (and that includes all computable ones) for all values of their arguments are all chain complete. We say no more here, but refer the interested reader to [stoy77] or [mann72] for further details.

9.9 PRACTICAL USE OF FIXED POINT INDUCTION

Fixed point induction is often used to prove the equality of two different implementations f and g, of the same function. This may be done in two steps, firstly to show that all approximations to f are ⊑ g (and hence $f ⊑ g$) and then the other way round to show that all approximations to g are ⊑ f (and hence $g ⊑ f$).

As an example consider the following two ways of defining the factorial function. The first is the straightforward way.

$$f\ n = if\ n=0\ then\ 1\ else\ n * f\ (n\text{-}1)$$

with solution *fix F* where

$$F\ f\ n = if\ n=0\ then\ 1\ else\ n * f\ (n\text{-}1)$$

The second method uses a tail-recursive method accumulating the result in one of the parameters:

$$g\ (m,n) = if\ n=0\ then\ m\ else\ g\ (m*n,n\text{-}1)$$

with solution *fix G* where

$$G\ g\ (m,n) = if\ n=0\ then\ m\ else\ g\ (m*n,n\text{-}1)$$

---

[1]See [stoy77] for further details.

THEOREM 9.7: $m*(f\ n) = g\ (m,n)$

As indicated above, we do this in two steps. First we show that

$$m*(f\ n) \sqsubseteq g\ (m,n)$$

and then we show that

$$m*(f\ n) \sqsubseteq g\ (m,n)$$

Proof of $m*(f\ n) \sqsubseteq g\ (m,n)$

Base: $f = \bot$

$$
\begin{aligned}
m*(\bot\ n) &= m*\bot \\
&= \bot \\
&\sqsubseteq g\ (m,n)
\end{aligned}
$$

Induction:

If $m * (f'\ n) \quad \sqsubseteq \quad g\ (m,n)$

then $m * (F f'\ n)$

$$
\begin{aligned}
&= m * [\ if\ n{=}0\ then\ 1\ else\ n * f'\ (n\text{-}1)] \\
&= if\ n{=}0\ then\ m\ else\ m * n * f'\ (n\text{-}1) \\
&\sqsubseteq if\ n{=}0\ then\ m\ else\ g\ (m*n,n\text{-}1) \quad \textbf{(Ex\ hyp.)} \\
&= G\ g\ (m,n) \\
&= g\ (m,n)
\end{aligned}
$$

Hence $m * (F f'\ n) \sqsubseteq g\ (m,n)$

and we get an infinite chain of f'_i

$$\bot,\ F \bot,\ F^2 \bot,\ldots$$

each of which satisfy the chain complete property

$$m * (f'_i\ n) \sqsubseteq g\ (m,n)$$

and their limit, $fix\ F = f$ also satisfies it

$$m * (f\ n) \sqsubseteq g\ (m,n)$$

The other half of the proof is very similar:

Proof of $m*(f\ n) \sqsubseteq g\ (m,n)$

Base: $g = \bot$

$$
\begin{aligned}
\bot\ (m,n) &= \bot \\
&\sqsubseteq m * (f\ n)
\end{aligned}
$$

Induction:

If $g'\ (m,n) \quad \sqsubseteq \quad m*f\ n$

then $G\ g'\ (m,n)$

$$\begin{aligned}
&= \quad \textit{if } n=0 \textit{ then } m \textit{ else } g'\ (m*n,n-1) \\
&\sqsubseteq \quad \textit{if } n=0 \textit{ then } m \textit{ else } m*n*f\ (n-1) \quad \textbf{(Ex hyp.)} \\
&= \quad m*[\textit{if } n=0 \textit{ then } 1 \textit{ else } n*f\ (n-1)] \\
&= \quad F\ f\ n \\
&= \quad m*f\ n
\end{aligned}$$

and we get an infinite chain of g'_i

$$\perp,\ G\perp,\ G^2\perp,\ldots$$

each of which satisfy

$$g'_i\ (m,n) \sqsubseteq m * (f\ n)$$

and their limit, *fix* $G = g$ also satisfies it.

$$g\ (m,n) \sqsubseteq m * (f\ n)$$

9.10 SUMMARY

In this chapter we have reviewed mathematical induction and seen how it and induction on lists are special cases of a more general concept, that of structural induction. An introduction to domains, discussing ordering by information content and concepts such as monotonicity and continuity has led us to look at a fixed point induction scheme which can be applied to cases where induction on functions is involved.

9.11 EXERCISES

1. Prove the associativity of the ++ function defined in 5.10.6 i.e. that

    $(x\ ++\ y)\ ++\ z = x\ ++\ (y\ ++\ z)$ for all x, y and z

2. Show that

    ```
    reverse( reverse x) = x
    ```

    where `reverse` is as defined in ??, the Haskell prelude.

3. If

    ```
    pour x []    = x
    pour x (h:t) = pour (h:x) t
    ```

    show that `reverse = pour []`.

4. Using the definitions of Fibonacci numbers given in section 9.2, show that

    $$fib(n+m) = fib(n-1) * fib(m-1) + fib\ n * fib\ m$$

    and hence express *fib(2n)* and *fib(2n+1)* in terms of *fib(n-1)* and *fib n*. Derive and prove correct an algorithm for the Fibonacci numbers which calculates pairs of consecutive numbers in terms of pairs with indices about half their size.

5.   Using the definitions in sections 9.4 and 4.4 show that

```
labels . reflect = reverse . labels
```

Chapter 10

Applicative Program Transformation

10.1 INTRODUCTION

In the introductory chapter, we cited as one of the advantages of functional programming that it was amenable to correctness proof and to transformation because of the referential transparency of its programs (the substitutivity of equals for equals) and the fact that mathematical techniques could be easily applied. In the last chapter we saw how to write some simple correctness proofs. Here we show how transformations can be used in a variety of ways, not least of which is to provide improved versions of programs by systematically changing them while guaranteeing that their semantics remain invariant.

This, however, is not the only use to which transformations can be and have been put. We shall show, as well, that transformations are of use in defining languages and that most compilers of functional languages make use of transformation techniques.

10.2 LANGUAGE DEFINITION

The Haskell language is defined by specifying a set of transformations which could be made to its programs to reduce them to programs in a simpler subset called the Haskell kernel. The kernel language is simpler than the full language which can be regarded as a sugaring of the kernel. Most of the effort in defining full Haskell can be thereby reduced to defining the meaning of constructs in the kernel only. The meaning of any Haskell program is given as the meaning of the kernel language program obtained by recursively applying transformations until no 'sugaring' remains. We adopted a similar position at the end of chapter 5 where we showed, albeit in a rather informal fashion, how to transform SASL programs into λ-expressions.

It should be pointed out that compiler writers of Haskell programs are not *required* to implement the language by performing these transformations (though they can do so if they want to). The transformations are purely to provide a defining framework to show in a rigorous way what the semantics of full Haskell programs are. Any compilation technique which produces *exactly the same effect* as the transformations will do.

We now show some of the features that full Haskell has in addition to those in the kernel and give a (sometimes simplified) version of some of the transformations used to define how a Haskell program may be reduced to a kernel language program.

To start with a simple example, the kernel language lacks some notation for lists, so that

```
[e1,e2,...,ek]
```

gets transformed into:

```
e1:(e2:(...(ek:[])...))
```

Similarly, the full Haskell language has an `if` conditional expression but the kernel only has a pattern matching `case`.

```
if e1 then e2 else e3
```

gets transformed into:

```
case e1 of
{    True   -> e2 ;
     False -> e3
}
```

A more complicated example shows how list comprehensions can be explained in terms of simpler constructs and a few functions defined in Haskell's standard prelude. Three transformations are involved (c.f. section 3.11.1). First a comprehension involving several qualifiers can be reduced to one involving only one as follows:

```
[ e | q1 , q2 ]
```

is transformed into a cascaded comprehension:

```
concat [[ e | q2 ] | q1 ]
```

where `concat` is a function defined in the Haskell standard prelude which takes a list of lists and concatenates them all together. Once all comprehensions are left with exactly one qualifier, we can apply the appropriate one of two transformations for dealing with generators and guards.

```
[ e | p <- l ]
```

is transformed into:

```
let ok p = True
    ok _ = False
in
 map (\p -> e) (filter ok l)
```

The `filter` selects all members of l that match the pattern and the `map` applies the appropriate function to each of them.

```
[ e | b ]
```

where b is a Boolean guard is transformed into:

```
if b then [e] else []
```

and this in turn transforms into:

```
case b of
{ True  -> [e] ;
  False -> []
}
```

using the transformation rule for `if` expressions given above.

Even small compete examples tend to be rather long-winded as the following shows. In section 3.10.2 we saw that the `quicksort` method consisted of partitioning a list into two lists: elements < than a pivot and elements ≥ the pivot. Each of these partitions is represented by a comprehension and the first is:

```
[ x | x <- t , x <= h ]
```

This transforms into:

```
concat ( let ok x = True
             ok _ = False || clearly redundant in this ex.
         in map ( \x -> case x <= h of
                          True  -> [x]
                          False -> []
                )
                (filter ok t)  || in fact the whole filter
                               || is redundant
       )
```

As can be seen, things can get quite complicated though optimisations are possible. They get even more so when pattern matching is concerned. We shall not give full details of all the transformations associated with patterns but we indicate the general strategy involved. The kernel does not include expressions with patterns in them and these have to be transformed away.

In full Haskell, patterns can appear in five different places:

- in `lambda` abstractions
- in function definitions
- in bindings of patterns to expressions
- in list comprehensions
- in `case` expressions

The first four all ultimately transform into `case` expressions. Indeed we saw how this was done for list comprehensions and the Haskell defining report [huda91] gives details for the others.

In fact `case` expressions only exist in a restricted form in the kernel and twelve different transformations are used to translate full `case` expressions into a simpler form.

The aim of this section has been to show how systematic use of transformations can reduce programs in a language to programs in a simple kernel subset of the original.

10.3 TRANSFORMATIONS IN COMPILERS

The whole aim of a compiler is to transform a source language program into an object language program with the same meaning, in fact a classic case of a semantics preserving transformation. A compiler, however, is usually divided into a number of phases and many of these involve transformations on the text. We talked about a number of these in chapter 8 when we discussed the implementation of lazy evaluation. They included

- The transformation of expressions to SKI combinators.
- Lambda lifting to convert functions to top level user combinators.
- Strictness analysis and path analysis to annotate a program with information about which functions need to evaluate their arguments.

There are other transformations which may be carried out in a compiler for a functional programming language. We will talk about two of them here.

The first of these involves dependency analysis to discover which definitions need to be regarded as recursive and also to solve a typing problem which sometimes arises. The second shows how a compiler can transform functions defined using pattern matching into ones defined using an efficient `case` expression.

10.3.1 Dependency Analysis

Consider the following Haskell definition:

```
let map f [] = []
    map f (h:t) = f h : map f t
    squares l = map square l
    square x = x*x
in squares [1,2,3]
```

A naive compiler would consider the three equations for `map`, `squares`, and `square` as mutually recursive. Although `squares` depends on both `square` and `map`, neither of the latter depend on `squares` and moreover, `map` is the only really recursive function in the group of definitions. This simple minded way of looking at these definitions has some unfortunate consequences.

Firstly recursive functions are generally slightly more inefficient to implement because some action corresponding to *fix* has to be carried out[1]. Although it does no harm to non-recursive definitions to fix them, we would like to implement them in a simpler way if possible.

Secondly, and more seriously, automatic type inference of the kind we described in section 4.7, may give rise to a more restricted type than necessary when applied to examples such as the one above if the definitions are considered to be mutually recursive. The type inferred for `map` above, for instance, would be constrained to:

```
(Int -> Int) -> [Int] -> [Int]
```

because of its application to `square`. In fact its more general type is:

```
(alpha -> beta) -> [alpha] -> [beta]
```

In this particular example this is not too serious because the definitions are all local ones and the scope rules would not allow `map` to be used anywhere else, but if the definitions had been made at the top level of a module so as to be available elsewhere, the monomorphic type would probably not be what was intended. In any case a mild extension to the example given above, such as:

```
let map f [] = []
    map f (h:t) = f h : map f t
    squares l = map square l
    square x = x*x
    evens l = map pos l
    pos x = x > 0
in ...
```

causes problems even with local definitions. This example will not type at all! One use of `map` is at type:

```
(Int -> Int) -> [Int] -> [Int]
```

and another at type:

```
(Int -> Bool) -> [Int] -> [Bool]
```

and these do not unify.

The answer to this problem is to analyse the *dependencies* in the program to discover which definitions depend on which others and then transform the program

---

[1]In case 9 of section 6.4 we saw the use of 'Fix', 'Fixup' and 'fixenv' to implement recursion on the simple SECD machine and in section 6.6 we saw how the special 'DECLGUESS' and 'TIEKNOT' instructions were needed for the second version of the SECD machine, while lazy implementations need their own methods of doing this, see for instance section 8.5.3.

into another with the same effect but where the definitions are made in a cascaded form rather than all in one mutually recursive block. In the above case, the program might be transformed into:

```
let square x = x*x
in let pos x = x>0
   in letrec map f [] = []
             map f (h:t) = f h : map f t
      in let squares l = map square l
             evens l = map pos l
         in ...
```

(where `letrec` indicates a recursive definition and `let` a non-recursive one). In the above, `map` will be typed in isolation and given its correct polymorphic type:

```
(alpha -> beta) -> [alpha] -> [beta]
```

It is pointed out in [peyt87], that, as well as providing information about recursive definitions and solving a typing problem, dependency analysis of this type leads to a considerably more efficient treatment of strictness analysis.

10.3.2 Transforming Pattern Matching Definitions

The other type of transformation that a compiler might carry out and which we discuss here is that used when pattern matching definitions are transformed into efficient `case` expressions.

Consider the following definition of a Haskell function:

```
interleave []    l        = l
interleave (h:t) []       = h:t
interleave (h:t) (h':t') = h:h':interleave t t'
```

which takes the elements of two lists turn about until one of them is exhausted and then finishes with the remainder of the other one. A version of the functional language SASL [camp79] would have implemented this function in the following way. Each clause would be considered in turn to see if it matched the arguments passed to it and when (and if) one finally did match, the appropriate right hand would be evaluated with the appropriate bindings. For instance, if `interleave [1,2,3] [4,5]` were to be called, the first equation would be tried, entailing matching [] against [1,2,3] and this would fail immediately. The second equation would then require (h:t) to be matched against [1,2,3] and this would succeed, but the second argument match of [] against [4,5] would fail. The third equation would then require the *rematching* of (h:t) against [1,2,3] before the second argument match which would this time succeed.

A much more efficient matching process would factor out the common match in the second and third equations transforming the definitions into something like:

```
interleave []    l = l
interleave (h:t) l =     interleave' l
where interleave' []      = h:t
      interleave' (h':t') = h:h':interleave t t'
```

leaving the subsidiary function, `interleave'` to deal with the second argument.

In languages with static type checking and algebraic types (such as Haskell) even more efficiency can be gained because by the time the matching process starts at run time it is already known that the arguments can only be lists and, (unlike SASL which uses dynamic types), no tests for other types of object need be compiled. Haskell, as we have seen, has static typing and a general pattern matching `case` expression and the transformation in this case would be to the following code:

```
interleave =
    \ p ->\ l ->
        case p of
        []    -> l
        (h:t) -> case l of
                 []      -> h:t
                 (h':t') -> h:h':interleave t t'
```

As empty lists will be distinguished from non-empty ones by a tag in a standard place in the representation of the list the cases can be very quickly selected by using the tag as an index into a jump table.

The example was chosen in the knowledge that the cascaded case expressions would contain mutually exclusive and exhaustive possibilities. This is not always the case and readers are referred to chapter 5 of [peyt87] for further details of how this kind of transformation can be organised.

10.4 SYSTEMATIC TRANSFORMATION

The examples of transformation we have discussed so far have been specific to particular tasks and consequently, special *ad-hoc* techniques specifically designed to suit these tasks can be brought into play. However, users faced with the prospect of using transformations to improve a program would like a methodology giving them some general principles and tools to help them make systematic changes. Such a methodology has been discovered by Burstall and Darlington [burs77, darl82b, darl91].

We start with an example given by Darlington in [darl82b]. Suppose we are given functions for appending lists and finding their lengths[1]:

```
length []    = 0                   || 1
length (h:t) = 1 + length t        || 2

append []    l = l                 || 3
append (h:t) l = h : append t l    || 4
```

and suppose we now wish to write a function which will join two lists and calculate the length of the result. An obvious way of doing this is to write:

```
lengthof2 l1 l2 = length(append l1 l2)   || 5
```

---

[1]It is likely that many functional programming systems will have these functions built-in in some sense. That is irrelevant to this argument which only requires knowledge of their defining equations.

and although this is a perfectly accurate and executable specification of the required function it contains some inefficiencies because it requires more list scanning than necessary. First `append` scans all of `l1` and then `length` scans the whole of the result.

To transform this solution into a more efficient one, let us take two instances of the defining equation for `lengthof2`. If `l1` is `[]`, we get:

```
lengthof2 [] 12 = length(append [] 12)   || 6
```

and by the first equation for `append` this simplifies to:

```
lengthof2 [] 12 = length 12              || 7
```

This provides a base case for a new definition of `lengthof2`. An inductive case is provided by a second instance of the specification, (5). If `l1` is not empty, we can write:

```
lengthof2 (h:t) 12 = length(append (h:t) 12)   || 8, by 5
                   = length(h : append t 12)    ||by 4
                   = 1 + length(append t 12)     ||by 2
                   = 1 + lengthof2 t 12          ||by 5
```

and bringing this result together with (7) we get a new definition of the function we specified:

```
lengthof2 []    12 = length 12
lengthof2 (h:t) 12 = 1 + lengthof2 t 12
```

which only scans each of the two lists `l1` and `l2` once.

Burstall and Darlington identify a number of basic tactical transformation types, some of which are used in the above example. They are

Definition At any time one can introduce a new equation which defines some completely new object. The left hand side of the equation must not be an instance of the left hand of any previously defined equation, otherwise this would redefine an existing object. This introduction of equations corresponds, in the proof of correctness domain, to the spark of genius[1] that has to be found for some proofs.

Although the previous example does not make use of new definitions, we shall see an example below.

Instantiation Any existing equation can be instantiated to a more specific one by substitution for its parameters.

We used instantiation twice in the above example to create equations 6 and 8, both of which are instances of equation 5.

Unfolding This technique uses an existing equation to rewrite its left hand side, where it appears on the right of some other equation, as its right hand side.

---

[1]Burstall and Darlington call this a *Eureka step*.

More formally, if $E = E'$ and $F = F'$ are two existing equations and there is an occurrence of an instance of E in F', replace it by the corresponding instance of E' obtaining F'' and add the equation $F = F''$. Unfolding is a kind of transformation time reduction where we make use of existing equations to simplify others.

We used unfolding in the above example to create equation 7 and to simplify equation 8.

Folding This is the opposite of unfolding and rewrites right hand sides as left hand sides.

We used it above in the last simplification step of equation 8.

Abstraction We can introduce a `let` or `where` clause to name a sub-expression, often one that is repeated.

We give an example below.

Laws If we know any theorems about the primitives used we can apply them to manipulate equations.

As another example which illustrates many of these points, we show (following [burs77]) how to produce an algorithm for the Fibonacci function similar to that proved correct in section 9.2. The simple version is:

```
f 0 = 1                     || 1
f 1 = 1                     || 2
f x = f(x-1) + f(x-2)       || 3
```

From these we derive:

```
g x = ( f(x+1) , f x )            || 4 definition. Eureka!
g 0 = ( f 1 , f 0 )               || instantiation of 4
    = ( 1 , 1 )                   || 5 unfolding twice
g x = ( f x + f(x-1) , f x )      || unfolding 4 using 3
    = let (u,v) = ( f x , f(x-1) )
      in ( u+v , u )              || abstracting
    = let (u,v) = g(x-1)
      in ( u+v , u )              || folding using 4
f x = let (u,v) = ( f(x-1) , f(x-2) )
      in u+v                      || abstracting 3
    = let (u,v) = g(x-2)
      in u+v                      || folding using 4
```

which gives a new definition for `f`.

The basic transformation types we have introduced above can effect improvements in a large number of ways but they are basically tactical in nature. Moreover it is clear that such a system must be user guided and would be very difficult to automate completely. Darlington's more recent work [darl89, darl91] has concentrated on providing a user guided system which provides the basic tactical tools given above and also a library of strategies which allow high level groups of transformations or transformation macros to be applied in appropriate circumstances. The method relies on the use of *skeletons* expressed as higher order functions for which efficient implementations exist, sometimes choosing the skeletons most appropriate to the hardware on which the functions are running.

10.5 OTHER TRANSFORMATIONS

A number of other uses have been made of transformation techniques. Sheeran [shee85] has shown that transformation techniques can be used for developing and improving VLSI designs of hardware. An algebraic approach has been used by a number of people, for instance Williams [will82, will88], based on the FP style of applicative programming developed by Backus [back78a] and others.

10.6 SUMMARY

We have shown that transformation techniques can be used for:

• Language Definition. We discussed the elimination of the square bracket notation for lists, the conversion of if expressions and list comprehensions to case form using explicit maps and filters and pointed out that pattern matching may also be eliminated in this way.

• Compiler Implementation in a number of ways including the transformation of expressions into combinator form, either to SKI combinators or, by lambda lifting to user combinator form and for strictness analysis, path analysis and dependency analysis. We pointed out in the latter case that this kind of transformation can be used to remove some typing problems.

• Program Improvement under user control. We saw that, under Burstall and Darlington's system, a number of tactics can be used to transform functional definitions. These were definition, instantiation, unfolding, folding, abstraction and laws.

10.7 EXERCISES

1. Carry out the transformations that reduce the comprehension

```
[ (n*n-m*m, 2*n*m, n*n+m*m) | n <- [2 .. 100] ,
                              m <- [1 .. n-1] ,
                              gcd n m = 1 ,
                              odd (m+n)
]
```

to case-map-filter form.

2. Perform dependency analysis (by hand) on the following expression and reduce the number of recursive lets (letrec) to a minimum:

```
let x       = fac z
    fac n   = if n=0 then 1 else n * fac(n-1)
    z       = 4
    sum x y = if x = 0 then y else sum (x-1) (y+1)
in sum x z
```

(This example is taken from [peyt87]).

3. From the following definitions:

```
ones 0 = []
ones n = 1 : ones (n-1)

length []    = 0
length (_:t) = 1 + length t

f = ones . length
```

produce, using the Burstall-Darlington approach, a new more efficient definition of f.

4. Use Burstall-Darlington techniques to transform the often quoted version of factorial:

```
fact 0 = 1
fact n = n * fact(n-1)
```

into a tail recursive form:

```
fact n        = factail n 1
factail 0 acc = acc
factail n acc = factail (n-1) (n*acc)
```

5. Use Burstall-Darlington techniques to transform the following program into a more efficient form:

```
average x = sum x / length x

sum []    = 0
sum (h:t) = h + sum t

length []    = 0
length (_:t) = 1 + length t
```

Chapter 11

Parallel Evaluation

11.1 INTRODUCTION

In this chapter we present a brief introduction to parallel evaluation of functional programs. Unlike the rest of the book, the majority of this material comes under the heading of current research. Much of the work is still under way and little of it is complete, and so what follows is a snapshot of the research position at this moment in time.

It was stated in the introductory chapter that one of the advantages of applicative systems is that we are free to evaluate expressions in any order, even in parallel, as there are no side effects. We have seen that, providing a program terminates, the order will not affect the final value obtained. We have also seen that normal order evaluation is guaranteed to terminate if any order does and that lazy evaluation is one way of implementing normal order. However, lazy evaluation, which constantly procrastinates and leaves things to the last moment, seems to be directly opposed to parallel evaluation which should strive towards eagerly evaluating everything in sight. In this chapter we show how to reconcile these two ideals and look at some architectures of systems which are being developed to carry out effective parallel functional programming.

11.2 EAGER EVALUATION

Let us review why lazy evaluation is a useful concept. As stated above, it has the useful property that it is guaranteed to terminate if any order does. In addition it allows us to use very large data structures and even potentially infinite ones without evaluating all of them at once, only working out the values of parts of the structure which are demanded by other parts of the computation. The aim of a parallel evaluation should therefore be to find an evaluation order which eagerly evaluates some things before they are needed and in parallel with other tasks, *without changing the semantics of the evaluation*. In other words we want to keep the effects of lazy evaluation, which is only an implementation technique, by substituting another such technique which takes advantage of parallelism without changing the meanings of programs.

The key to this is *strictness analysis* (see sections 5.9 and 8.9) which attempts to find out by static analysis of a program whether certain sub-expressions will inevitably need to be evaluated[1], regardless of the order of evaluation. Such expressions can clearly be evaluated as early as equipment is available to carry out their evaluation. All the simple arithmetic operators are strict, so clearly this provides a starting point and this in turn leads to the deduction that user defined functions which only do arithmetic are also strict. Analysis of this sort can be quite complicated and the reader is referred to [blos86, clac85 and wadl87b] for further details.

If a strictness analyser were not available programs might be annotated by users to show which expressions should be strictly evaluated ahead of time, but it should be remembered that users sometimes make mistakes and an annotation is not a guarantee that what it says is correct. An automatic system is really to be preferred whenever possible.

Although we do not go into strictness analysis in depth, it is useful to note one fact that is often not completely understood. A function which is not proved strict in isolation may be called strictly. Consider for example the function which applies its first argument to its second:

```
apply f x = f x
```

Nothing can be said about the strictness or otherwise of the second argument of apply (it is strict in f) but a call:

```
apply sqrt e
```

would be a provably strict example because sqrt is an arithmetic function. It would therefore be advantageous to evaluate e before entering apply or in parallel with it and other tasks. It is hoped that strictness analysis will enable us to uncover potential parallelism in cases where it exists. It should be noted, however, that it is the responsibility of users to choose algorithms which contain potential parallelism and this may be no light task, especially for traditional recursive programmers who are used to algorithms which iterate down lists and are inherently sequential. They will have to get used to seeking out methods such as 'divide and conquer' which splits tasks into two which can be independently carried out in parallel.

The duties of a parallel programming system must be to provide a means of generating tasks where potential for parallelism is found so that such tasks can be safely started without changing the semantics of the original program. The system's duties are also to provide proper scheduling and synchronisation of such tasks.

---

[1]Some researchers (e.g. [huda84]) have proposed *speculative* evaluation where expressions might be evaluated even if there is no proof that they will ever be required. This leads to the dangers of *runaway parallelism* where tasks are created faster than they can be stopped and it is certain that some sophisticated task garbage collector would be needed (see [peyt89]).

11.3 SPARKING NEW TASKS

Consider the strict expression:

```
a + b
```

The code generated for a lazy sequential SECD machine (see sections 6.6 and 8.3) would be:

```
LOOKUP a
STRICT
OVERWRITE
LOOKUP b
STRICT
OVERWRITE
PLUS
```

where the STRICT OVERWRITE pairs of instruction are there to evaluate the relevant objects (if necessary) and overwrite their suspensions with their weak head normal form values. In a parallel implementation, it should be the aim of code to calculate a and b at the same time. One way of doing this is for the processor executing the code to be made to *spark* new processes for calculating a and b and then to wait for these to complete before doing the addition. Alternatively the parent process can arrange for a to be sparked while calculating b itself. Thus code might be something like:

```
     EVAL a,L1
     EVAL b,L1
     STOP
L1   SYNCH
     PLUS
```

where the executing process attempts to spark two new processes (using EVAL and then stops. Each of the sparks is told where to come back to (L1) when finished and the SYNCH operation allows the stream to restart when all sparks have returned to it.

We will not go into the details of this kind of code but concentrate on the more general idea of tasks and sparking. Clack and Peyton Jones [clac86] have suggested that processes (tasks) have the following properties:

- Each task has access to the whole graph to be evaluated and is concerned with finding the values, in normal order, of a sequence of nodes in the graph.

- Each task can spark others to reduce subgraphs it will need to their values.

- Each available processor executes only one task at a time but may swap to others if held up.

11.4 STATES OF EVALUATION

In sequential graph reduction, we already know that nodes in the graph to be reduced can be in one of two different states. They can be suspended or evaluated (see section 8.2). In a parallel situation, a third state can arise because several processing elements (processors) may all want to consider the same node of a graph and it would be wasted effort for more than one to carry out the evaluation. Thus we need to be able to mark nodes as 'under evaluation' or *busy* and this gives rise to a second way in which processing elements may be blocked from further evaluation, besides that shown above. In [clac86] these states are called *node colours*.

We need to consider what action a processor must take when encountering each of these states.

- If the node is already evaluated, its value should be acquired immediately and no further action is needed.

- If a suspended node is encountered, a new process should be sparked to evaluate it to weak head normal form and the node marked as under consideration. A *wait queue* of processes trying to find the value of the node should be started and attached to the node. This will initially contain only the process which set up the queue. In the example above the entry might contain the label L1.

- If a node is found to be busy, the present process should be blocked and added to the queue of waiting processes attached to the node.

When the process actually evaluating a node under consideration finishes doing so, the value obtained should overwrite the node (as in the sequential case) and the processes in its wait queue should all be woken up again.

11.5 POOLS OF TASKS

We have mentioned that processes will be blocked when waiting for calculations they need to be completed. Clearly when a processing element has to wait like this, it should be given other work to do otherwise the available parallelism will not be fully utilised. Such a processor should queue the waiting task for later consideration and start or resume another task. The way this can be done is by having a *pool* of tasks waiting for processors. How this pool is implemented varies from system to system but it should be part of the job of a scheduler in the system and entirely transparent to users. We will suggest a particular method of our own for operating pools of tasks later in the chapter (see section 11.5).

It should be clear that it is desirable property of any scheduling method that there should always be work in the pools for available processors to carry out. It should also be clear that no processor should be overworked. Ideally no processor should ever be idle and the pools of waiting tasks should not grow too large. The allocation of tasks to processing elements should be arranged to be as fair as possible. This problem is known as *load balancing*.

11.6 PARALLEL PROJECTS

The following is a brief review of on-going research into parallel implementations of functional systems.

11.6.1 ALICE and Flagship

The ALICE project [darl81] at Imperial College, London University is a pioneering attempt at implementing parallel graph reduction on hardware. A transputer-based prototype has been built and evaluated [crip87]. This consists of up to 40 processors and a multistage switching network to provide communications. The

Flagship project [town87, wats88] grew out of and draws on the experiences of ALICE. It addresses questions of 'real-world' computing such as virtual memory, multi-user operation, distributed input/output and persistence. It is based on a distributed memory model with closely coupled processor/memory pairs rather than having a global memory which can be accessed by all processing elements. One of the advantages of this architecture is that it can support other varieties of declarative system such as logic programming and dataflow.

11.6.2 GRIP

The GRIP machine of Peyton Jones and his co-workers [clac86, peyt87b, peyt89b] is an advanced project which is showing considerable success in achieving really effective speed-ups. The model of evaluation was originally the 'Four Stroke Reduction Engine' described in the first of the above references but more recent work has been on the 'Spineless Tagless G-Machine' [peyt91] for implementing parallel Haskell which uses a highly efficient representation of objects reminiscent of the object-oriented technique of *methods*. Each object on the graph carries with it a pointer to a list of entry points of such methods to deal with different aspects of the object. For instance there are methods which allow the object to be garbage collected (see [sans91]) and, more pertinently for this chapter, a method which indicates the object's 'colour' (see 11.4). The point of such methods is that, rather than having to test a tag on the object to find its colour, all that has to be done is to jump straight to the method which will deal with the object in that particular state. For instance the method for an evaluated object will merely return the object, but if it is a suspension, it could be made to initiate a sparking of the object's own evaluation. When an object changes colour, all that is needed is to update the correct entry in the method table to an entry point to deal with the new colour.

11.6.3 The <ν-G> Machine

Johnsson and Augustsson have developed a parallel implementation [augu89, augu89b] of LML, a lazy purely functional version of the (nearly) functional programming language ML. The abstract machine which is used to implement this is called the *<ν-G> machine* and it runs on the commercially available Sequent Symmetry parallel hardware.

11.6.4 Monsoon

Monsoon [papa88] is a dataflow machine and is capable of scaling up by the addition of new processing elements but it has a fine grained model of parallelism (segments of executable code available for sparking are very small) and this leads, if appropriate steps are not taken (see P-RISC and STAR:DUST below), to a high amount of overhead in process scheduling and communication. A compiler for the non-strict (but non-lazy) language Id [nikh90] has been developed for Monsoon.

11.6.5 P-RISC

P-RISC [nikh89] is an architecture designed to try to reduce the overhead of fine-grained process management by merging dataflow techniques with established principles of sequential RISC processors. Many of the points mentioned above for the Monsoon machine still apply.

11.6.6 Other Projects

Parallelism in functional programming is an extremely fertile and volatile area at present and other research groups investigating parallel implementations include:

- Alfalfa and Buckwheat [gold86, gold88], Yale University
- PAM [loog89], Aachen and Olderberg Universities
- MaRS[cast86], Centre d'Etudes et de Récherches de Toulouse
- APERM[vree89], University of Amsterdam
- Clean[plas90], University of Nijmegen

Discussion of these projects are, however, beyond the scope of this chapter.

11.7 STAR:DUST

We end by describing some work being done by the author and colleagues at St. Andrews University. STAR:DUST (St. Andrews RISC: dataflow using sequential threads) [osth91] is a processor designed for efficient execution of sequential threads in parallel. It is applicable to other areas besides functional programming, but we concentrate on that area here. This project focuses on the generation of *scalable* parallel code which should be able to run on machines of arbitrary size and physical topology, automatically taking advantage of any parallelism available. Scalability is attractive because, superficially at least, a larger number of processing engines should mean a larger capacity for doing the work available.

Attention has been payed by researchers into parallel programming to increasing the *granularity* of parallelism. By this we mean the size of program sections which can be executed concurrently. There is a communications overhead associated with too fine a granularity because of the synchronisation needed to allow data to be shared between processors. Associated with this is another reason why the overheads have to be studied seriously. That is that communications multiply rapidly with the number of processors involved, in proportion to their square in the average case.

11.7.1 Requirements

If scalability of hardware is to be achieved, it is clear that we require a framework which can tolerate the inevitably increasing inter-processor communication latencies resulting from scaling up [arvi87].

Another need is for a simple means of communication which can deal with calling of functions, parameter passing and following pointers in the global data space.

In addition we need to be able to switch quickly between threads of control in order that any processor is kept doing useful work without spending time on the overhead of context switching. We have already seen that, for processors which may be frequently blocked waiting for results, it is essential that they have a stock of work ready to do instead and it is no use if that work cannot be started as quickly as possible.

We require that access to local working data be as fast as possible so that a process carrying out a sequential thread is not placed at a disadvantage.

11.7.2 Machine Architecture

STAR:DUST owes much to several other architectures. It is, as its acronym suggests, related both to RISC (reduced instruction set) machines and to dataflow machines.

Each processor is modelled after the Sun SPARC [garn88] and it has a number of directly addressable registers one of which is the program counter (PC). Instructions are executed sequentially (and can be pipelined) and a memory manager supplies a cache to speed up access to local memory which is by load and store instructions into registers while arithmetic is done directly on registers only. Figure 11.1 shows the RISC nature of a STAR:DUST processor.

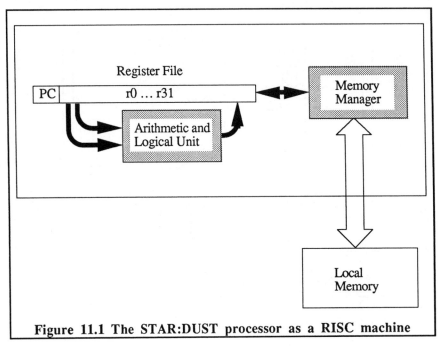

Figure 11.1 The STAR:DUST processor as a RISC machine

11.7.3 STAR:DUST as a Parallel Processor

The pool of tasks (see section 11.5) is distributed among all the available processors in a manner to be described in section 11.7.6 so that any given element has a queue of waiting tasks. Each of these is called a *thread* and is represented by a *context*, which is a program counter and eight values which are placed in registers r0 to r7 when the context is switched to that thread. Contexts also form the basis of the way we communicate with other processors in the network and we call a context in transit a *message*. There are two parallel control instructions in the instruction set.

The `term` instruction terminates the active thread and moves the next context in the queue of tasks into the machine registers so that the context is switched.

The `start pc` instruction starts a new thread on another processor, constructing a message from the `pc` operand and the values in registers c24 to c31. These are used as communications registers, one of which specifies to which processor the message is being sent. This new thread is queued on that processor to be started at location `pc`. All processors are initially loaded with a copy of the whole code to be executed and this address will presumably contain code to *answer* the message. All this can be illustrated as shown in figure 11.1

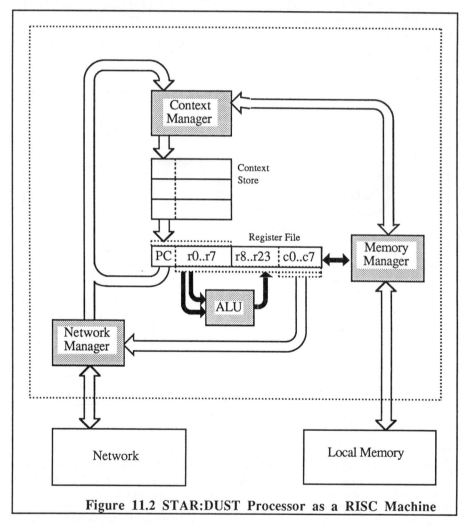

Figure 11.2 STAR:DUST Processor as a RISC Machine

11.7.4 Executing Sub-tasks in Parallel

Consider now an example of a process which wishes to spark two sub-processes in parallel. For simplicity, assume that these sub-processes are not called with any parameters but are each executed to produce a result which must be returned.

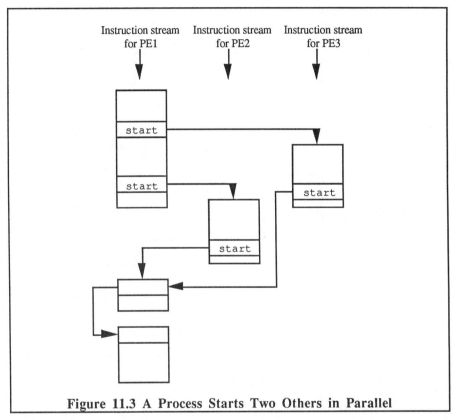

Figure 11.3 A Process Starts Two Others in Parallel

In figure 11.3, the parent (calling) process is represented by the three threads making up the stream for processing element 1 on the left and the two called processes (which operate in parallel) are in the middle and on the right executed by processors 2 and 3. The calling thread at the top starts the two sub-processes and then terminates itself. Both the sub-processes restart the caller at the same point (the middle of the three threads making up the calling stream) and then terminate themselves. At the common resumption point, the calling stream performs *synchronisation*, counting down until two replies have been received. If not, the thread terminates itself, but otherwise it jumps to the third thread to perform calculations on the two received results.

Consider now the call of a supercombinator with several arguments. These arguments will have to be placed in store local to the called process so that it can access them without further communication overheads.

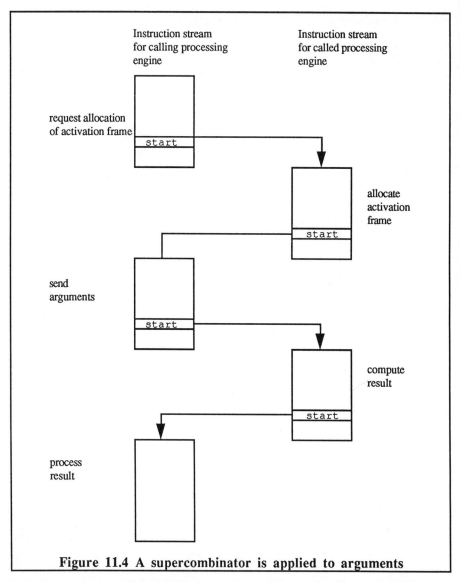

Figure 11.4 A supercombinator is applied to arguments

In figure 11.4, the calling process has therefore first to ask the called process to set up an *activation frame* where the parameters can be stored. The called process allocates the frame from its local heap space and terminates after returning the address of the frame back. The calling process then proceeds to send arguments to that frame and restarts the called process which can get on with its main work before returning its result in the way we have seen before.

11.7.5 Evaluating Suspensions

Requesting the value of a suspension requires sending a message to the processor holding the suspended object. If the object is already evaluated, this degenerates into a simple lookup. If the suspension is being evaluated elsewhere, the calling process is entered on a wait list and the called process terminated, thus blocking the calling process.

If the suspension has not yet been evaluated, the called process changes the object's state to busy and starts evaluation of the associated closure after entering the caller onto a new wait list. When the value arrives back, all the processes waiting for it must be notified and reactivated by scanning the wait list.

11.7.6 Load Distribution on STAR:DUST

We end by considering the problem of how to choose a processor to evaluate a newly sparked process. Ideally we would like to choose the one that is least heavily loaded. This needs, however, an expensive global synchronisation for each new task started. Theoretical results reported in [seid89] encouraged us to use the simple method of choosing a processor *at random*.

The second difficulty we have to overcome is that of a possible parallelism explosion. This can lead to overflow in the queue of contexts waiting to be executed by a processor. For fast context switching, it is essential that this queue be maintained in fast cached store and the problems of this overflowing into slower store would be very difficult to overcome and cause thrashing. Again it is appropriate to chose a probabilistic approach. Each processor sending any message to another, must inform it (as part of the message) of its current workload. This should be enough for each processor to maintain an approximation to the global workload of the whole machine. We can then, using a 'branch if busy' instruction, decide to execute certain tasks sequentially instead of in parallel if the estimated business of the whole machine exceeds a certain amount.

For further details of this and other aspects of STAR:DUST the interested reader should consult [osth91].

11.8 SUMMARY

In this chapter we have attempted to show how on-going research is making inroads into implementing functional programs on parallel hardware. We have shown how eager evaluation can be carried out by sparking tasks and how synchronisation of such tasks needs to be carried out. We have given a brief overview of a number of different projects pursuing parallelism implementations. We have concluded by giving some details of our own research into the problem.

Bibliography

ansi78   *Programming Language FORTRAN*, American National Standards Institute, 1978

arvi80   Arvind, Kathail, V. & Pingali, K. *A Dataflow Architecture with Tagged Tokens* Proc. Internat. Conf. on Circuits and Computers, 1980

acm80   *Proc 1980 ACM Conf. on LISP and Functional Programming* ACM, Stanford, California, 1980

acm82   *Proc 1982 ACM Conf. on LISP and Functional Programming* ACM, Pittsburg, Pennsylvania., 1982

acm84   *Proc 1984 ACM Conf. on LISP and Functional Programming* ACM, Austin, Texas., 1984

acm86   *Proc 1986 ACM Conf. on LISP and Functional Programming* ACM, Cambridge, Mass., 1988

acm88   *Proc 1988 ACM Conf. on LISP and Functional Programming* ACM, Salt Lake City, 1988

arvi87   Arvind & Iannucci, R.A. *Two Fundamental Issues in Multiprocessing* Proc. DFVLR Conf. in Parallel Processing in Science and Engineering, Bonn-Bad Godesberg, 1987

augu87   Augustsson, L. *Compiling Lazy Functional Languages, Part II* Ph.D. Thesis Chalmers University of Technology, 1987

augu89   Augustsson, L. & Johnsson, T. *The Chalmers Lazy-ML Compiler* Computer Journal, Vol. 32, 2, 1989

augu89b   Augustsson, L. & Johnsson, T., *Parallel Graph Reduction with the $< v - G >$ machine*, In [fpca89]

213

back78   Backus, J. *Can Programming be Liberated from the von Neumann Style? A Functional Style and its Algebra of Programs* Turing Award Lecture Communications of the ACM, Vol. 21 pp613 *et seq.*, 1978

bare84   Barendregt, H.P. *The Lambda Calculus: Its Syntax and Semantics*, (Revised Edn.) North Holland, 1984

bell71   Bell, C.G. & Newell, A. *Computer Structures: Readings & Examples* McGraw-Hill, 1971

bird86   Bird, R. *An Introduction to the Theory of Lists* Oxford University Programming Research Group Monograph PRG—56, 1986

bird88   Bird, R. & Wadler, P.L. *Introduction to Functional Programming* Prentice Hall, 1988

bitt84   Bitton, D.B., DeWitt, D.J., Hsaio, D.K. & Menon, J. A *Taxonomy of Parallel Sorting* Computer Surveys, Vol. 16, 1984

blos86   Bloss, A. & Hudak, P. *Variations on Strictness Analysis* In [acm86]

blos88   Bloss, A. *Path Analysis: Using Order-of-Evaluation Information to Optimize Lazy Functional Languages* Ph.D. Thesis, Yale University, 1988

blos89   Bloss, A. *Update Analysis and the Efficient Implementation of Functional Aggregates* In [fpca89]

bjor82   Bjørner, D. & Jones, C.B. *Formal Specification and Software Development* Prentice Hall, 1982

burg75a   Burge, W.H. *Recursive Programming Techniques* Addison Wesley, 1975

burg75b   Burge, W.H. *Stream Processing Functions* IBM Journal of Research and Development, Vol. 19,1, 1975

burk46   Burks, A.W., Goldstine, H.H & von Neumann, J. *Preliminary Discussion of the Logical Design of an Electronic Computing Instrument* U.S. Army Ordnance Dept. Report, 1946 — reprinted in [bell71]

burs77   Burstall, R.M., & Darlington, J. A *Transformation System for Developing Recursive Programs* Journal of the ACM, Vol. 24, pp44—67

burs80   Burstall, R.M., McQueen, D.B. & Sannella, D.T. *HOPE: An Experimental Applicative Language* University of Edinburgh, also In [acm80]

camp79   Campbell, W.A. *An Abstract Machine for a Purely Functional Language* St.Andrews Univ., Dept. Comp. Sci. Technical Rep. July 1979

card85   Cardelli, L. *Basic Polymorphic Typechecking* Polymorphism Volume II, 1, 1985

card86   Cardelli, L. & Wegner, P. *On Understanding Types, Data Abstraction and Polymorphism* Computer Surveys, Vol. 17, 4, 1986

cast86   Castan, M. et al. *Towards the Design of a Parallel Graph Reduction Machine: The MaRS Project* Proc. Workshop on Graph Reduction, Santa Fé Lecture Notes in Computer Science, Vol. 279 Springer-Verlag, 1986

char86   Charlesworth, A.E. & Gustafson, J.L *Introducing Replicated VLSI to Supercomputing: The FPS—164/MAX Scientific Computer* IEEE Computing, Vol. 19, 3 pp10—23, 1986

chur41   Church, A. *The Calculi of Lambda-Conversion* Annals of Mathematical Studies, Volume 6, Princeton University Press, 1941 and Kraus Reprint, 1971

clac85   Clack, C. & Peyton Jones, S.L *Strictness Analysis — A Practical Approach* In [fpca85]

clac86   Clack, C. & Peyton Jones, S.L *The Four Stroke Reduction Engine* In [acm86]

clar84   Clark, K.L. & McCabe, F.G. *micro-PROLOG: Programming in Logic* Prentice Hall, 1984

cloc81   Clocksin, W.F. & Mellish, C.S. *Programming in PROLOG* Springer-Verlag 1981

cole76   Cole, A.J. *Macro Processors* Cambridge University Press, 1976

comp89   Computer Journal, Vol. 32, 2, 1989

curr58   Curry, H.B., Feys, R. & Craig, W. *Combinatory Logic, Volume I* North Holland, 1958

crip87   Cripps, M.D., Darlington, J. et al. *The Design and Implementation of ALICE: A Parallel Graph Reduction Machine* Proc. Workshop on Graph Reduction, Springer-Verlag, 1987

curr72   Curry, H.B., Hindley, J.R. & Seldin, J.P. *Combinatory Logic, Volume II* North Holland 1972

darl81   Darlington, J. & Reeve, M. *ALICE, a Multi-Processor Reduction Machine for the Parallel Evaluation of Applicative Languages* In [fpca81] pp 65—76

darl82a   Ed. Darlington, J., Henderson, P. & Turner, D.A. *Functional Programming and its Applications* Cambridge University Press, 1982

darl82b   Darlington, J. *Program Transformation* In [darl82a] and in [turn82]

darl89   Darlington, J. et al., *A Functional Programming Environment Supporting Execution, Partial Evaluation and Transformation* In PARLE '89 Parallel Architectures and Languages Europe Lecture Notes in Computer Science Vol. 365/366, Springer Verlag, 1989

darl91   Darlington, J. et al. *Structured Parallel Functional Programming*, In [glas91], pp31—51, 1991

davi79   Davie, A.J.T. *Variable Access in Languages in which Procedures are First Class Citizens* St.Andrews University Department of Computational Science Report CS/79/2, 1979

davi81   Davie, A.J.T. & Morrison, R. *Recursive Descent Compiling* Ellis-Horwood, 1981

davi89   Davie, A.J.T. & McNally, D. *CASE – A Lazy Version of an SECD Machine with a Flat Environment* Proceedings IEEE TENCON '89, Bombay, India, 1989

denn80   Dennis, J.B. *Data Flow Supercomputers* IEEE Computing, Vol. 13,11, pp48—56

dijk76   Dijkstra, E.W. *A Discipline of Programming* Prentice Hall, 1976

fike70   Fike, C.T. *PL/1 for Scientific Programmers* Prentice Hall, 1970

flan77   Flanders, P.M., Hunt, D.J., Reddaway, S.F. & Parkinson, D. *Efficient High Speed Computing with the Distributed Array Processor* in [kuck77]

fpca81   *Conference on Functional Programming Languages and Computer Architecture* ACM, Portsmouth, New Hampshire. October, 1981

fpca85   *Conference on Functional Programming Languages and Computer Architecture* Nancy, Lecture Notes in Computer Science Vol. 201, Springer-Verlag, 1985

fpca87   *Conference on Functional Programming Languages and Computer Architecture* Portland, Oregon, Lecture Notes in Computer Science Vol. 274, Springer-Verlag, 1987

fpca89   *Conference on Functional Programming Languages and Computer Architecture* Imperial College, London September, ACM Press, 1989

frae53   Fraenkel, A. *Abstract Set Theory* North Holland, 1953

frie76   Friedman, D.P. & Wise, D.S. *CONS Should not Evaluate its Arguments* In 'Automata, Languages and Programming' Eds. Michaelson & Milner, Edinburgh Univ. Press, 1976

garn88   Garner, R.B. *The Scalable Processor Architecture (SPARC)* Proc. Compcon 88, IEEE Computer Science Press, pp278, 1988

glas91   Glaser, H. & Hartel, P., (Eds.), *Proceedings of the Workshop on the Parallel Implementation of Functional Languages*, University of Southampton Department of Electronics and Computer Science, report CSTR 91-07, June 1991

gold86   Goldberg, P. & Hudak, P. *Alfalfa: Distributed Graph Reduction on a Hypercube Multiprocessor* Proc. Workshop on Graph Reduction, Santa Fé Lecture Notes on Computer Science, Vol. 279 pp 94 - 113, Springer-Verlag, 1986

gold88   Goldberg, P. *Buckwheat: Graph Reduction on a Shared Memory Multiprocessor* In [acm88]

grie81   Gries, D. *The Science of Programming* Springer-Verlag, 1981

harp86   Harper, R. & Mitchell, K. *Introduction to Standard ML* Laboratory for Foundations of Computer Science, Edinburgh University 1986

haye85   Hayes, I. *Specification Case Studies* Oxford University Computing Laboratory, Programming Research Group, Monograph PRG46, 1985

hend76   Henderson, P. & Morris, J.H. *A Lazy Evaluator* Proc. 3rd Annual ACM Symposium on Principles of Programming Languages, Atlanta, 1976

hend80   Henderson, P. *Functional Programming, Application and Implementation*, Prentice-Hall, 1980

hend86   Henderson, P. *Functional Programming, Formal Specification and Rapid Prototyping*, IEEE Transactions on Software Engineering, SE-12, 2, pp241-250, 1986

hill86a   Hillis, W.D. & Steele Jr., G.L. *Data Parallel Algorithms* Communications of the ACM, Vol. 29, 12, 1986

hill86b   Hillis, W.D. *The Connection Machine* M.I.T. Press, 1986 hind86   Hindley, J.R. & Seldin, J.P. *An Introduction to Combinators and the λ-Calculus* Cambridge University Press, 1986

hoar69   Hoare, C.A.R. *An axiomatic Basis for Computer Programming* Communications of the ACM, Vol. 12, 10, 1969

hoar62   Hoare, C.A.R. *Quicksort* Computer Journal, Vol. 5, pp10—15, 1962

huda84   Hudak, P. *Distributed Applicative Processing Systems* Yale University Department of Computer Science , YALEU/DCS/TR— 317, May 1985

huda85   Hudak, P. *Functional Programming on Multiprocessor Architectures* — Research in Progress Yale University Department of Computer Science report, November 1985

huda89   Hudak, P. *Conception, Evolution, and Application of Functional Programming Languages* Computer Surveys, Vol. 21, 3, pp359— 411, 1989

huda91   Hudak, P. et al. *Report on the Programming Language Haskell*, Version 1.1 Glasgow and Yale Universities, 1991. A version of the report with all known outstanding errors and omissions corrected is to be published in SIGPLAN notices in early 1992.

hugh82   Hughes, R.J.M. *Super-Combinators: A New Implementation Method for Applicative Languages* In [acm82]

hugh83   Hughes, R.J.M. *The Design and Implementation of Programming Languages* Ph.D. Thesis published as Oxford University Computing Laboratory, Programming Research Group, Monograph PRG40, 1983

hugh87   Hughes, R.J.M. *Backwards Analysis of Functional Programs* Department of Computer Science , Univ. of Glasgow, 1987 and in Proc. Workshop on Partial Evaluation and Mixed Computation, Eds. Bjørner, D. & Ershov, A.P. North Holland, 1987

hugh89   Hughes, R.J.M. *Why Functional Programming Matters* Computer Journal, Vol. 32, 2, 1989

ieee82   Special Edition on Data Flow Systems IEEE Computing, Vol. 15,2, 1982

inge61   Ingerman, P.Z. *Thunks* Communications of the ACM, Vol. 4, 1, 1961

jens78   Jensen, K. & Wirth, N. *Pascal User Manual and Report* Revised Edition, Springer-Verlag, 1978

john84   Johnsson, T. *Efficient Compilation of Lazy Evaluation* Proc. SIGPLAN '84 Symposium on Compiler Construction, ACM, Montreal 1984

john85   Johnsson, T. *Lambda Lifting: Transforming Programs to Recursive Equations* In [fpca85] — Also Aspenäs Workshop on Implementation of Functional Languages, Göteborg 1985

john86   Johnsson, T. *Target Code Generation from G-Machine Code* Proc. Workshop on Graph Reduction, Santa Fé Lecture Notes on Computer Science, Vol. 279 pp 119 - 159, Springer-Verlag, 1986

john87   Johnsson, T. *Compiling Lazy Functional Languages* Ph.D. Thesis, Chalmers University of Technology, 1987 — incorporates [john84], [john85] and [john86]

jone84   Jones, S.B. *A Range of Operating Systems written in a Purely Functional Style* Stirling University Dept. Comp. Sci. TR.16, 1984 — also Oxford University Computing Laboratory, Programming Research Group, Monograph PRG42

jone89   Jones, S.B. *Functional Programming and Operating Systems* Computer Journal, Vol. 32, 2, 1989

joos89a   Joosten, S.M.M. *The use of functional programming in software development* Ph.D. Thesis, University of Twente, ISBN 90 9002729 7, 1989.

joos89b   Joosten, S.M.M. *Public Transport in Frankfurt: an Experiment in Functional Programming* STAPLE(ESPRIT 891) Report Staple/Twe/89 Twente University, 1989

kell79   Keller, R.M. et al. *A Loosely-Coupled Applicative Multi-Processing System* AFIPS National Computer Conference, Volume 48 1979

kell83   Keller, R.M. & Lindstrom, G. *Rediflow: A Multiprocessing Architecture Combining Reduction and Dataflow* In PAW 83: Visuals used at the Parallel Architecture Workshop, Office of Basic Energy Sciences, Univ. Colorado, 1983

kell85   Keller, R.M. & Lindstrom, G. *Rediflow Project Publications* University of Utah, Department of Computer Science , 1985

klee52   Kleene, S.C. *Introduction to Meta-Mathematics* North Holland, 1952

klop80   Klop, J.W. *Combinatory Reduction Systems* Thesis, University of Utrecht, Mathematische Centrum Kruislaan 413, Amsterdam, 1980

kogg81   Kogge, P.M. *The Architecture of Pipelined Computers* McGraw-Hill, 1981 kowa79   Kowalski, R. *Logic for Problem Solving* North Holland, 1979

kuck77   Kuck, D.J., Lawrie, D.H. & Sameh, A.H. (eds.) *High Speed Computer and Algorithm Organisation* Academic Press, 1977

land65   Landin, P.J. *The Mechanical Evaluation of Expressions* Computer Journal, Vol. 6,4, 1964

lawd62   Lawden D.F. *Introduction to Tensor Calculus and Relativity* Methuen;Wiley, 1962

loog89   Loogen, R., Kuchen, H. & Indermark, K. *Distributed Implementation of Programmed Graph Reduction* PARLE '89, Lecture Notes in Computer Science Vols. 365/366 Springer Verlag, 1989

mann72   Manna, Z., Ness, S. & Vuillemin, J.E. *Inductive Methods for Proving Properties of Programs* Communications of the ACM, Vol. 16, 8, pp 491—502,1973

mann83   Manna, Z. & Pnueli, A. *Verification of Concurrent Programs: A Temporal Proof System* Report No. STAN—CS—83—967, Department of Computer Science , Stanford University, June 1983

mcca62   McCarthy, J. et al. *LISP 1.5 Programmer's Manual* MIT Press, Cambridge, Mass., 1962

mich68   Michie, D. `Memo' Functions and Machine Learning* Nature Volume 218, 1968

miln78   Milner, R. *A Theory of Type Polymorphism in Programming* J. Computer and System Sciences Volume 17,3, 1978

morr77   Morrison, R. *A Method of Implementing Procedure Entry and Exit in Block Structured High Level Languages* Software Practice and Experience, Vol. 9,5 pp535—537, 1977

morr79   Morrison, R. *On the Development of Algol* Ph.D. Thesis, University of St. Andrews, 1979

morr82   Morrison, R. *The String as a Simple Data Type* SIGPLAN Notices, Vol. 17, 3, 1982

naur63   Naur, P. , ed *Revised Report on the Algorithmic Language ALGOL 60* Communications of the ACM, Vol. 6, 1, 1963

nikh89   Nikhil, R. *Can Dataflow Subsume von Neumann Computing?* Proc. 16th Annual International Symposium on Computer Architecture, Jerusalem, 1989

nikh90   Nikhil, R. *The Parallel Programming Language Id and its Compilation for Parallel Machines* MIT Laboratory for Computer Science, Computational Structures Group Memo. 313, Cambridge, Mass., 1990

nils71   Nilsson, N.J. *Problem Solving Methods in Artificial Intelligence* McGraw-Hill, 1971

papa88   Papadopoulos, G.M. *Implementation of a General Purpose Dataflow Multiprocessor* MIT Laboratory for Computer Science, Technical Report 432 (Ph.D. Thesis), August 1988

peyt84   Peyton Jones, S. *Arbitrary Precision Arithmetic Using Continued Fractions* INDRA Note 1530, Department of Computer Science, University College, London,1984

peyt87   Peyton Jones, S. *The Implementation of Functional Programming Languages* Prentice Hall, 1987

peyt87b   Peyton Jones, S., *GRIP: A High Performance Architecture for Parallel Graph Reduction*, In [fpca87]

peyt89   Peyton Jones, S. *Parallel Implementations of Functional Programming Languages* Computer Journal, Vol. 32, 2, pp175—186

peyt89b   Peyton Jones, S., Clack, C. & Salkild, J., High Performance Parallel Graph Reduction, In PARLE '89 Parallel Architectures and Languages Europe Lecture Notes in Computer Science Vol. 365/366, Springer Verlag, 1989

peyt91   Peyton Jones, S., *The Spineless Tagless G-machine: Second Attempt*, In [glas91] — also to be published in Journal of Functional Programming

ping86   Pingali, K. & Arvind *Efficient Demand-Driven Evaluation. Parts 1 & 2* TOPLAS Vol. 7,2, 1985 & TOPLAS Vol. 8,1, 1986

plas90   Plasmeyer, R. & v. Eekelen, M. *Concurrent Functional Programming* University of Nijmegen, 1990

quin60   Quine, W. v O. *Word and Object* MIT Press, 1960

rand64   Randell, B. & Russell, L.J. *ALGOL 60 Implementation* Academic Press, 1964

rama77   Ramamoorthy, C.V. & Li, H.F. *Pipeline Architecture* Computer Surveys, Vol. 9, 1977

reyn72   Reynolds, J.C. *Definitional Interpreters for Higher-Order Programming Languages* Proc. ACM Nat. Conf. 1972 rich82   Richards, H. *The Pragmatics of SASL Programming Applications* Burroughs Austin Research Center Report ARC 82—15, 1982

rich83   Rich, E. *Artificial Intelligence* McGraw-Hill, 1983

rich84a   Richards, H. *An Overview of ARC SASL* SIGPLAN Notices, Vol. 19,10, 1984

rich84b   Richards, H. *Programming in SASL* Burroughs Austin Research Center Report ARC 84—21, 1984

robi65   Robinson, J.A. *A Machine-Oriented Logic Based on the Resolution Principle* Journal of the ACM, Vol. 12,1, 1965

robi83   Robinson, J.A. *A Proposal to Develop a ``Fifth Generation'' Programming System Based on Logic Programming, Functional Programming and a Highly Parallel Reduction Machine* Logic Programming Research Center School of Computer and Information Science, Syracuse Univ., New York 13210, USA, 1983

sans91   Sansom, P.M., Dual-Mode Garbage Collection, In [glas91]

schm86   Schmidt, D.A. *Denotational Semantics* Allyn and Bacon, Inc., Massachusetts, 1986

schn84   Schneider, E.A. *A Formal Definition of SASL for Verification Proofs* Burroughs Austin Research Center Report ARC 84—04, 1984

schö24   Schönfinkel, M. *Über die Bausteine der Mathematischen Logik* Math. Ann. Volume 92, 1924 — English Translation — On the Building Blocks of Mathematical Logic In From Frege to Gödel, Ed. van Heijenoort, J., Harvard Univ. Press, 1967

scot76   Scott, D. *Data Types as Lattices* SIAM Journal of Computing Vol. 5,3, 1976

sebe89   Sebesta, R.W. *Concepts of Programming Languages* Benjamin/Cummings, 1989

seid89   Seidl, H. & Wilhelm, R. *Probabilistic Load Balancing for Parallel Graph Reduction* Proc. IEEE TENCON '89 Conference, Bombay, 1989

seth89   Sethi, R. *Programming Languages: Concepts and Constructs* Addison Wesley, 1989

shee85   Sheeran, M. *Designing Regular Array Architectures using Higher Order Functions* In [fpca85]

slee80   Sleep, M.R. & Burton, F.W. *Towards a Zero Assignment Parallel Processor* Proc. 2nd Int. Conf. on Distributed Computing Systems 1980

some87   Sommerville, I. & Morrison, R. *Software Development with Ada* Addison Wesley, 1987

stee87   Steele Jr., G.L. & Sussman, G.J. *The Revised Report on SCHEME: A Dialect of LISP* AI Memo 452, MIT Artificial Intelligence Lab. Cambridge, Mass., 1987

stem89   Stemple, D., et al. *Exceeding the Limits of Polymorphism in Database Programming Languages* Department of Computer Science University of Massachusetts, Amherst, 1989

ston87   Stone, H.S. *High-Performance Computer Architecture* Addison Wesley, 1987

stoy77   Stoy, J.E. *Denotational Semantics: The Scott-Strachey Approach to Programming Language Theory* MIT Press, 1977

stra67   Strachey, C. *Fundamental Concepts in Programming Languages* NATO Summer School in Programming, Copenhagen, 1967

stro86   Stroustrup, B. *The C++ Programming Language* Addison Wesley, 1986

tenn81   Tennant, R.D. *Principles of Programming Languages* Prentice Hall, 1981

thom85   Thompson, S. *Laws in Miranda* University of Kent at Canterbury Computing Lab. Report 35, 1985

thom86a   Thompson, S. *Writing Interactive Programs in Miranda* University of Kent at Canterbury Computing Lab. Report 40, 1986

thom86b   Thompson, S. *Proving Properties of Functions Defined on Lawful Types* University of Kent at Canterbury Computing Lab. Report 37, 1986

town87   Townsend, P. *Flagship Hardware and Implementation* ICL Technical Journal, May 1987

turn75   Turner, D.A. *Implementation of SASL* St.Andrews University Department of Computer Science\ Report TR/75/4, 1975

turn76   Turner, D.A. *SASL Language Manual* St.Andrews University Department of Computer Science \ Report CS/75/1, 1975, Revised 1976

turn79a   Turner, D.A. *SASL Language Manual* St.Andrews University Department of Computer Science \ Report CS/79/3, 1979

turn79b   Turner, D.A. *A New Implementation Technique for Applicative Languages* Software Practice and Experience Vol. 9, 1979

turn79c   Turner, D.A. *Another Algorithm for Bracket Abstraction* Journal of Symbolic Logic Vol. 44,2, 1979

turn81a   Turner, D.A. *The Semantic Elegance of Applicative Languages* In [fpca81] — also in [turn82]

turn81b   Turner, D.A. *The Future of Applicative Programming* In Trends in Information Processing Systems — Proc. 3rd Conf. of the European Cooperation in Informatics, Springer-Verlag, 1981 — also in [turn82]

turn82a   Turner, D.A. *Recursion Equations as a Programming Language* In [darl82]

turn82b   Turner, D.A. & Darlington, J. *Applicative Programming — An Emerging Technology* Annual Open Lecture Course, Department of Computer Science , Univ. St.Andrews 1982

turn85a   Turner, D.A. *Programs as Executable Specifications* In "Mathematical Logic and Programming Languages", Ed. Hoare, C.A.R. & Shepherdson, J.C. Prentice Hall, 1985

turn85b   Turner, D.A. *Miranda: A Non-Strict Functional Language with Polymorphic Types* In [fpca85]

veen86   Veen, J. *Dataflow Machine Architecture* Computer Surveys, Vol. 18, 1986

vneu45   von Neumann, A.H. *First Draft of a Report on the EDVAC* Moore School of Electrical Engineering University of Pennsylvania, Philadelphia (report) June 1945

vree89   Vree, W.G. *Design Considerations for a Parallel Reduction Machine* Ph. D. Thesis, Department of Mathematics and Computer Science, University of Amsterdam, 1989

wadl87   Wadler, P.L. *Fixing Some Space Leaks with a Garbage Collector* Software Practice and Experience Vol. 17,9, 1987

wadl87b   Wadler, P.L. & Hughes, R.J.M. *Contexts Made Simple* University of Glasgow Department of Computer Science 1987

wadl88   Wadler, P.L. & Blott, S. *How to make ad-hoc polymorphism less ad-hoc* Proc. 16th ACM Symp. on Priciples of Programming Languages, 1989

wadl90   Wadler, P.L. *Comprehending Monads* Proc. ACM Conference on Lisp and Functional Programming, Nice, 1990

wats79   Watson, I. & Gurd, J. *A Prototype Dataflow Computer with Token Labelling* Proc. Nat. Comp. Conf. Volume 48, 1979

wats88   Watson, I. et al. *Flagship: A Parallel Architecture for Declarative Programming* Proc. 15th Annual International Symposium on Computer Architecture, Honolulu, Hawaii, p124, 1988

wegn68   Wegner, P. *Programming Languages, Information Structures and Machine Organisation* McGraw-Hill, 1968

will82   Williams, J.H. *On the Development of the Algebra of Functional Programs* TOPLAS Vol. 4, 1982

will88   Williams, J.H., *Sacrificing Simplicity for Convenience: Where do You Draw the Line?* Proc. 15th ACM SIGACT-SIGPLAN Symposium on Principles of Programming Languages, San Diego, 1988

Appendix A

Predefined Haskell Operators

Operators in Haskell have three kinds of *fixity*, left-associative (like + and -), right-associative (like && and | |) and non-associative (like < and >). Each has, in addition, a *precedence level* which specifies its syntactic precedence with respect to other operators in the absence of round brackets. A higher precedence means an operator binds more tightly. Thus a+b*c is taken to mean a+(b*c) because + has precedence 6 and * has precedence 7. Operators defined by users can be given precedences and fixities using fixity declarations as specified in the Haskell report, but the operators predeclared in the various Haskell prelude modules have fixities and precedences as follows:

Precedence	Fixity	Operators
9	left	!, !!, //
9	right	.
8	right	**, ^, ^^
7	left	%, :%, *
7	none	/ `div`, `mod`, `rem`
6	left	+, -
6	none	:+
5	right	:, ++
5	none	\\
4	none	==, /=, <, >, <=, >=, `elem`, `notElem`
3	right	&&
2	right			
1	none	:=

Appendix B

The Haskell Preludes

This appendix contains the Haskell preludes complete. The functions and values defined here provide a wealth of further examples of Haskell programming. One or two advanced features of Haskell, such as the mechanism for *deriving* default instances of certain classes and the full import/export mechanisms for modules, have not been discussed in the main text of the book. For these the reader is referred to the Haskell report [huda91].

Haskell has several preludes, the main one of which is called `Prelude`. This and another called `PreludeCore` are basic to Haskell and may not be redefined by the user. The `Prelude` module imports and re-exports others which are:

`PreludeCore`	All the algebraic datatypes, type synonyms, classes and instance declarations which are basic to Haskell.
`PreludeBuiltin`	Things that cannot be specified in Haskell itself like the type `Int` and addition of `Int`s and `Float`s.
`PreludeRatio`	Standard functions on `Rational` numbers.
`PreludeComplex`	Standard functions on `Complex` numbers.
`PreludeList`	Standard functions on lists
`PreludeArray`	Standard functions on arrays
`PreludeText`	Standard functions for manipulating text
`PreludeIO`	Standard functions for Input/Output

Prelude

```
-- Standard value bindings

module Prelude (
    PreludeCore.., PreludeRatio.., PreludeComplex.., PreludeList..,
    PreludeArray.., PreludeText.., PreludeIO..,
    nullBin, isNullBin, appendBin,
    (&&), (||), not, otherwise,
    minChar, maxChar, ord, chr,
    isAscii, isControl, isPrint, isSpace,
    isUpper, isLower, isAlpha, isDigit, isAlphanum,
    toUpper, toLower,
    minInt, maxInt, subtract, gcd, lcm, (^), (^^),
    truncate, round, ceiling, floor, fromIntegral, fromRealFrac, atan2,
    fst, snd, id, const, (.), flip, ($), until, asTypeOf, error ) where

import PreludeBuiltin
import PreludeCore
import PreludeList
import PreludeArray
import PreludeRatio
import PreludeComplex
import PreludeText
import PreludeIO

infixr 9  .
infixr 8  ^, ^^
infixr 3  &&
infixr 2  ||
infixr 0  $


-- Binary functions

nullBin             :: Bin
nullBin             =  primNullBin

isNullBin           :: Bin -> Bool
isNullBin           =  primIsNullBin

appendBin           :: Bin -> Bin -> Bin
appendBin           =  primAppendBin

-- Boolean functions

(&&), (||)          :: Bool -> Bool -> Bool
True  && x          =  x
False && _          =  False
True  || _          =  True
False || x          =  x

not                 :: Bool -> Bool
not True            =  False
not False           =  True

otherwise           :: Bool
otherwise           =  True
```

```
-- Character functions

minChar, maxChar        :: Char
minChar                 = '\0'
maxChar                 = '\255'

ord                     :: Char -> Int
ord                     = primCharToInt

chr                     :: Int -> Char
chr                     = primIntToChar

isAscii, isControl, isPrint, isSpace        :: Char -> Bool
isUpper, isLower, isAlpha, isDigit, isAlphanum    :: Char -> Bool

isAscii c               = ord c < 128
isControl c             = c < ' ' || c == '\DEL'
isPrint c               = c >= ' ' && c <= '~'
isSpace c               = c == ' ' || c == '\t' || c == '\n' ||
                          c == '\r' || c == '\f' || c == '\v'
isUpper c               = c >= 'A' && c <= 'Z'
isLower c               = c >= 'a' && c <= 'z'
isAlpha c               = isUpper c || isLower c
isDigit c               = c >= '0' && c <= '9'
isAlphanum c            = isAlpha c || isDigit c


toUpper, toLower            :: Char -> Char
toUpper c | isLower c       = chr ((ord c - ord 'a') + ord 'A')
          | otherwise       = c

toLower c | isUpper c       = chr ((ord c - ord 'A') + ord 'a')
          | otherwise       = c

-- Numeric functions

minInt, maxInt          :: Int
minInt                  = primMinInt
maxInt                  = primMaxInt

subtract        :: (Num a) => a -> a -> a
subtract        = flip (-)

gcd             :: (Integral a) => a -> a -> a
gcd 0 0         = error "gcd{Prelude}: gcd 0 0 is undefined"
gcd x y         = gcd' (abs x) (abs y)
                    where gcd' x 0  = x
                          gcd' x y  = gcd' y (x `rem` y)

lcm             :: (Integral a) => a -> a -> a
lcm _ 0         = 0
lcm 0 _         = 0
lcm x y         = abs ((x `div` (gcd x y)) * y)

(^)             :: (Num a, Integral b) => a -> b -> a
x ^ 0           = 1
x ^ (n+1)       = f x n x
                    where f _ 0 y = y
                          f x n y = g x n where
                                      g x n | even n     = g (x*x) (n`div`2)
                                            | otherwise  = f x (n-1) (x*y)
_ ^ _           = error "(^){Prelude}: negative exponent"
```

```
(^^)               :: (Fractional a, Integral b) => a -> b -> a
x ^^ n             =  if n >= 0 then x^n else 1/x^(-n)

truncate           :: (RealFrac a, Integral b) => a -> b
truncate x         =  m  where (m,_) = properFraction x

round              :: (RealFrac a, Integral b) => a -> b
round x            =  let (n,r) = properFraction x
                          m     = if r < 0 then n - 1 else n + 1
                      in case signum (abs r - 0.5) of
                              -1 -> n
                               0 -> if even n then n else m
                               1 -> m

ceiling            :: (RealFrac a, Integral b) => a -> b
ceiling x          =  if r > 0 then n + 1 else n
                      where (n,r) = properFraction x

floor              :: (RealFrac a, Integral b) => a -> b
floor x            =  if r < 0 then n - 1 else n
                      where (n,r) = properFraction x

fromIntegral       :: (Integral a, Num b) => a -> b
fromIntegral       =  fromInteger . toInteger

fromRealFrac       :: (RealFrac a, Fractional b) => a -> b
fromRealFrac       =  fromRational . toRational

atan2              :: (RealFloat a) => a -> a -> a
atan2 y x          =  case (signum y, signum x) of
                          ( 0, 1) ->  0
                          ( 1, 0) ->  pi/2
                          ( 0,-1) ->  pi
                          (-1, 0) ->  -pi/2
                          ( _, 1) ->  atan (y/x)
                          ( _,-1) ->  atan (y/x) + pi
                          ( 0, 0) ->  error "atan2{Prelude}: atan2 of origin"


-- Some standard functions:
-- component projections for pairs:
fst                     :: (a,b) -> a
fst (x,y)               =  x

snd                     :: (a,b) -> b
snd (x,y)               =  y

-- identity function
id                      :: a -> a
id x                    =  x

-- constant function
const                   :: a -> b -> a
const x _               =  x

-- function composition
(.)                     :: (b -> c) -> (a -> b) -> a -> c
(f . g) x               =  f (g x)
```

```
-- flip f  takes its (first) two arguments in the reverse order of f.
flip                   :: (a -> b -> c) -> b -> a -> c
flip f x y             = f y x


-- right-associating infix application operator (useful in continuation-
-- passing style)
($)                    :: (a -> b) -> a -> b
f $ x                  = f x


-- until p f  yields the result of applying f until p holds.
until                  :: (a -> Bool) -> (a -> a) -> a -> a
until p f x | p x      = x
            | otherwise = until p f (f x)


-- asTypeOf is a type-restricted version of const.  It is usually used
-- as an infix operator, and its typing forces its first argument
-- (which is usually overloaded) to have the same type as the second.
asTypeOf               :: a -> a -> a
asTypeOf               = const
```

PreludeBuiltin

```
interface PreludeBuiltin  where

infixr 5 :

-- The following are algebraic types with special syntax.  All of their
-- standard instances are derived here, except for class Text, for
-- which the special syntax must be taken into account.  See PreludeText
-- for the Text instances of lists and the trivial type and a scheme
-- for Tuple Text instances.
--
-- data [a] = [] | a : [a]  deriving (Eq, Ord, Binary)        Lists
-- data () = ()  deriving (Eq, Ord, Ix, Enum, Binary)         Trivial Type
-- data (a,b) = (a,b)  deriving (Eq, Ord, Ix, Binary)         Pairs
-- data (a,b,c) = (a,b,c)  deriving (Eq, Ord, Ix, Binary)    Triples
-- et cetera                                                  Other Tuples


-- The primitive types:

data Char
data Int
data Integer
data Float
data Double
data Bin

instance Binary Char
instance Binary Int
instance Binary Integer
instance Binary Float
instance Binary Double

primMinInt, primMaxInt          :: Int
primCharToInt                   :: Char -> Int
primIntToChar                   :: Int -> Char
primIntToInteger                :: Int -> Integer
primIntegerToInt                :: Integer -> Int

primEqInt, primLeInt            :: Int -> Int -> Bool
primPlusInt, primMulInt         :: Int -> Int -> Int
```

```
primNegInt                             :: Int -> Int
primDivRemInt                          :: Int -> Int -> (Int,Int)

primEqInteger, primLeInteger           :: Integer -> Integer -> Bool
primPlusInteger, primMulInteger        :: Integer -> Integer -> Integer
primNegInteger                         :: Integer -> Integer
primDivRemInteger                      :: Integer -> Integer -> (Integer,Integer)

primFloatRadix                         :: Integer
primFloatDigits, primFloatMinExp,
    primFloatMaxExp                    :: Int
primDecodeFloat                        :: Float -> (Integer,Int)
primEncodeFloat                        :: Integer -> Int -> Float
primEqFloat, primLeFloat               :: Float -> Float -> Bool
primPlusFloat, primMulFloat,
    primDivFloat                       :: Float -> Float -> Float
primNegFloat                           :: Float -> Float

primPiFloat                            :: Float
primExpFloat, primLogFloat,
    primSqrtFloat, primSinFloat,
    primCosFloat, primTanFloat,
    primAsinFloat, primAcosFloat,
    primAtanFloat, primSinhFloat,
    primCoshFloat, primTanhFloat,
    primAsinhFloat, primAcoshFloat,
    primAtanhFloat                     :: Float -> Float

primDoubleRadix                        :: Integer
primDoubleDigits, primDoubleMinExp,
    primDoubleMaxExp                   :: Int
primDecodeDouble                       :: Double -> (Integer,Int)
primEncodeDouble                       :: Integer -> Int -> Double
primEqDouble, primLeDouble             :: Double -> Double -> Bool
primPlusDouble, primMulDouble,
    primDivDouble                      :: Double -> Double -> Double
primNegDouble                          :: Double -> Double
primPiDouble                           :: Double
primExpDouble, primLogDouble,
    primSqrtDouble, primSinDouble,
    primCosDouble, primTanDouble,
    primAsinDouble, primAcosDouble,
    primAtanDouble, primSinhDouble,
    primCoshDouble, primTanhDouble,
    primAsinhDouble, primAcoshDouble,
    primAtanhDouble                    :: Double -> Double

primNullBin                            :: Bin
primIsNullBin                          :: Bin -> Bool
primAppendBin                          :: Bin -> Bin -> Bin
```

```
-- error is applied to a string, returns any type, and is everywhere undefined.
-- Operationally, the intent is that its application terminate execution of
-- the program and display the argument string in some appropriate way.
error                   :: String -> a
```

PreludeCore

```
-- Standard types, classes, and instances

module PreludeCore (
    Eq((==), (/=)),
    Ord((<), (<=), (>=), (>), max, min),
    Num((+), (-), (*), negate, abs, signum, fromInteger),
    Integral(divRem, div, rem, mod, even, odd, toInteger),
    Fractional((/), fromRational),
    Floating(pi, exp, log, sqrt, (**), logBase,
            sin, cos, tan, asin, acos, atan,
            sinh, cosh, tanh, asinh, acosh, atanh),
    Real(toRational),
    RealFrac(properFraction, approxRational),
    RealFloat(floatRadix, floatDigits, floatRange,
            encodeFloat, decodeFloat, exponent, significand, scaleFloat),
    Ix(range, index, inRange),
    Enum(enumFrom, enumFromThen, enumFromTo, enumFromThenTo),
    Text(readsPrec, showsPrec, readList, showList), ReadS, ShowS,
    Binary(readBin, showBin),
--  List type: [_]((:), [])
--  Tuple types: (_,_), (_,_,_), etc.
--  Trivial type: ()
    Bool(True, False),
    Char, Int, Integer, Float, Double, Bin,
    Ratio, Complex((:+)), Assoc((:=)), Array,
    String, Rational ) where

import PreludeBuiltin
import Prelude(iterate)
import PreludeText(Text(readsPrec, showsPrec, readList, showList))
import PreludeRatio(Ratio, Rational)
import PreludeComplex(Complex((:+)))
import PreludeArray(Assoc((:=)), Array)
import PreludeIO(Name, Request, Response, IOError,
            Dialogue, SuccCont, StrCont, BinCont, FailCont)

infixr 8  **
infixl 7  *
infix  7  /, `div`, `rem`, `mod`
infixl 6  +, -
infix  4  ==, /=, <, <=, >=, >


-- Equality and Ordered classes

class  Eq a  where
    (==), (/=)        :: a -> a -> Bool

    x /= y            = not (x == y)

class  (Eq a) => Ord a  where
    (<), (<=), (>=), (>):: a -> a -> Bool
    max, min           :: a -> a -> a

    x <  y             = x <= y && x /= y
    x >= y             = y <= x
    x >  y             = y < x
```

```
    -- The following default methods are appropriate for partial orders.
    -- Note that the second guards in each function can be replaced
    -- by "otherwise" for total orders.
    max x y | x >= y  =  x
            | y >= x  =  y
            |otherwise      =  error "max{PreludeCore}: no ordering relation"
    min x y | x <= y  =  x
            | y <= x  =  y
            |otherwise      =  error "min{PreludeCore}: no ordering relation"


-- Numeric classes

class  (Eq a, Text a) => Num a   where
    (+), (-), (*)    :: a -> a -> a
    negate           :: a -> a
    abs, signum      :: a -> a
    fromInteger      :: Integer -> a

    x - y            =  x + negate y

class  (Num a, Ord a) => Real a      where
    toRational       ::  a -> Rational

class  (Real a) => Integral a   where
    div, rem, mod    :: a -> a -> a
    divRem           :: a -> a -> (a,a)
    even, odd        :: a -> Bool
    toInteger        :: a -> Integer

    x `div` y        =  q  where (q,r) = divRem x y
    x `rem` y        =  r  where (q,r) = divRem x y
    x `mod` y        =  if signum r == - signum y then r + y else r
                        where r = x `rem` y
    even x           =  x `rem` 2 == 0
    odd              =  not . even

class  (Num a) => Fractional a   where
    (/)              :: a -> a -> a
    fromRational     :: Rational -> a

class  (Fractional a) => Floating a   where
    pi               :: a
    exp, log, sqrt   :: a -> a
    (**), logBase    :: a -> a -> a
    sin, cos, tan    :: a -> a
    asin, acos, atan :: a -> a
    sinh, cosh, tanh :: a -> a
    asinh, acosh, atanh :: a -> a

    x ** y           =  exp (log x * y)
    logBase x y             =  log y / log x
    sqrt x           =  x ** 0.5
    tan  x           =  sin  x / cos  x
    tanh x           =  sinh x / cosh x

class  (Real a, Fractional a) => RealFrac a   where
    properFraction   :: (Integral b) => a -> (b,a)
    approxRational   :: a -> a -> Rational
```

```
class  (RealFrac a, Floating a) => RealFloat a  where
    floatRadix              :: a -> Integer
    floatDigits             :: a -> Int
    floatRange              :: a -> (Int,Int)
    decodeFloat             :: a -> (Integer,Int)
    encodeFloat             :: Integer -> Int -> a
    exponent                :: a -> Int
    significand             :: a -> a
    scaleFloat              :: Int -> a -> a

    exponent x              = if m == 0 then 0 else n + floatDigits x
                                 where (m,n) = decodeFloat x

    significand x    = encodeFloat m (- floatDigits x)
                          where (m,_) = decodeFloat x

    scaleFloat k x   = encodeFloat m (n+k)
                          where (m,n) = decodeFloat x


-- Index and Enumeration classes

class  (Ord a) => Ix a  where
    range          :: (a,a) -> [a]
    index          :: (a,a) -> a -> Int
    inRange        :: (a,a) -> a -> Bool

class  (Ord a) => Enum a     where
    enumFrom              :: a -> [a]           -- [n..]
    enumFromThen          :: a -> a -> [a]       -- [n,n'..]
    enumFromTo            :: a -> a -> [a]       -- [n..m]
    enumFromThenTo        :: a -> a -> a -> [a] -- [n,n'..m]

    enumFromTo n m    = takeWhile (<= m) (enumFrom n)
    enumFromThenTo n n' m
                      = takeWhile (if n' >= n then (<= m) else (>= m))
                             (enumFromThen n n')


-- Text class

type  ReadS a = String -> [(a,String)]
type  ShowS   = String -> String

class  Text a  where
    readsPrec :: Int -> ReadS a
    showsPrec :: Int -> a -> ShowS
    readList  :: ReadS [a]
    showList  :: [a] -> ShowS

    readList      = readParen False (\r -> [pr | ("[",s) <- lex r,
                                            pr        <- readl s])
                      where readl  s = [([],t)   | ("]",t) <- lex s] ++
                                       [(x:xs,u) | (x,t)   <- reads s,
                                                   (xs,u)  <- readl' t]
                            readl' s = [([],t)   | ("]",t) <- lex s] ++
                                       [(x:xs,v) | (",",t) <- lex s,
                                                   (x,u)   <- read t,
                                                   (xs,v)  <- readl' u]
```

```
        showList []      = showString "[]"
        showList (x:xs)
                  = showChar '[' . shows x . showl xs
                    where showl []      = showChar ']'
                          showl (x:xs) = showChar ',' . shows x . showl xs

-- Binary class

class  Binary a   where
    readBin             :: Bin -> (a,Bin)
    showBin             :: a -> Bin -> Bin


-- Boolean type

data  Bool  = False | True  deriving (Eq, Ord, Ix, Enum, Text, Binary)


-- Character type

instance  Eq Char   where
    c == c'            = ord c == ord c'

instance  Ord Char   where
    c <= c'            = ord c <= ord c'

instance  Ix Char   where
    range (c,c')       = [c..c']
    index (c,c') ci  = ord ci - ord c
    inRange (c,c') ci      = ord c <= i && i <= ord c'
                       where i = ord ci

instance  Enum Char   where
    enumFrom c              = map chr [ord c .. ord maxChar]
    enumFromThen c c'       = map chr [ord c, ord c' .. ord maxChar]

type  String = [Char]


-- Standard Integral types

instance  Eq Int   where
    (==)               = primEqInt

instance  Eq Integer   where
    (==)               = primEqInteger

instance  Ord Int   where
    (<=)               = primLeInt

instance  Ord Integer   where
    (<=)               = primLeInteger

instance  Num Int   where
    (+)                = primPlusInt
    negate             = primNegInt
    (*)                = primMulInt
    abs                = absReal
    signum             = signumReal
    fromInteger            = primIntegerToInt
```

```
instance  Num Integer  where
    (+)                 =  primPlusInteger
    negate              =  primNegInteger
    (*)                 =  primMulInteger
    abs                 =  absReal
    signum              =  signumReal
    fromInteger x       =  x

absReal x  | x >= 0         =  x
           | otherwise =  - x

signumReal x | x == 0          =  0
             | x > 0   =  1
             | otherwise = -1

instance  Real Int  where
    toRational x        =  toInteger x % 1

instance  Real Integer  where
    toRational x        =  x % 1

instance  Integral Int  where
    divRem              =  primDivRemInt
    toInteger           =  primIntToInteger

instance  Integral Integer  where
    divRem              =  primDivRemInteger
    toInteger x         =  x

instance  Ix Int  where
    range (m,n)         =  [m..n]
    index (m,n) i       =  i - m
    inRange (m,n) i     =  m <= i && i <= n

instance  Ix Integer  where
    range (m,n)         =  [m..n]
    index (m,n) i       =  fromInteger (i - m)
    inRange (m,n) i     =  m <= i && i <= n

instance  Enum Int  where
    enumFrom            =  numericEnumFrom
    enumFromThen        =  numericEnumFromThen

instance  Enum Integer  where
    enumFrom            =  numericEnumFrom
    enumFromThen        =  numericEnumFromThen

numericEnumFrom                 ::  (Real a) => a -> [a]
numericEnumFromThen             ::  (Real a) => a -> a -> [a]
numericEnumFrom                 =  iterate (+1)
numericEnumFromThen n m         =  iterate (+(m-n)) n

-- Standard Floating types

instance  Eq Float  where
    (==)                =  primEqFloat

instance  Eq Double  where
    (==)                =  primEqDouble
```

```haskell
instance  Ord Float  where
    (<=)                = primLeFloat

instance  Ord Double  where
    (<=)                = primLeDouble

instance  Num Float  where
    (+)                 = primPlusFloat
    negate              = primNegFloat
    (*)                 = primMulFloat
    abs                 = absReal
    signum              = signumReal
    fromInteger n       = encodeFloat n 0

instance  Num Double  where
    (+)                 = primPlusDouble
    negate              = primNegDouble
    (*)                 = primMulDouble
    abs                 = absReal
    signum              = signumReal
    fromInteger n       = encodeFloat n 0

instance  Real Float  where
    toRational          = floatingToRational

instance  Real Double  where
    toRational          = floatingToRational

floatingToRational x  =   (m%1)*(b%1)^^n
                          where (m,n) = decodeFloat x
                                b     = floatRadix  x

instance  Fractional Float  where
    (/)                 = primDivFloat
    fromRational        = rationalToFloating

instance  Fractional Double  where
    (/)                 = primDivDouble
    fromRational        = rationalToFloating

rationalToFloating x  =   fromInteger (numerator x)
                              / fromInteger (denominator x)

instance  Floating Float  where
    pi                  = primPiFloat
    exp                 = primExpFloat
    log                 = primLogFloat
    sqrt                = primSqrtFloat
    sin                 = primSinFloat
    cos                 = primCosFloat
    tan                 = primTanFloat
    asin                = primAsinFloat
    acos                = primAcosFloat
    atan                = primAtanFloat
    sinh                = primSinhFloat
    cosh                = primCoshFloat
    tanh                = primTanhFloat
    asinh               = primAsinhFloat
    acosh               = primAcoshFloat
    atanh               = primAtanhFloat
```

```
instance Floating Double where
    pi          = primPiDouble
    exp         = primExpDouble
    log         = primLogDouble
    sqrt        = primSqrtDouble
    sin         = primSinDouble
    cos         = primCosDouble
    tan         = primTanDouble
    asin        = primAsinDouble
    acos        = primAcosDouble
    atan        = primAtanDouble
    sinh        = primSinhDouble
    cosh        = primCoshDouble
    tanh        = primTanhDouble
    asinh       = primAsinhDouble
    acosh       = primAcoshDouble
    atanh       = primAtanhDouble


instance RealFrac Float where
    properFraction   = floatProperFraction
    approxRational   = floatApproxRational

instance RealFrac Double where
    properFraction   = floatProperFraction
    approxRational   = floatApproxRational

floatProperFraction x       = let (m,n) = decodeFloat x
                                  b     = floatRadix x
                              in if n >= 0
                                 then (fromInteger m * fromInteger b ^ n, 0)
                                 else let d      = b ^ (-n)
                                          (m',k) = divRem m d
                                      in (fromInteger m',
                                            fromInteger k / fromInteger d)

floatApproxRational x eps =
    let (m,n) = decodeFloat x
        b     = floatRadix x
        (p,q) = if n < 0 then (m, b^(-n)) else (m*b^n, 1)
    in case dropWhile (\r -> abs (fromRational r - x) > eps)
                      (approximants p q)
       of (_:r:_) | denominator r == 1 -> r
          (r:_)                        -> r


instance RealFloat Float where
    floatRadix _     = primFloatRadix
    floatDigits _    = primFloatDigits
    floatRange _     = (primFloatMinExp,primFloatMaxExp)
    decodeFloat      = primDecodeFloat
    encodeFloat      = primEncodeFloat

instance RealFloat Double where
    floatRadix _     = primDoubleRadix
    floatDigits _    = primDoubleDigits
    floatRange _     = (primDoubleMinExp,primDoubleMaxExp)
    decodeFloat      = primDecodeDouble
    encodeFloat      = primEncodeDouble
```

```
instance  Enum Float  where
    enumFrom          =  numericEnumFrom
    enumFromThen      =  numericEnumFromThen

instance  Enum Double  where
    enumFrom          =  numericEnumFrom
    enumFromThen      =  numericEnumFromThen
```

PreludeRatio

```
-- Standard functions on rational numbers

module  PreludeRatio (
    Ratio, Rational, (%), numerator, denominator,
    approximants, partialQuotients ) where

infixl 7  %, :%

prec = 7

data  (Integral a)    => Ratio a = a :% a   deriving (Eq, Binary)
type  Rational            =  Ratio Integer

(%)                        :: (Integral a) => a -> a -> Ratio a
numerator, denominator       :: (Integral a) => Ratio a -> a
approximants               :: (Integral a) => a -> a -> [Ratio a]
partialQuotients           :: (Integral a) => a -> a -> [a]


reduce _ 0                =  error "(%){PreludeRatio}: zero denominator"
reduce x y                =  (x `div` d) :% (y `div` d)
                             where d = gcd x y


x % y                     =  reduce (x * signum y) (abs y)

numerator (x:%y)          =  x

denominator (x:%y)        =  y

approximants p q          =  zipWith (:%) ps qs
                             where
                             ps       = gen unit (unit*a)
                             qs       = gen 0 1
                             unit     = signum p * signum q
                             (a:as)   = partialQuotients (abs p) (abs q)
                             gen x x' = xs where
                                        xs = x' : zipWith3 next as (x:xs) xs
                             next a x x' = x'*a + x

partialQuotients p q  =  a : (if r==0 then [] else partialQuotients q r)
                         where (a,r) = divRem p q


instance  (Integral a)        => Ord (Ratio a)   where
    (x:%y) <=  (x':%y')       =  x * y' <= x' * y
    (x:%y) <   (x':%y')       =  x * y' <  x' * y
```

```
instance  (Integral a)        => Num (Ratio a)  where
    (x:%y) + (x':%y')         =  reduce (x*y' + x'*y) (y*y')
    (x:%y) * (x':%y')         =  reduce (x * x') (y * y')
    negate (x:%y)             =  (-x) :% y
    abs (x:%y)                =  abs x :% y
    signum (x:%y)             =  signum x :% 1
    fromInteger x             =  fromInteger x :% 1

instance  (Integral a)        => Real (Ratio a)  where
    toRational (x:%y)         =  toInteger x :% toInteger y

instance  (Integral a)        => Fractional (Ratio a)  where
    (x:%y) / (x':%y')         =  (x*y') % (y*x')
    fromRational (x:%y)       =  fromInteger x :% fromInteger y

instance  (Integral a)        => RealFrac (Ratio a)  where
    properFraction (x:%y)     =  (fromIntegral q, r:%y)
                                    where (q,r) = divRem x y

    approxRational x@(p:%q) eps = toRational approx
        where approx    = case dropWhile (\r -> abs (r-x) > eps)
                                         (approximants p q)  of
                              _:r@(_:%1):_  -> r
                              r:_           -> r

instance  (Integral a)        => Enum (Ratio a)  where
    enumFrom          =  iterate ((+)1)
    enumFromThen n m  =  iterate ((+)(m-n)) n

instance  (Integral a) => Text (Ratio a)  where
    readsPrec p   =  readParen (p > prec)
                          (\r -> [(x%y,u) | (x,s)   <- reads r,
                                            ("%",t) <- lex s,
                                            (y,u)   <- reads t ])

    showsPrec p (x:%y)      =  showParen (p > prec)
                          (shows x . showString " % " . shows y)
```

PreludeComplex

```
-- Complex Numbers

module PreludeComplex where

infix  6  :+

data  (RealFloat a)     => Complex a = a :+ a  deriving (Eq,Binary,Text)

instance  (RealFloat a)      => Num (Complex a)  where
    (x:+y) + (x':+y')        =  (x+x') :+ (y+y')
    (x:+y) - (x':+y')        =  (x-x') :+ (y-y')
    (x:+y) * (x':+y')        =  (x*x'-y*y') :+ (x*y'+y*x')
    negate (x:+y)            =  negate x :+ negate y
    abs z                    =  magnitude z :+ 0
    signum 0                 =  0
    signum z@(x:+y)          =  x/r :+ y/r  where r = magnitude z
    fromInteger n            =  fromInteger n :+ 0
```

```haskell
instance  (RealFloat a) => Fractional (Complex a)  where
    (x:+y) / (x':+y')         =  (x*x''+y*y'') / d :+ (y*x''-x*y'') / d
                         where x'' = scaleFloat k x'
                               y'' = scaleFloat k y'
                               k   = - max (exponent x') (exponent y')
                               d   = x'*x'' + y'*y''

    fromRational a    =  fromRational a :+ 0

instance  (RealFloat a) => Floating (Complex a)     where
    pi              =  pi :+ 0
    exp (x:+y)      =  expx * cos y :+ expx * sin y
                       where expx = exp x
    log z           =  log (magnitude z) :+ phase z

    sqrt 0          =  0
    sqrt z@(x:+y)   =  u :+ (if y < 0 then -v else v)
                       where (u,v) = if x < 0 then (v',u') else (u',v')
                             v'    = abs y / (u'*2)
                             u'    = sqrt ((magnitude z + abs x) / 2)

    sin (x:+y)      =  sin x * cosh y :+ cos x * sinh y
    cos (x:+y)      =  cos x * cosh y :+ sin x * sinh y
    tan (x:+y)      =  (sinx*coshy:+cosx*sinhy)/(cosx*coshy:+sinx*sinhy)
                       where sinx  = sin x
                             cosx  = cos x
                             sinhy = sinh y
                             coshy = cosh y

    sinh (x:+y)     =  cos y * sinh x :+ sin  y * cosh x
    cosh (x:+y)     =  cos y * cosh x :+ (- sin y * sinh x)
    tanh (x:+y)     =  (cosy*sinhx:+siny*coshx)/(cosy*coshx:+(-siny*sinhx))
                       where siny  = sin y
                             cosy  = cos y
                             sinhx = sinh x
                             coshx = cosh x

    asin z@(x:+y)   =  y':+(-x')
                       where  (x':+y') = log ((-y:+x) + sqrt (1 - z*z))
    acos z@(x:+y)   =  y'':+(-x'')
                       where (x'':+y'') = log (z + ((-y'):+x'))
                             (x':+y')   = sqrt (1 - z*z)
    atan z@(x:+y)   =  y':+(-x')
                       where
                       (x':+y') = log (((-y+1):+x) * sqrt (1/(1+z*z)))

    asinh z         =  log (z + sqrt (1+z*z))
    acosh z         =  log (z + (z+1) * sqrt ((z-1)/(z+1)))
    atanh z         =  log ((z+1) * sqrt (1 - 1/(z*z)))


realPart, imagPart :: (RealFloat a) => Complex a -> a
realPart (x:+y)          =  x
imagPart (x:+y)          =  y

conjugate         :: (RealFloat a) => Complex a -> Complex a
conjugate (x:+y) =  x :+ (-y)

mkPolar           :: (RealFloat a) => a -> a -> Complex a
mkPolar r theta          =  r * cos theta :+ r * sin theta
```

```
cis                 :: (RealFloat a) => a -> Complex a
cis theta           =  cos theta :+ sin theta

polar               :: (RealFloat a) => Complex a -> (a, a)
polar z             =  (magnitude z, phase z)

magnitude, phase :: (RealFloat a) => Complex a -> a
magnitude (x:+y) =  scaleFloat k
                        (sqrt ((scaleFloat mk x)^2 + (scaleFloat mk y)^2))
                    where k  = max (exponent x) (exponent y)
                          mk = - k

phase (x:+y)    =  atan2 y x
```

PreludeList

```
-- Standard list functions

module PreludeList  where

infixl 9  !!
infix  5  \\
infixr 5  ++
infix  4 `elem`, `notElem`

-- head and tail extract the first element and remaining elements,
-- respectively, of a list, which must be non-empty. last and init
-- are the dual functions working from the end of a finite list,
-- rather than the beginning.

head                :: [a] -> a
head (x:_)          =  x
head []             =  error "head{PreludeList}: head []"

last                :: [a] -> a
last [x]            =  x
last (_:xs)         =  last xs
last []             =  error "last{PreludeList}: last []"

tail                :: [a] -> [a]
tail (_:xs)         =  xs
tail []             =  error "tail{PreludeList}: tail []"

init                :: [a] -> [a]
init [x]            =  []
init (x:xs)         =  x : init xs
init []             =  error "init{PreludeList}: init []"

-- null determines if a list is empty.
null                :: [a] -> Bool
null []             =  True
null (_:_)          =  False

-- list concatenation (right-associative)
(++)                :: [a] -> [a] -> [a]
xs ++ ys            =  foldr (:) ys xs
```

```
-- list difference (non-associative).  In the result of xs \\ ys,
-- the first occurrence of each element of ys in turn (if any)
-- has been removed from xs.  Thus, (xs ++ ys) \\ xs == ys.
(\\)                        :: (Eq a) => [a] -> [a] -> [a]
(\\)                        =  foldl del
                              where []      `del` _   = []
                                    (x:xs) `del` y
                                      | x == y    = xs
                                      | otherwise = x : xs `del` y

-- length returns the length of a finite list as an Int; it is an instance
-- of the more general genericLength, the result type of which may be
-- any kind of number.

genericLength               :: (Num a) => [b] -> a
genericLength               =  foldl (\n _ -> n+1) 0

length                      :: [a] -> Int
length                      =  genericLength

-- List index (subscript) operator, 0-origin
(!!)                        :: (Integral a) => [b] -> a -> b
(x:_)  !! 0                 =  x
(_:xs) !! (n+1)                 =  xs !! n
(_:_)  !!  _                =  error "(!!){PreludeList}: negative index"
[]     !! (_+1)                 =  error "(!!){PreludeList}: index too large"

-- map f xs applies f to each element of xs; i.e., map f xs == [f x | x <- xs].
map                         :: (a -> b) -> [a] -> [b]
map f []                    =  []
map f (x:xs)                =  f x : map f xs

-- filter, applied to a predicate and a list, returns the list of those
-- elements that satisfy the predicate; i.e.,
-- filter p xs == [x | x <- xs, p x].
filter                      :: (a -> Bool) -> [a] -> [a]
filter p                    =  foldr (\x xs -> if p x then x:xs else xs) []

-- partition takes a predicate and a list and returns a pair of lists:
-- those elements of the argument list that do and do not satisfy the
-- predicate, respectively; i.e.,
-- partition p xs == (filter p xs, filter (not . p) xs).
partition                   :: (a -> Bool) -> [a] -> ([a],[a])
partition p                 =  foldr select ([],[])
                              where select x (ts,fs) | p x       = (x:ts,fs)
                                                     | otherwise = (ts,x:fs)

-- foldl, applied to a binary operator, a starting value (typically the
-- left-identity of the operator), and a list, reduces the list using
-- the binary operator, from left to right:
--      foldl f z [x1, x2, ..., xn] == (...((z `f` x1) `f` x2) `f`...) `f` xn
-- foldl1 is a variant that has no starting value argument, and  thus must
-- be applied to non-empty lists.  scanl is similar to foldl, but returns
-- a list of successive reduced values from the left:
--      scanl f z [x1, x2, ...] == [z, z `f` x1, (z `f` x1) `f` x2, ...]
-- Note that  last (scanl f z xs) == foldl f z xs.
-- scanl1 is similar, again without the starting element:
--      scanl1 f [x1, x2, ...] == [x1, x1 `f` x2, ...]

foldl                       :: (a -> b -> a) -> a -> [b] -> a
foldl f z []                =  z
foldl f z (x:xs)            =  foldl f (f z x) xs
```

```
foldl1                  :: (a -> a -> a) -> [a] -> a
foldl1 f (x:xs)              =  foldl f x xs
foldl1 _ []             = error "foldl1{PreludeList}: empty list"

scanl                   :: (a -> b -> a) -> a -> [b] -> [a]
scanl f q xs            = q : (case xs of
                                []   -> []
                                x:xs -> scanl f (f q x) xs)

scanl1                  :: (a -> a -> a) -> [a] -> [a]
scanl1 f (x:xs)             =  scanl f x xs
scanl1 _ []             = error "scanl1{PreludeList}: empty list"
```

-- foldr, foldr1, scanr, and scanr1 are the right-to-left duals of the
-- above functions.

```
foldr                   :: (a -> b -> b) -> b -> [a] -> b
foldr f z []            = z
foldr f z (x:xs)        = f x (foldr f z xs)

foldr1                  :: (a -> a -> a) -> [a] -> a
foldr1 f [x]            = x
foldr1 f (x:xs)             = f x (foldr1 f xs)
foldr1 _ []             = error "foldr1{PreludeList}: empty list"

scanr                   :: (a -> b -> b) -> b -> [a] -> [b]
scanr f q0 []           = [q0]
scanr f q0 (x:xs)       = f x q : qs
                          where qs@(q:_) = scanr f q0 xs

scanr1                  :: (a -> a -> a) -> [a] -> [a]
scanr1 f  [x]           = [x]
scanr1 f  (x:xs)        = f x q : qs
                          where qs@(q:_) = scanr1 f xs
scanr1 _ []             = error "scanr1{PreludeList}: empty list"
```

-- iterate f x returns an infinite list of repeated applications of f to x:
-- iterate f x == [x, f x, f (f x), ...]
```
iterate                 :: (a -> a) -> a -> [a]
iterate f x             = x : iterate f (f x)
```

-- repeat x is an infinite list, with x the value of every element.
```
repeat                  :: a -> [a]
repeat x                = xs where xs = x:xs
```

-- cycle ties a finite list into a circular one, or equivalently,
-- the infinite repetition of the original list. It is the identity
-- on infinite lists.

```
cycle                   :: [a] -> [a]
cycle xs                = xs' where xs' = xs ++ xs'
```

-- take n, applied to a list xs, returns the prefix of xs of length n,
-- or xs itself if n > length xs. drop n xs returns the suffix of xs
-- after the first n elements, or [] if n > length xs. splitAt n xs
-- is equivalent to (take n xs, drop n xs).

```
take                    :: (Integral a) => a -> [b] -> [b]
take  0     _           = []
take  _     []          = []
take (n+1) (x:xs)       = x : take n xs
```

```
drop                    :: (Integral a) => a -> [b] -> [b]
drop  0    xs              = xs
drop  _    []             = []
drop (n+1) (_:xs)       = drop n xs

splitAt                 :: (Integral a) => a -> [b] -> ([b],[b])
splitAt  0    xs          = ([],xs)
splitAt  _    []          = ([],[])
splitAt (n+1) (x:xs)    = (x:xs',xs'') where (xs',xs'') = splitAt n xs
```

-- takeWhile, applied to a predicate p and a list xs, returns the longest
-- prefix (possibly empty) of xs of elements that satisfy p. dropWhile p xs
-- returns the remaining suffix. Span p xs is equivalent to
-- (takeWhile p xs, dropWhile p xs), while break p uses the negation of p.

```
takeWhile               :: (a -> Bool) -> [a] -> [a]
takeWhile p []              = []
takeWhile p (x:xs)
           | p x        = x : takeWhile p xs
           | otherwise = []

dropWhile               :: (a -> Bool) -> [a] -> [a]
dropWhile p []              = []
dropWhile p xs@(x:xs')
           | p x        = dropWhile p xs'
           | otherwise = xs

span, break             :: (a -> Bool) -> [a] -> ([a],[a])
span p []               = ([],[])
span p xs@(x:xs')
           | p x        = let (ys,zs) = span p xs' in (x:ys,zs)
           | otherwise     = ([],xs)
break p                 = span (not . p)
```

-- lines breaks a string up into a list of strings at newline characters.
-- The resulting strings do not contain newlines. Similary, words
-- breaks a string up into a list of words, which were delimited by
-- white space. unlines and unwords are the inverse operations.
-- unlines joins lines with terminating newlines, and unwords joins
-- words with separating spaces.

```
lines                   :: String -> [String]
lines ""                = []
lines s                 = let (l, s') = break (== '\n') s
                          in  l : case s' of
                                        []      -> []
                                        (_:s'') -> lines s''

words                   :: String -> [String]
words s                 = case dropWhile isSpace s of
                               "" -> []
                               s' -> w : words s''
                                     where (w, s'') = break isSpace s'

unlines                 :: [String] -> String
unlines                 = concat . map (++ "\n")

unwords                 :: [String] -> String
unwords []              = ""
unwords ws              = foldr1 (\w s -> w ++ ' ':s) ws
```

```
-- nub (meaning "essence") removes duplicate elements from its list argument.
nub                  :: (Eq a) => [a] -> [a]
nub []               = []
nub (x:xs)           = x : nub (filter (/= x) xs)

-- reverse xs returns the elements of xs in reverse order.  xs must be finite.
reverse              :: [a] -> [a]
reverse              = foldl (flip (:)) []

-- and returns the conjunction of a Boolean list.  For the result to be
-- True, the list must be finite; False, however, results from a False
-- value at a finite index of a finite or infinite list.  or is the
-- disjunctive dual of and.
and, or              :: [Bool] -> Bool
and                  = foldr (&&) True
or                   = foldr (||) False

-- Applied to a predicate and a list, any determines if any element
-- of the list satisfies the predicate.  Similarly, for all.
any, all             :: (a -> Bool) -> [a] -> Bool
any p                = or . map p
all p                = and . map p

-- elem is the list membership predicate, usually written in infix form,
-- e.g., x `elem` xs.  notElem is the negation.
elem, notElem        :: (Eq a) => a -> [a] -> Bool
elem                 = any . (==)
notElem              = all . (/=)

-- sum and product compute the sum or product of a finite list of numbers.
sum, product         :: (Num a) => [a] -> a
sum                  = foldl (+) 0
product              = foldl (*) 1

-- sums and products give a list of running sums or products from
-- a list of numbers.  For example,  sums [1,2,3] == [0,1,3,6].
sums, products          :: (Num a) => [a] -> [a]
sums                 = scanl (+) 0
products             = scanl (*) 1

-- maximum and minimum return the maximum or minimum value from a list,
-- which must be non-empty, finite, and of an ordered type.
maximum, minimum     :: (Ord a) => [a] -> a
maximum              = foldl1 max
minimum              = foldl1 min

-- concat, applied to a list of lists, returns their flattened concatenation.
concat               :: [[a]] -> [a]
concat               = foldr (++) []

-- transpose, applied to a list of lists, returns that list with the
-- "rows" and "columns" interchanged.  The input need not be rectangular
-- (a list of equal-length lists) to be completely transposable, but can
-- be "triangular": Each successive component list must be not longer
-- than the previous one; any elements outside of the "triangular"
-- transposable region are lost.  The input can be infinite in either
-- dimension or both.
transpose            :: [[a]] -> [[a]]
transpose            = foldr
                          (\xs xss -> zipWith (:) xs (xss ++ repeat []))
                          []
```

```
-- zip takes two lists and returns a list of corresponding pairs.  If one
-- input list is short, excess elements of the longer list are discarded.
-- zip3 takes three lists and returns a list of triples, etc.  Versions
-- of zip producing up to septuplets are defined here.

zip                  :: [a] -> [b] -> [(a,b)]
zip                  =  zipWith (\a b -> (a,b))

zip3                 :: [a] -> [b] -> [c] -> [(a,b,c)]
zip3                 =  zipWith3 (\a b c -> (a,b,c))

zip4                 :: [a] -> [b] -> [c] -> [d] -> [(a,b,c,d)]
zip4                 =  zipWith4 (\a b c d -> (a,b,c,d))

zip5                 :: [a] -> [b] -> [c] -> [d] -> [e] -> [(a,b,c,d,e)]
zip5                 =  zipWith5 (\a b c d e -> (a,b,c,d,e))

zip6                 :: [a] -> [b] -> [c] -> [d] -> [e] -> [f]
                        -> [(a,b,c,d,e,f)]
zip6                 =  zipWith6 (\a b c d e f -> (a,b,c,d,e,f))

zip7                 :: [a] -> [b] -> [c] -> [d] -> [e] -> [f] -> [g]
                        -> [(a,b,c,d,e,f,g)]
zip7                 =  zipWith7 (\a b c d e f g -> (a,b,c,d,e,f,g))

-- The zipWith family generalises the zip family by zipping with the
-- function given as the first argument, instead of a tupling function.
-- For example, zipWith (+) is applied to two lists to produce the list
-- of corresponding sums.

zipWith              :: (a->b->c) -> [a]->[b]->[c]
zipWith z (a:as) (b:bs)     =  z a b : zipWith z as bs
zipWith _ _ _        =  []

zipWith3             :: (a->b->c->d) -> [a]->[b]->[c]->[d]
zipWith3 z (a:as) (b:bs) (c:cs)
                     =  z a b c : zipWith3 z as bs cs
zipWith3 _ _ _ _     =  []

zipWith4             :: (a->b->c->d->e) -> [a]->[b]->[c]->[d]->[e]
zipWith4 z (a:as) (b:bs) (c:cs) (d:ds)
                     =  z a b c d : zipWith4 z as bs cs ds
zipWith4 _ _ _ _ _   =  []

zipWith5             :: (a->b->c->d->e->f)
                        -> [a]->[b]->[c]->[d]->[e]->[f]
zipWith5 z (a:as) (b:bs) (c:cs) (d:ds) (e:es)
                     =  z a b c d e : zipWith5 z as bs cs ds es
zipWith5 _ _ _ _ _ _ =  []

zipWith6             :: (a->b->c->d->e->f->g)
                        -> [a]->[b]->[c]->[d]->[e]->[f]->[g]
zipWith6 z (a:as) (b:bs) (c:cs) (d:ds) (e:es) (f:fs)
                     =  z a b c d e f : zipWith6 z as bs cs ds es fs
zipWith6 _ _ _ _ _ _ _    =  []

zipWith7             :: (a->b->c->d->e->f->g->h)
                        -> [a]->[b]->[c]->[d]->[e]->[f]->[g]->[h]
zipWith7 z (a:as) (b:bs) (c:cs) (d:ds) (e:es) (f:fs) (g:gs)
                     =  z a b c d e f g : zipWith7 z as bs cs ds es fs gs
zipWith7 _ _ _ _ _ _ _ _ =  []
```

```
-- unzip transforms a list of pairs into a pair of lists.  As with zip,
-- a family of such functions up to septuplets is provided.

unzip                 :: [(a,b)] -> ([a],[b])
unzip                 = foldr (\(a,b) (as,bs) -> (a:as,b:bs)) ([],[])

unzip3                :: [(a,b,c)] -> ([a],[b],[c])
unzip3                = foldr (\(a,b,c) (as,bs,cs) -> (a:as,b:bs,c:cs))
                              ([],[],[])

unzip4                :: [(a,b,c,d)] -> ([a],[b],[c],[d])
unzip4                = foldr (\(a,b,c,d) (as,bs,cs,ds) ->
                                  (a:as,b:bs,c:cs,d:ds))
                              ([],[],[],[])

unzip5                :: [(a,b,c,d,e)] -> ([a],[b],[c],[d],[e])
unzip5                = foldr (\(a,b,c,d,e) (as,bs,cs,ds,es) ->
                                  (a:as,b:bs,c:cs,d:ds,e:es))
                              ([],[],[],[],[])

unzip6                :: [(a,b,c,d,e,f)] -> ([a],[b],[c],[d],[e],[f])
unzip6                = foldr (\(a,b,c,d,e,f) (as,bs,cs,ds,es,fs) ->
                                  (a:as,b:bs,c:cs,d:ds,e:es,f:fs))
                              ([],[],[],[],[],[])

unzip7                :: [(a,b,c,d,e,f,g)] -> ([a],[b],[c],[d],[e],[f],[g])
unzip7                = foldr (\(a,b,c,d,e,f,g) (as,bs,cs,ds,es,fs,gs) ->
                                  (a:as,b:bs,c:cs,d:ds,e:es,f:fs,g:gs))
                              ([],[],[],[],[],[],[])
```

PreludeArray

```
module PreludeArray ( Array, Assoc((:=)), array, listArray, (!), bounds,
                      indices, elems, assocs, accumArray, (//), accum, amap,
                      ixmap
                    ) where

-- This module specifies the semantics of arrays only: it is not
-- intended as an efficient implementation.

infixl 9  !
infixl 9  //
infix  1  :=

data  Assoc a b =  a := b  deriving (Eq, Ord, Ix, Text, Binary)
data  (Ix a)    => Array a b = MkArray (a,a) (a -> b) deriving ()

array         :: (Ix a) => (a,a) -> [Assoc a b] -> Array a b
listArray     :: (Ix a) => (a,a) -> [b] -> Array a b
(!)           :: (Ix a) => Array a b -> a -> b
bounds        :: (Ix a) => Array a b -> (a,a)
indices       :: (Ix a) => Array a b -> [a]
elems         :: (Ix a) => Array a b -> [b]
assocs        :: (Ix a) => Array a b -> [Assoc a b]
accumArray    :: (Ix a) => (b -> c -> b) -> b -> (a,a) -> [Assoc a c]
                            -> Array a b
(//)          :: (Ix a) => Array a b -> [Assoc a b] -> Array a b
accum         :: (Ix a) => (b -> c -> b) -> Array a b -> [Assoc a c]
                            -> Array a b
amap          :: (Ix a) => (b -> c) -> Array a b -> Array a c
ixmap         :: (Ix a, Ix b) => (a,a) -> (a -> b) -> Array b c
                            -> Array a c
```

```
array b ivs =
    if and [inRange b i | i:=_ <- ivs]
        then MkArray b
                        (\j -> case [v | (i := v) <- ivs, i == j] of
                            [v]    -> v
                            []     -> error "(!){PreludeArray}: \
                                            \undefined array element"
                            _      -> error "(!){PreludeArray}: \
                                            \multiply defined array element")
        else error "array{PreludeArray}: out-of-range array association"

listArray b vs               = array b (zipWith (:=) (range b) vs)

(!) (MkArray _ f)     = f

bounds (MkArray b _)  = b

indices               = range . bounds

elems a               = [a!i | i <- indices a]

assocs a              = [i := a!i | i <- indices a]

a // us               = array (bounds a)
                            ([i := a!i | i <- indices a \\ [i | i:=_ <- us]]
                            ++ us)

accum f               = foldl (\a (i := v) -> a // [i := f (a!i) v])

accumArray f z b      = accum f (array b [i := z | i <- range b])

amap f a              = array b [i := f (a!i) | i <- range b]
                            where b = bounds a

ixmap b f a           = array b [i := a ! f i | i <- range b]

instance (Ix a, Eq b)  => Eq (Array a b)  where
    a == a'            =  assocs a == assocs a'

instance (Ix a, Ord b) => Ord (Array a b)  where
    a <=  a'           =  assocs a <= assocs a'

instance (Ix a, Text a, Text b) => Text (Array a b)  where
    showsPrec p a = showParen (p > 9) (
                    showString "array " .
                    shows (bounds a) . showChar ' ' .
                    shows (assocs a)                    )

    readsPrec p = readParen (p > 9)
            (\r -> [(array b as, u) | ("array",s) <- [lex r],
                                    (b,t)        <- reads s,
                                    (as,u)       <- reads t    ]
                ++
                [(listArray b xs, u) | ("listArray",s) <- [lex r],
                                    (b,t)            <- reads s,
                                    (xs,u)           <- reads t ])

instance (Ix a, Binary a, Binary b) => Binary (Array a b)  where
    showBin a = showBin (bounds a) . showBin (elems a)
```

```
    readBin bin = (listArray b vs, bin'')
            where (b,bin')  = readBin bin
                  (vs,bin'') = readBin bin'
```

PreludeText

```
module  PreludeText (
        reads, shows, show, read, lex,
        showChar, showString, readParen, showParen ) where

reads               :: (Text a) => ReadS a
reads               = readsPrec 0

shows               :: (Text a) => a -> ShowS
shows               = showsPrec 0

read                :: (Text a) => String -> a
read s              = case [x | (x,t) <- reads s, ("","") <- lex t] of
                        [x] -> x
                        []  -> error "read{PreludeText}: no parse"
                        _   -> error "read{PreludeText}: ambiguous parse"

show                :: (Text a) => a -> String
show x              = shows x ""

showChar            :: Char -> ShowS
showChar            = (:)

showString          :: String -> ShowS
showString          = (++)

showParen           :: Bool -> ShowS -> ShowS
showParen b p          = if b then showChar '(' . p . showChar ')' else p

readParen           :: Bool -> ReadS a -> ReadS a
readParen b g = if b then mandatory else optional
                where optional r = g r ++ mandatory r
                      mandatory r = [(x,u) | ("(",s) <- lex r,
                                             (x,t)   <- optional s,
                                             (")",u) <- lex t    ]

lex                     :: ReadS String
lex ""                  = [("","")]
lex (c:s) | isSpace c      = lex (dropWhile isSpace s)
lex ('-':'-':s)             = case dropWhile (/= '\n') s of
                            '\n':t -> lex t
                            _      -> [] -- unterminated end-of-line
                                         -- comment

lex ('{':'-':s)              = lexNest lex s
                        where
                        lexNest f ('-':'}':s) = f s
                        lexNest f ('{':'-':s) = lexNest (lexNest f) s
                        lexNest f (c:s)       = lexNest f s
                        lexNest _ ""          = [] -- unterminated
                                                   -- nested comment

lex ('<':'-':s)            = [("<-",s)]
lex ('\'':s)           = [('\'':ch++"'", t) | (ch,t) <- lexLitChar s,
                                                ch /= "'"            ]
```

```
lex ('"':s)              = [('"':str, t)        | (str,t) <- lexString s]
                           where
                           lexString ('"':s) = [("\"",s)]
                           lexString s = [(ch++str, u)
                                                | (ch,t)  <- lexStrItem s,
                                                  (str,u) <- lexString t  ]

                           lexStrItem ('\\':'&':s) = [("\\&",s)]
                           lexStrItem ('\\':c:s) | isSpace c
                              = [("\\&",t) | '\\':t <- [dropWhile isSpace s]]
                           lexStrItem s              = lexLitChar s

lex (c:s) | isSingle c       = [([c],s)]
          | isSym1 c         = [(c:sym,t)        | (sym,t) <- [span isSym s]]
          | isAlpha c        = [(c:nam,t)        | (nam,t) <- [span isIdChar s]]
          | isDigit c        = [(c:ds++fe,t)     | (ds,s)  <- [span isDigit s],
                                                   (fe,t)  <- lexFracExp s     ]
          | otherwise        = []    -- bad character
              where
              isSingle c  =   c `elem` ",;()[]{}_`"
              isSym1 c    =   c `elem` "-~" || isSym c
              isSym c     =   c `elem` "!@#$%&*+./<=>?\\^|:"
              isIdChar c  =   isAlphanum c || c `elem` "_'"

              lexFracExp ('.':s) = [('.':ds++e,u) | (ds,t) <- lexDigits s,
                                                    (e,u)  <- lexExp t     ]
              lexFracExp s       = [("",s)]

              lexExp (e:s) | e `elem` "eE"
                   = [(e:c:ds,u) | (c:t)  <- [s], c `elem` "+-",
                                   (ds,u) <- lexDigits t] ++
                     [(e:ds,t)   | (ds,t) <- lexDigits s]
              lexExp s = [("",s)]

lexDigits                 :: ReadS String
lexDigits                 =  nonnull isDigit

nonnull                   :: (Char -> Bool) -> ReadS String
nonnull p s               =  [(cs,t) | (cs@(_:_),t) <- [span p s]]

lexLitChar                :: ReadS String
lexLitChar ('\\':s)       =  [('\\':esc, t) | (esc,t) <- lexEsc s]
              where
              lexEsc (c:s)     | c `elem` "abfnrtv\\\"'" = [([c],s)]
              lexEsc ('^':c:s) | c >= '@' && c <= '_'    = [(['^',c],s)]
              lexEsc s@(d:_)   | isDigit d               = lexDigits s
              lexEsc ('o':s) = [('o':os, t) | (os,t) <- nonnull isOctDigit s]
              lexEsc ('x':s) = [('x':xs, t) | (xs,t) <- nonnull isHexDigit s]
              lexEsc s@(c:_)   | isUpper c
                   = case [(mne,s') | mne <- "DEL" : elems asciiTab,
                                      ([],s') <- [match mne s]             ]
                     of (pr:_) -> [pr]
                        []     -> []
              lexEsc _         = []
lexLitChar (c:s)          =  [([c],s)]

isOctDigit c = c >= '0' && c <= '7'
isHexDigit c = isDigit c || c >= 'A' && c <= 'F'
                         || c >= 'a' && c <= 'f'

match                     :: (Eq a) => [a] -> [a] -> ([a],[a])
```

```
match (x:xs) (y:ys) | x == y  =  match xs ys
match xs    ys                =  (xs,ys)

asciiTab = listArray ('\NUL', ' ')
            ["NUL", "SOH", "STX", "ETX", "EOT", "ENQ", "ACK", "BEL",
             "BS",  "HT",  "LF",  "VT",  "FF",  "CR",  "SO",  "SI",
             "DLE", "DC1", "DC2", "DC3", "DC4", "NAK", "SYN", "ETB",
             "CAN", "EM",  "SUB", "ESC", "FS",  "GS",  "RS",  "US",
             "SP"]


-- Trivial type

instance  Text ()  where
    readsPrec p    = readParen False
                         (\r -> [((),t) | ("(",s) <- lex r,
                                          (")",t) <- lex s ] )
    showsPrec p () = showString "()"


-- Binary type

instance  Text Bin  where
    readsPrec p s = error "readsPrec{PreludeText}: Cannot read Bin."
    showsPrec p b =  showString "<<Bin>>"


-- Character type

instance  Text Char  where
    readsPrec p     = readParen False
                          (\r -> [(c,t) | ('\'':s,t)<- lex r,
                                          (c,_)     <- readLitChar s])

    showsPrec p '\'' = showString "'\\''"
    showsPrec p c    = showChar '\'' . showLitChar c . showChar '\''

    readList = readParen False (\r -> [pr | ('"':s, t) <- lex r,
                                            pr          <- readl s    ])
               where readl ('"':s)      = [("",s)]
                     readl ('\\':'&':s) = readl s
                     readl s            = [(c:cs,u) | (c ,t) <- readLitChar s,
                                                      (cs,u) <- readl t       ]

    showList cs = showChar '"' . showl cs
                where showl ""       = showChar '"'
                      showl ('"':cs) = showString "\\\"" . showl cs
                      showl (c:cs)   = showLitChar c . showl cs

readLitChar          :: ReadS Char
readLitChar ('\\':s) =  readEsc s
        where
        readEsc ('a':s)    = [('\a',s)]
        readEsc ('b':s)    = [('\b',s)]
        readEsc ('f':s)    = [('\f',s)]
        readEsc ('n':s)    = [('\n',s)]
        readEsc ('r':s)    = [('\r',s)]
        readEsc ('t':s)    = [('\t',s)]
        readEsc ('v':s)    = [('\v',s)]
        readEsc ('\\':s)   = [('\\',s)]
        readEsc ('"':s)    = [('"',s)]
        readEsc ('\'':s)   = [('\'',s)]
```

```
        readEsc ('^':c:s) | c >= '@' && c <= '_'
                            = [(chr (ord c - ord '@'), s)]
        readEsc s@(d:_) | isDigit d
                            = [(chr n, t) | (n,t) <- readDec s]
        readEsc ('o':s)   = [(chr n, t) | (n,t) <- readOct s]
        readEsc ('x':s)   = [(chr n, t) | (n,t) <- readHex s]
        readEsc s@(c:_) | isUpper c
                        = let table = ('\DEL' := "DEL") : assocs asciiTab
                          in case [(c,s') | (c := mne) <- table,
                                            ([],s')    <- [match mne s]]
                              of (pr:_) -> [pr]
                                 []     -> []
        readEsc _         = []
readLitChar (c:s)    = [(c,s)]

showLitChar                    :: Char -> ShowS
showLitChar c | c > '\DEL' =  protectEsc isDigit (show (ord c))
showLitChar '\DEL'         =  showString "\\DEL"
showLitChar '\\'           =  showString "\\\\"
showLitChar c | c >= ' '   =  showChar c
showLitChar '\a'           =  showString "\\a"
showLitChar '\b'           =  showString "\\b"
showLitChar '\f'           =  showString "\\f"
showLitChar '\n'           =  showString "\\n"
showLitChar '\r'           =  showString "\\r"
showLitChar '\t'           =  showString "\\t"
showLitChar '\v'           =  showString "\\v"
showLitChar '\SO'          =  protectEsc (== 'H') (showString "\\SO")
showLitChar c              =  showString ('\\' : asciiTab!c)

protectEsc p f                 = f . cont
                      where cont s@(c:_) | p c = "\\&" ++ s
                            cont s             = s

readDec, readOct, readHex :: (Integral a) => ReadS a
readDec = readInt 10 isDigit (\d -> ord d - ord '0')
readOct = readInt  8 isOctDigit (\d -> ord d - ord '0')
readHex = readInt 16 isHexDigit hex
            where hex d = ord d - (if isDigit d then ord '0'
                                   else ord (if isUpper d then 'A' else 'a')
                                      - 10)

readInt :: (Integral a) => a -> (Char -> Bool) -> (Char -> Int) -> ReadS a
readInt radix isDig digToInt s =
    [(foldl1 (\n d -> n * radix + d) (map (fromIntegral . digToInt) ds), r)
        | (ds,r) <- nonnull isDig s ]

showInt :: (Integral a) => a -> ShowS
showInt n r = let (n',d) = divRem n 10
                  r'     = chr (ord '0' + fromIntegral d) : r
              in if n' == 0 then r' else showInt n' r'

-- Standard integral types

instance  Text Int  where
    readsPrec p = readSigned readDec
    showsPrec   = showSigned showInt

instance  Text Integer  where
    readsPrec p = readSigned readDec
    showsPrec   = showSigned showInt
```

```
readSigned:: (Real a) => ReadS a -> ReadS a
readSigned readPos = readParen False read'
                where read' r  = read'' r ++
                                 [(-x,t) | ("-",s) <- lex r,
                                           (x,t)   <- read'' s]
                      read'' r = [(n,s)  | (str,s) <- lex r,
                                           (n,"")   <- readPos str]

showSigned:: (Real a) => (a -> ShowS) -> Int -> a -> ShowS
showSigned showPos p x = if x < 0 then showParen (p > 6)
                                       (showChar '-' . showPos (-x))
                             else showPos x


-- Standard real floating-point types

instance  Text Float  where
    readsPrec p = readSigned readFloat
    showsPrec   = showSigned showFloat

instance  Text Double  where
    readsPrec p = readSigned readFloat
    showsPrec   = showSigned showFloat

-- The functions readFloat and showFloat below use rational arithmetic
-- to insure correct conversion between the floating-point radix and
-- decimal.  It is often possible to use a higher-precision floating-
-- point type to obtain the same results.

readFloat r = [(fromRational ((n%1)*10^^(k-d)), t) | (n,d,s) <- readFix r,
                                                     (k,t)    <- readExp s]
              where readFix r = [(read (ds++ds'), length ds', t)
                                  | (ds,'.':s) <- lexDigits r,
                                    (ds',t)     <- lexDigits s ]

                    readExp (e:s) | e `elem` "eE" = readExp' s
                    readExp s                     = [(0,s)]

                    readExp' ('-':s) = [(-k,t) | (k,t) <- readDec s]
                    readExp' ('+':s) = readDec s
                    readExp' s       = readDec s

-- The number of decimal digits m below is chosen to guarantee
-- read (show x) == x.  See
--      Matula, D. W.  A formalization of floating-point numeric base
--      conversion.  IEEE Transactions on Computers C-19, 8 (1970 August),
--      681-692.

showFloat x =
    if x == 0 then showString ("0." ++ take (m-1) (repeat '0'))
              else if e >= m-1 || e < 0 then showSci else showFix
    where
    showFix      = showString whole . showChar '.' . showString frac
                   where (whole,frac) = splitAt (e+1) (show sig)
    showSci      = showChar d . showChar '.' . showString frac
                   . showChar 'e' . show e
                   where (d:frac) = show sig
    (m, sig, e)  = if b == 10 then (w,        s,    n+w-1)
                              else (m', sig', e'   )
    m'           = ceiling ((fromInt w * log (fromInteger b))/log 10) + 1
    (sig', e')   = if    sig1 >= 10^m'     then (round (t/10), e1+1)
```

```
                        else if sig1 <   10^(m'-1) then (round (t*10), e1-1)
                                           else (sig1,          e1  )
    sig1          = round t
    t             = s%1 * (b%1)^^n * 10^^(m'-e1-1)
    e1            = floor (logBase 10 x)
    (s, n)        = decodeFloat x
    b             = floatRadix x
    w             = floatDigits x


-- Lists

instance  (Text a) => Text [a]   where
    readsPrec p = readList
    showsPrec p = showList


-- Tuples

instance  (Text a, Text b) => Text (a,b)   where
    readsPrec p = readParen False
                            (\r -> [((x,y),  w) | ("(",s) <- lex r,
                                                  (x,t)   <- reads s,
                                                  (",",u) <- lex t,
                                                  (y,v)   <- reads u,
                                                  (")",w) <- lex v ] )

    showsPrec p (x,y) = showChar '(' . shows x . showChar ',' .
                                shows y . showChar ')'
-- et cetera


-- Functions

instance  Text (a -> b)   where
    readsPrec p s  =  error "readsPrec{PreludeText}: Cannot read functions."
    showsPrec p f  =  showString "<<function>>"
```

PreludeIO

```
-- I/O functions and definitions

module PreludeIO  where

-- File and channel names:

stdin     = "stdin"
stdout    = "stdout"
stderr    = "stderr"
stdecho   = "stdecho"


-- Requests and responses:

data Request =        -- file system requests:
                      ReadFile        String
                   | WriteFile       String String
                   | AppendFile      String String
                   | ReadBinFile     String
                   | WriteBinFile    String Bin
                   | AppendBinFile   String Bin
                   | DeleteFile      String
```

```
                        | StatusFile    String
                -- channel system requests:
                        | ReadChan      String
                        | AppendChan    String String
                        | ReadBinChan   String
                        | AppendBinChan String Bin
                        | StatusChan    String
                -- environment requests:
                        | Echo          Bool
                        | GetArgs
                        | GetEnv        String
                        | SetEnv        String String
                deriving Text

data Response =         Success
                | Str String
                | StrList [String]
                | Bn  Bin
                | Failure IOError
                deriving Text

data IOError =          WriteError   String
                | ReadError    String
                | SearchError  String
                | FormatError  String
                | OtherError   String
                deriving Text


-- Continuation-based I/O:

type Dialogue     = [Response] -> [Request]
type SuccCont     =                Dialogue
type StrCont      = String      -> Dialogue
type StrListCont  = [String]    -> Dialogue
type BinCont      = Bin         -> Dialogue
type FailCont     = IOError     -> Dialogue

done         ::                                           Dialogue
readFile     :: String ->               FailCont -> StrCont      -> Dialogue
writeFile    :: String -> String -> FailCont -> SuccCont     -> Dialogue
appendFile   :: String -> String -> FailCont -> SuccCont     -> Dialogue
readBinFile  :: String ->               FailCont -> BinCont      -> Dialogue
writeBinFile :: String -> Bin    -> FailCont -> SuccCont     -> Dialogue
appendBinFile :: String -> Bin   -> FailCont -> SuccCont     -> Dialogue
deleteFile   :: String ->               FailCont -> SuccCont     -> Dialogue
statusFile   :: String ->               FailCont -> StrCont      -> Dialogue
readChan     :: String ->               FailCont -> StrCont      -> Dialogue
appendChan   :: String -> String -> FailCont -> SuccCont     -> Dialogue
readBinChan  :: String ->               FailCont -> BinCont      -> Dialogue
appendBinChan :: String -> Bin   -> FailCont -> SuccCont     -> Dialogue
statusChan   :: String ->               FailCont -> StrCont      -> Dialogue
echo         :: Bool   ->               FailCont -> SuccCont     -> Dialogue
getArgs      ::                         FailCont -> StrListCont -> Dialogue
getEnv       :: String ->               FailCont -> StrCont      -> Dialogue
setEnv       :: String -> String -> FailCont -> SuccCont     -> Dialogue

done resps   = []

readFile name fail succ resps =
     (ReadFile name) : strDispatch fail succ resps
```

```
writeFile name contents fail succ resps =
    (WriteFile name contents) : succDispatch fail succ resps

appendFile name contents fail succ resps =
    (AppendFile name contents) : succDispatch fail succ resps

readBinFile name fail succ resps =
    (ReadBinFile name) : binDispatch fail succ resps

writeBinFile name contents fail succ resps =
    (WriteBinFile name contents) : succDispatch fail succ resps

appendBinFile name contents fail succ resps =
    (AppendBinFile name contents) : succDispatch fail succ resps

deleteFile name fail succ resps =
    (DeleteFile name) : succDispatch fail succ resps

statusFile name fail succ resps =
    (StatusFile name) : strDispatch fail succ resps

readChan name fail succ resps =
    (ReadChan name) : strDispatch fail succ resps

appendChan name contents fail succ resps =
    (AppendChan name contents) : succDispatch fail succ resps

readBinChan name fail succ resps =
    (ReadBinChan name) : binDispatch fail succ resps

appendBinChan name contents fail succ resps =
    (AppendBinChan name contents) : succDispatch fail succ resps

statusChan name fail succ resps =
    (StatusChan name) : strDispatch fail succ resps

echo bool fail succ resps =
    (Echo bool) : succDispatch fail succ resps

getArgs fail succ resps =
        GetArgs : strListDispatch fail succ resps

getEnv name fail succ resps =
        (GetEnv name) : strDispatch fail succ resps

setEnv name val fail succ resps =
        (SetEnv name val) : succDispatch fail succ resps


strDispatch fail succ (resp:resps) =
            case resp of Str val     -> succ val resps
                         Failure msg -> fail msg resps

strListDispatch fail succ (resp:resps) =
            case resp of StrList val -> succ val resps
                         Failure msg -> fail msg resps

binDispatch fail succ (resp:resps) =
            case resp of Bn val      -> succ val resps
                         Failure msg -> fail msg resps

succDispatch fail succ (resp:resps) =
```

```
                case resp of Success     -> succ resps
                             Failure msg -> fail msg resps


abort           :: FailCont
abort err       =  done

exit            :: FailCont
exit err        =  appendChan stdout msg abort done
                   where msg = case err of ReadError s    -> s
                                           WriteError s   -> s
                                           SearchError s  -> s
                                           FormatError s  -> s
                                           OtherError s   -> s

print           :: (Text a) => a -> Dialogue
print x         =  appendChan stdout (show x) abort done
prints          :: (Text a) => a -> String -> Dialogue
prints x s      =  appendChan stdout (shows x s) abort done

interact        :: (String -> String) -> Dialogue
interact f      =  readChan stdin abort
                           (\x -> appendChan stdout (f x) abort done)
```

Appendix C

Haskell Syntax

C.1 Notational Conventions

These notational conventions are used for presenting syntax:

[*pattern*]	optional
{*pattern*}	zero or more repetitions
(*pattern*)	grouping
$pat_1 \mid pat_2$	choice
$pat_{\{pat'\}}$	difference—elements generated by *pat* except those generated by *pat'*
`fibonacci`	terminal syntax in typewriter font

BNF-like syntax is used throughout, with productions having form:

$$nonterm \quad \rightarrow \quad alt_1 \mid alt_2 \mid ... \mid alt_n$$

There are some families of nonterminals indexed by precedence levels (written as a superscript). Similarly, the nonterminals *op*, *varop*, and *conop* have a double index: a letter *l*, *r*, or *n* for left-, right- or nonassociativity and a precedence level. Thus, for example

$$aexp^i \quad \rightarrow \quad (\ exp^{i+1}\ op^{(a,i)}\ )$$

actually stands for 30 productions, with 10 substitutions for *i* and three for *a*.

In both the lexical and the context-free syntax, there are some ambiguities that are to be resolved by making grammatical phrases as long as possible, proceeeding from left to right (in shift-reduce parsing, resolving shift/reduce conflicts by shifting). In the lexical syntax, this is the "consume longest lexeme" rule. In the context-free syntax, this means that conditionals, let-expressions and lambda-abstractions extend to the right as far as possible.

C.2 Lexical Syntax

program   → { *lexeme* | *whitespace* }

lexeme   → *varid* | *conid* | *varsym* | *consym* | *literal* | *special* | *reservedop* |
                reservedid

literal   → *integer* | *float* | *char* | *string*

special   → (|) | , | ; | [|] | _ | ` | { | }

whitespace → *whitestuff* {*whitestuff*}

whitestuff → *whitechar* | *comment* | *ncomment*

whitechar → *newline* | *space* | *tab* | *vertab* | *formfeed*

newline   → a newline (system dependent)

space   → a space

tab   → a horizontal tab

vertab   → a vertical tab

formfeed   → a form feed

comment   → -- {*any*} *newline*

ncomment   → {- *ANYseq* {*ncomment ANYseq*} -}

ANYseq   → {*ANY*}{*ANY*} ({- | -}) {*ANY*}

ANY   → *any* | *newline* | *vertab* | *formfeed*

any   → *graphic* | *space* | *tab*

graphic   → *large* | *small* | *digit*
         | ! | " | # | $ | % | & | ' | (|) | * | +
         | , | - | . | / | : | ; | < | = | > | ? | @
         | [| \ |] | ^ | _ | ` | { | | | } | ~

small   → a | b | ... | z

large   → A | B | ... | z

digit   → 0 | 1 | ... | 9

varid	→	(*small* {*small* | *large* | *digit* | ' | _}){*reservelil*}
conid	→	*large* {*small* | *large* | *digit* | ' | _}
reservedid	→	case | class | data | default | deriving | else | hiding | if
	|	import | in | infix | infixl | infixrl | instance | interface
	|	let | module | of | renaming | then | to | type | where

varsym	→	((*symbol* | *presymbol*) {*symbol* | : }){*reservelop*}
consym	→	(: {*symbol* | : }){*reservelop*}
conop	→	*aconop* | ` *aconid* `
presymbol	→	- | ~
symbol	→	! | # | $ | % | & | * | + | . | / | < | = | > | ? | @ | \ | ^ | |
reservedop	→	.. | :: | => | = | @ | \ | | | ~ | <- | ->

tyvar	→	*avarid*	(*type variables*)
tycon	→	*aconid*	(*type constructors*)
tycls	→	*aconid*	(*type classes*)
modid	→	*aconid*	(*modules*)

integer	→	*digit*{*digit*}
float	→	*integer* . *integer* [(e | E)[- | +] *integer*]

char	→	' (*graphic* {' | \} | *space* | *escape*{\&}) '
string	→	" {*graphic*{" | \} | *space* | *escape* | *gap*} "
escape	→	\ (*charesc* | *ascii* | *integer* | o *octit*{*octit*} | x *hexit*{*he~it*})
charesc	→	a | b | f | n | r | t | v | \ | " | ' | &
ascii	→	^ *cntrl* | NUL | SOH | STX | ETX | EOT | ENQ | ACK
	|	BEL | BS | HT | LF | VT | FF | CR | SO | SI | DLE
	|	DC1 | DC2 | DC3 | DC4 | NAK | SYN | ETB | CAN
	|	EM | SUB | ESC | FS | GS | RS | US | SP | DEL
cntrl	→	*large* | @ | [| \ |] | ^ | _
gap	→	\ *whitechar* {*whitechar*} \
hexit	→	*digit* | A | B | C | D | E | F | a | b | c | d | e | f
octit	→	0 | 1 | 2 | 3 | 4 | 5 | 6 | 7

C.3 Layout

Definitions: The indentation of a lexeme is the column number indicating the start of that lexeme; the indentation of a line is the indentation of its leftmost lexeme. To determine the column number, assume a fixed-width font with this tab convention: tab stops are 8 characters apart, and a tab character causes the insertion of enough spaces to align the current position with the next tab stop.

In the syntax given in the other parts of the report, *declaration lists* are always preceded by the keyword `where`, `let` or `of`, and are enclosed within curly braces ({ }) with the individual declarations separated by semicolons (;). For example, the syntax of a `let` expression is:

$$\texttt{let } \{ \ decl_1 \ ; \ decl_2 \ ; \ ...; \ decl_n \ [;] \ \} \ \texttt{in } exp$$

Haskell permits the omission of the braces and semicolons by using *layout* to convey the same information. This allows both layout-sensitive and -insensitive styles of coding, which can be freely mixed within one program. Because layout is not required, Haskell programs can be straightforwardly produced by other programs.

The layout (or "off-side") rule takes effect whenever the open brace is omitted after the keyword `where`, `let` or `of`. When this happens, the indentation of the next lexeme (whether or not on a new line) is remembered and the omitted open brace is inserted (the whitespace preceding the lexeme may include comments). For each subsequent line, if it contains only whitespace or is indented more, then the previous item is continued (nothing is inserted); if it is indented the same amount, then a new item begins (a semicolon is inserted); and if it is indented less, then the declaration list ends (a close brace is inserted). A close brace is also inserted whenever the syntactic category containing the declaration list ends; that is, if an illegal lexeme is encountered at a point where a close brace would be legal, a close brace is inserted. The layout rule will match only those open braces that it has inserted; an open brace that the user has inserted must be matched by a close brace inserted by the user.

Given these rules, a single newline may actually terminate several declaration lists. Also, these rules permit:

```
f x = let a = 1; b = 2
          g y = exp2 in exp 1
```

making a, b and g all part of the same declaration list.

To facilitate the use of layout at the top level of a module (several modules may reside in one file), the keywords `module` and `interface` and the end-of-file token are assumed to occur in column 0 (whereas normally the first column is 1). Otherwise, all top-level declarations would have to be indented.

C.4 Context-Free Syntax

module	→	`module` *modid* [*exports*] `where` *body*	
	|	*body*	
body	→	{ [*impdecls* ;] [[*fixdecls* ;] *topdecls* [;]] }	
	|	{ *impdecls* [;] }	
impdecls	→	*impdecl₁* ; ... ; *impdecl_n*	*(n ≥ 1)*
exports	→	(*export₁* , ... , *export_n*)	*(n ≥ 1)*
export	→	*entity*	
	|	*modid* ..	
impdecl	→	`import` *modid* [*impspec*] [`renaming` *renamings*]	
impspec	→	(*import₁* , ... , *import_n*)	*(n ≥ 0)*
	|	`hiding` (*import₁* , ... , *import_n*)	*(n ≥ 1)*
import	→	*entity*	
renamings	→	(*renaming₁* , ... , *renaming_n*)	*(n ≥ 1)*
renaming	→	*var₁* `to` *var₂*	
	|	*con₁* `to` *con₂*	
entity	→	*varid*	
	|	*tycon*	
	|	*tycon* (..)	
	|	*tycon* (*con₁* , ... , *con_n*)	*(n ≥ 1)*
	|	*tycls* (..)	
	|	*tycls* (*var₁* , ... , *var_n*)	*(n ≥ 0)*
fixdecls	→	*fix₁* ; ... ; *fix_n*	*(n ≥ 1)*
fix	→	`infixl` [*digit*] *ops*	
	|	`infixr` [*digit*] *ops*	
	|	`infix` [*digit*] *ops*	
ops	→	*op₁* , ... , *op_n*	*(n ≥ 1)*
topdecls	→	*topdecl₁* ; ... ; *topdecl_n*	*(n ≥ 1)*

topdecl	→	type *simple* = *type*
	|	data [*context* =>] *simple* = *constrs* [deriving (*tycls* | (*tyclses*))]
	|	class [*context* =>] *class* [where { *cbody* [;] }]
	|	instance [*context* =>] *tycls inst* [where { *valdefs* [;] }]
	|	default (*type* | (*type₁*, ... , *typeₙ*)) ($n \geq 0$)
	|	*decl*

decls	→	*decl₁*; ... ; *declₙ*	($n \geq 0$)
decl	→	*vars* :: [*context* =>] *type*	
	|	*valdef*	

type	→	*btype* [-> *type*]	
btype	→	*ttycon atype₁*... *atypeₖ*	(arity *tycon* = $k \geq 1$)
	|	*atype*	

atype	→	*tyvar*	
	|	*tycon*	(arity *tycon* = 0)
	|	()	(unit type)
	|	(*type*)	(parenthesised type)
	|	(*type₁*, ... , *typeₖ*)	(tuple type, $k \geq 2$)
	|	[*type*]	

context	→	*class*	
	|	(*class₁*, ... , *classₙ*)	($n \geq 1$)
class	→	*tycls tyvar*	

cbody	→	*csigns* [; *valdef* [; *valdefs*]	
	|	*valdefs*	
csigns	→	*csign₁*; ... ; *csignₙ*	($n \geq 1$)
csign	→	*vars* :: [*context* =>] *type*	

vars	→	*var₁* , ... , *varₙ*	($n \geq 1$)

simple	$\to$	*tycon tyvar$_1$* ... *tyvar$_k$*	(arity *tycon* = $k \geq 0$)
constrs	$\to$	*constr$_1$* | ... | *constr$_n$*	($n \geq 1$)
constr	$\to$	*con atype$_1$* ... *atype$_k$*	(arity *con* = $k \geq 0$)
	|	*btype$_1$ conop btype$_2$*	(infix *conop*)
tyclses	$\to$	*tycls$_1$* , ... , *tycls$_n$*	($n \geq 0$)
inst	$\to$	*tycon*	(arity *tycon* = 0)
	|	(*tycon tyvar$_1$*... *tyvar$_k$*)	($k \geq 1$ *tyvars* distinct)
	|	(*tyvar$_1$*, ... , *tyvar$_k$*)	($k \geq 2$ *tyvars* distinct)
	|	( )	
	|	[*tyvar*]	
	|	(*tyvar$_1$*-> *tyvar$_2$*)	*tyvar$_1$* and *tyvar$_2$* distinct
valdefs	$\to$	*valdef$_1$*; ... ; *valdef$_n$*	($n \geq 0$)
valdef	$\to$	*lhs* = *exp* [where { *decls* [;] }]	
	|	*lhs gdrhs* [where { *decls* [;] }]	
lhs	$\to$	*apat*	
	|	*funlhs*	
funlhs	$\to$	*afunlhs*	
	|	*pat^{i+1} varop*$^{(\,a,i)}$ *pat^{i+1}*	
	|	*lpat^i varop*$^{(\,l,i)}$ *pat^{i+1}*	
	|	*pat^{i+1} varop*$^{(\,r,i)}$ *rpat^i*	
afunlhs	$\to$	*var apat*	
	|	(*funlhs*) *apat*	
	|	*afunlhs apat*	
gdrhs	$\to$	*gd* = *exp* [*gdrhs*]	
gd	$\to$	| *exp^0*	

exp	$\rightarrow$	exp^0 :: [*context* =>] *type*	(expression type signature)
	|	exp^0	
exp^i	$\rightarrow$	exp^{i+1} [$op^{(\text{n},i)}exp^{i+1}$]	
	|	$lexp^i$	
	|	$rexp^i$	
$lexp^i$	$\rightarrow$	($lexp^i \mid exp^{i+1}$)$op^{(1,i)}$ exp^{i+1}	
$lexp^6$	$\rightarrow$	- exp^7	
$rexp^i$	$\rightarrow$	exp^{i+1} $op^{(\text{r},i)}$ ($rexp^i \mid exp^{i+1}$)	
exp^{10}	$\rightarrow$	\ $apat_1$... $apat_n$ -> *exp*	(lambda abstraction, $n \geq 1$)
	|	let { *decls* [;] } in *exp*	(let expression)
	|	if *exp* then *exp* else *exp*	(conditional)
	|	case *exp* of { *alts* [;] }	(case expression)
	|	*fexp*	
fexp	$\rightarrow$	exp^{10} *aexp*	(function application)
	|	*aexp*	
aexp	$\rightarrow$	*var*	(variable)
	|	*con*	(constructor)
	|	*literal*	
	|	()	(unit)
	|	(*exp*)	(parenthesised expression)
	|	(exp_1, ... , exp_k)	(tuple, $k \geq 2$)
	|	[exp_1, ... , exp_k]	(list, $k \geq 0$)
	|	[exp_1 [, exp_2] .. [exp_3]]	(arithmetic sequence)
	|	[*exp* | $qual_1$, ... , $qual_n$]	(list comprehension, $n \geq 1$)
	|	($exp^{i+1}op^{(a,i)}$)	(left section)
	|	($op^{(a,i)}$ exp^{i+1})	(right section)
qual	$\rightarrow$	*pat* <- *exp*	
	|	*exp*	
alts	$\rightarrow$	alt_1; ... ; alt_n	($n \geq 1$)
alt	$\rightarrow$	*pat* -> *exp* [where { *decls* [;] }]	
	|	*pat gdpat* [where { *decls* [;] }]	

gdpat	$\rightarrow$	*gd -> exp* [*gdpat*]	
pat	$\rightarrow$	*pat^0*	
pat^i	$\rightarrow$	*pat^{i+1}*[*conop*$^{(n,i)}$ *pat^{i+1}*]	
	|	*lpat^i*	
	|	*rpat^i*	
lpat^i	$\rightarrow$	(*lpat^i* | *pat^{i+1}*)*conop*$^{(l,i)}$] *pat^{i+1}*	
lpat^6	$\rightarrow$	(*var* | _) + *integer*	(successor pattern)
	|	- {*integer* | *float*}	(negative literal)
rpat^i	$\rightarrow$	*pat^{i+1}conop*$^{(r,i)}$ (*rpat^i* | *pat^{i+1}*)	
pat^{10}	$\rightarrow$	*apat*	
	|	*con apat$_1$ ... apat$_k$*	(arity *con* = *k* $\geq$ *1*)
apat	$\rightarrow$	*var* [@ *apat*]	(as pattern)
	|	*con*	(arity *con* = *0*)
	|	*literal*	
	|	_	(wildcard)
	|	( )	(unit pattern)
	|	(*pat*)	(parenthesised pattern)
	|	(*pat$_1$*, ... , *pat$_k$*)	(tuple pattern, *k* $\geq$ 2)
	|	[*pat$_1$*, ... , *pat$_k$*]	(list pattern, *k* $\geq$ 0)
	|	~ *apat*	(irrefutable pattern)
var	$\rightarrow$	*varid* | (*varsym*)	(variable)
con	$\rightarrow$	*conid* | (*consym*)	(constructor)
varop	$\rightarrow$	*varsym* | \`*varid*\`	(variable operator)
conop	$\rightarrow$	*consym* | \`*conid*\`	(constructor operator)
op	$\rightarrow$	*varop* | *conop*	(operator)

C.5 Interface Syntax

interface	$\rightarrow$	`interface` *modid* `where` *ibody*	
ibody	$\rightarrow$	{ [*iimpdecls* ;] [*fixdecls* ;] *itopdecls* [;] }	
	|	{ *iimpdecls* [;] }	
iimpdecls	$\rightarrow$	*iimpdecl$_1$* ; ... ; *iimpdecl$_n$*	(*n* $\geq$ *1*)

iimpdecl	→	`import` *modid* (*import₁*, ... , *importₙ*)	
		[`renaming` *renamings*]	($n \geq 1$)
itopdecls	→	*itopdecl₁*; ... ; *itopdeclₙ*	($n \geq 1$)
itopdecl	→	`type` *simple* = *type*	
	|	`data` [*context* =>] *simple* [= *constrs*] [`deriving` (*tycls* | (*tyclses*))]]	
	|	`class` [*context* =>] *class* [`where` { *icdecls* [;] }]	
	|	`instance` [*context* =>] *tycls inst*	
	|	*vars* :: [*context* =>] *type*	
icdecls	→	*icdecl₁*; ... ; *icdeclₙ*	($n \geq 0$)
icdecl	→	*vars* :: *type*	

Appendix D

Haskell Class Structure

The following diagram represents the class structure of the predeclared numeric classes of Haskell (shown in **Chicago** font) and shows the principle operators and functions (in `Courier` font) associated with each class (its *methods*). It also shows the predeclared types (boxed) belonging to the classes. All the information shown here (and more) can be gleaned from the class declarations in the prelude. Information about classes `Binary`, `Ix` and `Enum` are not displayed.

A line descending from one class to another indicates that the second is an immediate sub-class of the first. Thus a class is a subclass of another if it may be reached from it by a series of descending lines. A subclass *inherits* all the methods from its superclasses. Thus the methods for a given type can be found by looking at the node at which the type appears boxed and all the nodes reachable from it by tracing an upward path.

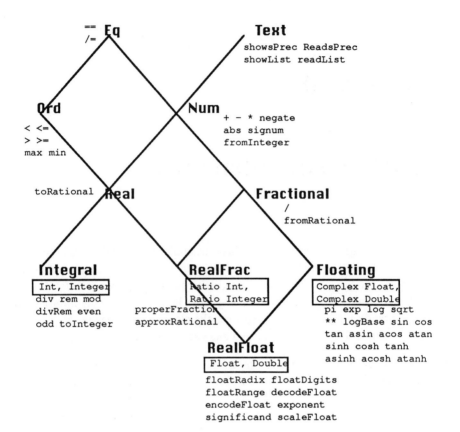

Index